PART 1

Paper 1.1

Preparing Financial Statements

REVISION SERIES

Official Publisher

FOULKS LYNCH
PUBLICATIONS

British Library Cataloguing-in-Publication Data

A catalogue record for this book is available from the British Library.

Published by Foulks Lynch Ltd
4, The Griffin Centre
Staines Road
Feltham
Middlesex
TW14 0HS

ISBN 0 7483 5995 8

© AT Foulks Lynch Ltd, 2003

Printed and bound in Great Britain.

Acknowledgements

The past ACCA examination questions are the copyright of the Association of Chartered Certified Accountants. The original answers to the questions from June 1994 onwards were produced by the examiners themselves and have been adapted by Foulks Lynch Ltd.

We are grateful to the Chartered Institute of Management Accountants and the Institute of Chartered Accountants in England and Wales for permission to reproduce past examination questions. The answers have been prepared by AT Foulks Lynch Ltd.

CONTENTS

This book includes a wide selection of questions from past ACCA exams, including the latest papers. In addition, there are full answers, many prepared by the examiner. This is the ONLY publication to include actual questions and official answers from the previous four sittings of the examination (at the date of publication).

Section

INDEX TO QUESTIONS AND ANSWERS

OBJECTIVE TEST QUESTIONS

PRACTICE QUESTIONS

Page number

SYLLABUS AND EXAMINATION FORMAT

Format of the paper-based examination

		Number of marks
Section A:	25 compulsory multiple choice questions (2 marks each)	50
Section B:	5 compulsory short form questions (8 – 12 marks each)	50
		100
Total time allowed: 3 hours		

Format of the computer-based examination

	Number of marks
Objective test questions	100

Total time allowed: 3 hours

Aim

To develop knowledge and understanding of the techniques used to prepare year-end financial statements, including necessary underlying records, and the interpretation of financial statements for incorporated enterprises, partnerships and sole traders.

Objectives

On completion of this paper candidates should be able to:

- describe the role and function of external financial reports and identify their users
- explain the accounting concepts and conventions present in generally accepted accounting principles
- record and summarise accounting data
- maintain records relating to fixed asset acquisition and disposal
- prepare basic financial statements for sole traders, partnerships, incorporated enterprises and simple groups
- appraise financial performance and the position of an organisation through the calculation and review of basic ratios
- demonstrate the skills expected in Part 1.

Position of the paper in the overall syllabus

No prior knowledge is required before commencing study for Paper 1.1. There is some connection with Paper 1.2 Financial Information for Management in the areas of performance management and data recording. There are no links with Paper 1.3 Managing People.

The basic financial accounting in Paper 1.1 is developed in Paper 2.5 Financial Reporting and Paper 3.6 Advanced Corporate Reporting. Knowledge from Paper 1.1 provides the background to Paper 2.6 Audit and Internal Review.

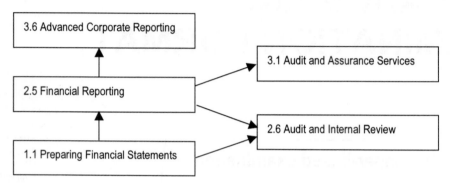

Syllabus content

1 General framework

(a) Types of business entity – limited companies, partnerships and sole traders.

(b) Forms of capital and capital structures in limited companies.

(c) The role of the Financial Reporting Council (FRC), the Finance Reporting Review Panel (FRRP), Accounting Standards Board (ASB) and the Urgent Issues Task Force (UITF).

(d) Application of Financial Reporting Standards (FRSs) and Statements of Standard Accounting Practice (SSAPs) to the preparation and presentation of financial statements.

(e) The ASB's Statement of Principles for Financial Reporting (Chapters 1, 2 and 3 only).

2 Accounting concepts and principles

(a) Basic accounting concepts and principles as stated in the ASB's Statement of Principles for Financial Reporting.

(b) Other accounting concepts:

    (i) historical cost

    (ii) money measurement

    (iii) entity

    (iv) dual aspect

    (v) time interval.

3 Double-entry bookkeeping and accounting systems

(a) Double-entry bookkeeping and accounting systems:

    (i) form and content of accounting records (manual and computerised)

    (ii) books of original entry, including journals

    (iii) sales and purchase ledgers

    (iv) cash book

    (v) general ledger

    (vi) trial balance

    (vii) accruals, prepayments and adjustments

    (viii) asset registers

    (ix) petty cash.

(b) Confirming and correcting mechanisms:

    (i) control accounts

    (ii) bank reconciliations

    (iii) suspense accounts and the correction of errors.

(c) General principles of the operation of a value added tax

(d) Computerised accounting systems.

4   Accounting treatments

(a)   Fixed assets, tangible and intangible:

  (i)   distinction between capital and revenue expenditure

  (ii)   accounting for acquisitions and disposals

  (iii) depreciation - definition, reasons for and methods, including straight line, reducing balance and sum of digits

  (iv)   research and development

  (v)   elementary treatment of goodwill.

(b)   Current assets:

  (i)   stock (excluding long-term contracts)

  (ii)   debtors, including accounting for bad and doubtful debts

  (iii) cash.

(c)   Current liabilities and accruals.

(d)   Shareholders' equity.

(e)   Post balance sheet events.

(f)   Contingencies.

5   Financial statements

(a)   Objectives of financial statements.

(b)   Users and their information needs.

(c)   Key features of financial statements:

  (i)   balance sheet

  (ii)   profit and loss account

  (iii) cash flow statement

  (iv)   notes to the financial statements (examined to a limited extent - see (d) (iii) below).

(d)   Preparation of financial statements for:

(i)   sole traders, including incomplete records techniques

(ii)   partnerships

(iii) limited companies, including profit and loss accounts and balance sheet for internal purposes and for external purposes in accordance with Companies Act 1985 formats and preparation of basic cash flow statements for limited companies (excluding group cash flow statements). The following notes to the financial statements will be examinable and no others:

  -    The ASB requirements governing reporting financial performance including the analysed profit and loss account and the additional statements and notes required by standards.

  -    Statement of movements in reserves

  -    Fixed assets

  -    Exceptional and extraordinary items

  -    Post balance sheet events

  -    Contingent liabilities and contingent assets

  -    Research and development expenditure

(iv)   groups of companies - preparation of a basic consolidated balance sheet for a company with one subsidiary.

6   Interpretation

(a)   Ratio analysis of accounting information and basic interpretation.

Excluded topics

The syllabus content outlines the area for assessment. No areas of knowledge are specifically excluded from the syllabus. No questions will be asked on: clubs and societies or partnerships other than the preparation of financial statements for partnerships.

Key areas of the syllabus

The objective of Paper 1.1 Preparing Financial Statements, is to ensure that candidates have the necessary basic accounting knowledge and skill to progress to the more advanced work of Paper 2.5 Financial Reporting. The two main skills required are:

•   the ability to prepare basic financial statements and the underlying accounting records on which they are based

•   an understanding of the principles on which accounting is based.

The key topic areas are as follows:

- preparation of financial statements for limited companies for internal purposes or for publication

- preparation of financial statements for partnerships and sole traders (including incomplete records)

- basic group accounts - consolidated balance sheet for a company with one subsidiary

- basic bookkeeping and accounting procedures

- accounting conventions and concepts

- interpretation of financial statements

- cash flow statements

- accounting standards

  - SSAPs 9, 13, and 17 plus FRSs 1, 3, 18 and relevant sections of FRSs 12 and 15.

  - FRS 15: the following paragraphs are examinable in so far as they relate to tangible fixed assets: 1-7, 34-36, 42-46, 61, 63, 72, 77-82 and 93. In relation to paragraph 2, only the following definitions are examinable: current value, depreciable amount, depreciation, recoverable amount, residual value, tangible fixed assets and useful economic life.

  - FRS 12: the following paragraphs are examinable in so far as they relate to contingent liabilities and contingent assets: 2, 3, 27-33, 91, 94, 96, 97, Appendix 2. The measurement rules in paragraphs 36-55 are not examinable.

Additional information

Candidates need to be aware that questions involving knowledge of new examinable regulations will not be set until at least six months after the last day of the month in which the regulation was issued.

Examinable documents are listed in the 'Exam Notes' section of the *Student Accountant*, usually appearing in the March and September issues three months before each examination.

ANALYSIS OF PAST PAPERS (PAPER-BASED EXAMINATIONS)

Section A questions

Section A will always consist of 25 compulsory multiple-choice questions covering a variety of syllabus topics.

Section B questions

Pilot paper 2001

1   Accounting concepts: materiality, substance over form, money measurement
2   Interpretation and ratio analysis
3   Cash flow statements
4   Current assets; liabilities; FRS12, SSAP17 and SSAP9
5   Limited company accounts: balance sheet

December 2001

1   Limited company accounts: profit and loss account
2   Sole traders: incomplete records
3   Groups of companies: balance sheet
4   Accounting concepts and principles: materiality, prudence, accounting standards
5   Interpretation and ratio analysis

June 2002

1   Indirect and direct methods of calculating cash flow
2   Basic book-keeping
3   Company balance sheet
4   Basic accounting concepts
5   Calculating and interpretation of ratios

December 2002

1   Company profit and loss account
2   Journal entries and suspense account
3   Consolidated balance sheet
4   Depreciation/amortisation
5   Correct treatment of accounting items

June 2003

1   Partnership's trading profit and loss account and appropriation account. Partners' current account.

2   Cash flow statement.

3   Balance sheet equation. Double entry bookkeeping.

4   Calculating ratios. Interpreting ratios.

5   Reserves. Issue of shares.

December 2003

1   Preparation of company's financial statements – balance sheet. Notes to the balance sheet – SSAP13.

2   Accounting treatment of fixed assets: valuation, depreciation and disposal.

3   Consolidated balance sheet.

4   SSAP9. FRS12. SSAP17.

5   Historical cost accounting.

REVISION GUIDANCE

Planning your revision

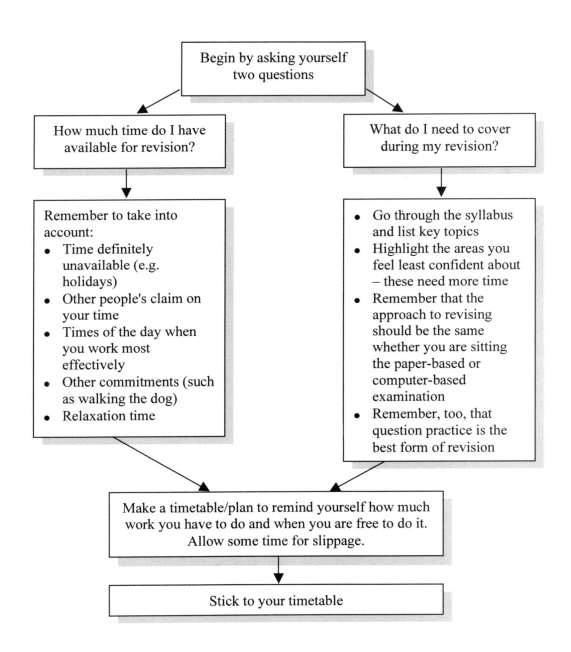

Begin by asking yourself two questions

How much time do I have available for revision?

What do I need to cover during my revision?

Remember to take into account:
- Time definitely unavailable (e.g. holidays)
- Other people's claim on your time
- Times of the day when you work most effectively
- Other commitments (such as walking the dog)
- Relaxation time

- Go through the syllabus and list key topics
- Highlight the areas you feel least confident about – these need more time
- Remember that the approach to revising should be the same whether you are sitting the paper-based or computer-based examination
- Remember, too, that question practice is the best form of revision

Make a timetable/plan to remind yourself how much work you have to do and when you are free to do it. Allow some time for slippage.

Stick to your timetable

Revision techniques

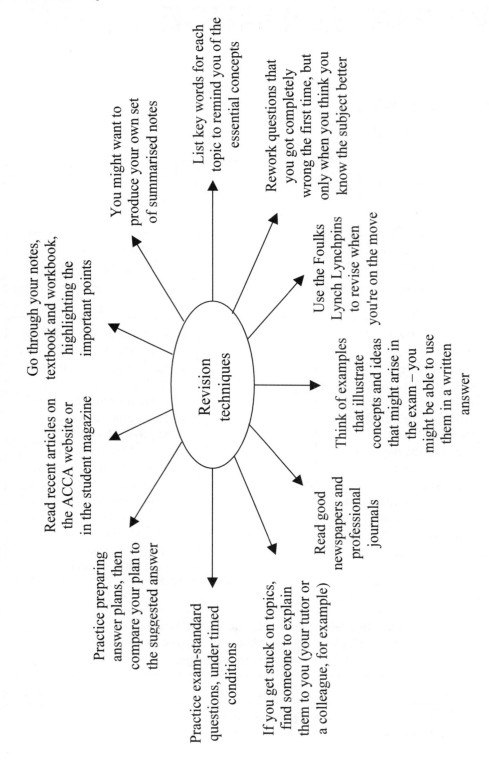

Revision techniques

List key words for each topic to remind you of the essential concepts

Rework questions that you got completely wrong the first time, but only when you think you know the subject better

You might want to produce your own set of summarised notes

Use the Foulks Lynch Lynchpins to revise when you're on the move

Go through your notes, textbook and workbook, highlighting the important points

Think of examples that illustrate concepts and ideas that might arise in the exam – you might be able to use them in a written answer

Read recent articles on the ACCA website or in the student magazine

Read good newspapers and professional journals

Practice preparing answer plans, then compare your plan to the suggested answer

Practice exam-standard questions, under timed conditions

If you get stuck on topics, find someone to explain them to you (your tutor or a colleague, for example)

EXAMINATION TECHNIQUES

Paper-based examinations – tips

- You might want to spend the first few minutes of the examination **reading the paper**.

- Where you have a **choice of question**, decide which questions you will do.

- Unless you know exactly how to answer the question, spend some time **planning** your answer.

- **Divide the time** you spend on questions in proportion to the marks on offer. One suggestion is to allocate 1½ minutes to each mark available, so a 10 mark question should be completed in 15 minutes.

- Spend the last **five minutes** reading through your answers and **making any additions or corrections**.

- **Essay questions**: Your essay should have a clear structure. It should contain a brief introduction, a main section and a conclusion. Be concise. It is better to write a little about a lot of different points than a great deal about one or two points.

- If you **get completely stuck** with a question, leave space in your answer book and **return to it later.**

- Stick to the question and **tailor your answer** to what you are asked. Pay particular attention to the verbs in the question.

- If you do not understand what a question is asking, **state your assumptions**. Even if you do not answer in precisely the way the examiner hoped, you should be given some credit, if your assumptions are reasonable.

- You should do everything you can to make things easy for the marker. The marker will find it easier to identify the points you have made if your **answers are legible**.

- **Multiple-choice questions**: don't treat these as an easy option – you could lose marks by rushing into your answer. Read the questions carefully and work through any calculations required. If you don't know the answer, eliminate those options you know are incorrect and see if the answer becomes more obvious.

- **Objective test questions** might ask for numerical answers, but could also involve paragraphs of text which require you to fill in a number of missing blanks, or for you to write a definition of a word or phrase. Others may give a definition followed by a list of possible key words relating to that description. Whatever the format, these questions require that you have *learnt* definitions, *know* key words and their meanings and importance, and *understand* the names and meanings of rules, concepts and theories.

- **Computations**: It is essential to include all your workings in your answers. Many computational questions require the use of a standard format: company profit and loss account, balance sheet and cash flow statement for example. Be sure you know these formats thoroughly before the examination and use the layouts that you see in the answers given in this book and in model answers.

- **Case studies**: to write a good case study, first identify the area in which there is a problem, outline the main principles/theories you are going to use to answer the question, and then apply the principles/theories to the case.

- **Reports, memos and other documents**: some questions ask you to present your answer in the form of a report or a memo or other document. So use the correct format - there could be easy marks to gain here.

Computer-based examinations – tips

- Be sure you understand how to use the **software** before you start the exam. If in doubt, ask the assessment centre staff to explain it to you.

- Questions are **displayed on the screen** and answers are entered using keyboard and mouse. At the end of the examination, you are given a certificate showing the result you have achieved.

- In addition to the traditional multiple-choice question type, CBEs might also contain **other types of questions**, such as number entry questions, formula entry questions, and stem questions with multiple parts. There are also questions that carry several marks.

- You need to be sure you **know how to answer questions** of this type before you sit the exam, through practice.

- Do not attempt a CBE until you have **completed all study material** relating to it.

- **Do not skip any of the material** in the syllabus.

- **Read each question** *very* carefully.

- **Double-check your answer** before committing yourself to it.

- Answer *every* question – if you do not know an answer, you don't lose anything by guessing. Think carefully before you **guess**.

- If you are answering a multiple-choice question, eliminate first those answers that you know are wrong. Then choose the most appropriate answer from those that are left.

- Remember that **only one answer to a multiple-choice question can be right**. After you have eliminated the ones that you know to be wrong, if you are still unsure, guess. But only do so after you have double-checked that you have only eliminated answers that are *definitely* wrong.

- **Don't panic** if you realise you've answered a question incorrectly. Getting one question wrong will not mean the difference between passing and failing.

Section 1

OBJECTIVE TEST QUESTIONS

GENERAL FRAMEWORK, ACCOUNTING CONCEPTS AND PRINCIPLES

1   **The MAIN aim of accounting is to:**

    A   maintain ledger accounts for every asset and liability

    B   provide financial information to users of such information

    C   produce a trial balance

    D   record every financial transaction individually.

2   **If the owner of a business takes goods from stock for his own personal use, which of the following accounting concepts would be relevant to how the transaction is accounted for?**

    A   Prudence concept

    B   Capitalisation concept

    C   Accruals concept

    D   Separate entity concept

3   **The accounting concept which dictates that fixed assets should be valued at cost less accumulated depreciation, rather than at their enforced saleable value, is the:**

    A   Net realisable value concept

    B   Prudence concept

    C   Realisation concept

    D   Going concern concept.

4   **Stocks should be valued at the lower of cost and net realisable value. Which ONE of the following accounting concepts governs this?**

    A   Consistency concept

    B   Accruals concept

    C   Prudence concept

    D   Money measurement concept

5   The term 'capital maintenance' refers to:

A   the cost of maintaining fixed assets in good condition

B   the cost of replacing fixed assets

C   the raising of new capital by the issue of shares

D   retaining sufficient profits to ensure that closing net assets are at least equal in value to net assets at the beginning of the period.

6   The Accounting Standards Board's 'Statement of Principles for Financial Reporting' gives five qualitative characteristics which make financial information reliable.

These five characteristics are:

A   relevance, reliability, comparability, understandability, materiality

B   accruals basis, going concern concept, consistency, prudence, true and fair view

C   faithful representation, neutrality, substance over form, completeness, consistency

D   freedom from material error, prudence, faithful representation, neutrality, completeness.

7   Which of the following four statements about accounting concepts or principles are correct?

Statement 1   The money measurement concept is that items in accounts are initially measured at their historical cost.

Statement 2   Comparability usually implies consistency in accounting policies from one period to another.

Statement 3   Information in financial statements needs to be neutral.

Statement 4   Gains are increases in ownership interest resulting from contributions from owners.

A   Statements 1 and 3 only

B   Statements 2 and 4 only

C   Statements 2 and 3 only

D   Statement 3 only

8   Which one of the following statements most closely expresses the meaning of 'true and fair'?

A   There is only one true and fair view of a company's financial statements.

B   True and fair is determined by compliance with accounting standards.

C   True and fair is determined by compliance with company law.

D   True and fair is largely determined by reference to generally accepted accounting practice.

9   Listed below are some comments on accounting concepts.

(1)   Financial information should not be provided until it is reliable.

(2)   Materiality means that only items having a physical existence may be recognised as assets.

(3)   The substance over form convention means that the legal form of a transaction must always be shown in financial statements, even if this differs from the commercial effect.

Which, if any, of these comments is correct, according to the ASB's *Statement of Principles for Financial Reporting*?

A   1 only

B   2 only

C   3 only

D   None of them.

10   Which of the following explanations of the prudence concept most closely follows that in FRS 18 *Accounting Policies*?

A   The application of a degree of caution in exercising judgement under conditions of uncertainty.

B   Revenue and profits are not recognised until realised, and provision is made for all known liabilities.

C   All legislation and accounting standards have been complied with.

D   Understatement of assets or gains and overstatement of liabilities or losses.

11   Listed below are some characteristics of financial information.

(1)   Neutrality

(2)   Prudence

(3)   Completeness

(4)   Timeliness

Which of these characteristics contribute to reliability, according to the ASB's *Statement of Principles for Financial Reporting*?

A   (1), (2) and (3) only

B   (1), (2) and (4) only

C   (1), (3) and (4) only

D   (2), (3) and (4) only

12   Which of the following statements about accounting concepts are correct?

(1)   The money measurement concept is that only items capable of being measured in monetary terms can be recognised in financial statements.

(2)   The prudence concept means that understating of assets and overstating of liabilities is desirable in preparing financial statements.

(3)   The historical cost concept is that assets are initially recognised at their transaction cost.

(4)   The substance over form convention is that, whenever legally possible, the economic substance of a transaction should be reflected in financial statements rather than simply its legal form.

A   (1), (2) and (3)

B   (1), (2) and (4)

C   (1), (3) and (4)

D   (2), (3) and (4)

13   The historical cost convention:

A   fails to take account of changing price levels over time

B   records only past transactions

C   values all assets at their cost to the business, without any adjustment for depreciation

D   has been replaced in accounting records by a system of current cost accounting.

14   In times of rising prices, what effect does the use of the historical cost concept have on a company's asset values and profit?

A   Asset values and profit both understated.

B   Asset values and profit both overstated.

C   Asset values understated and profit overstated.

D   Asset values overstated and profit understated.

15   The accounting concept or convention which, in times of rising prices, tends to understate asset values and overstate profits, is the:

A   going concern concept

B   prudence concept

C   realisation concept

D   historical cost convention.

16   In times of rising prices, the historical cost convention has the effect of:

A   valuing all assets at their cost to the business

B   recording goods sold at their cost price, even if they are worth less than that cost

C   understating profits and overstating balance sheet asset values

D   overstating profits and understating balance sheet asset values.

17   An employee of Madd plc developed a new product that has just been patented. The development costs of this product were negligible, but the patent rights are almost certainly worth many millions of pounds.

Which accounting concept would prevent the company from recognising the value of this patent as a fixed asset in its balance sheet?

A   Going concern

B   Materiality

C   Money measurement

D   Prudence

18   The profit of a business may be calculated by using which one of the following formulae?

   A   Opening capital – drawings + capital introduced – closing capital

   B   Closing capital + drawings – capital introduced – opening capital

   C   Opening capital + drawings – capital introduced – closing capital

   D   Closing capital – drawings + capital introduced – opening capital

19   A company includes in the valuation of its closing stock some goods that were received before the year end, but for which invoices were not received until after the year end. This is in accordance with:

   A   the historical cost convention

   B   the accruals concept

   C   the consistency concept

   D   the materiality concept.

20   Why should financial statements be prepared on a consistent basis?

   A   To make it easier to compare results from one year to the next.

   B   To ensure that the capital of the business is maintained.

   C   To ensure that no material error occurs in the financial statements.

   D   To make the financial statements easier to understand.

21   In times of falling prices, the historical cost convention:

   A   understates asset values and profits

   B   understates asset values and overstates profits

   C   overstates asset values and profits

   D   overstates asset values and understates profits.

22   A retail business has the following two items of stock at its year end.

Item	Cost	Net realisable value
	£	£
X	800	750
Y	600	640

Applying the prudence concept, what should be the valuation of this stock in the balance sheet of the business?

£ [   ]

23   The closing stock at cost of a company at 31 January 20X3 amounted to £284,700.

The following items were included at cost in the total:

   (1)   400 coats, which had cost £80 each and normally sold for £150 each. Owing to a defect in manufacture, they were all sold after the balance sheet date at 50% of their normal price. Selling expenses amounted to 5% of the proceeds.

   (2)   800 skirts, which had cost £20 each. These too were found to be defective. Remedial work in February 20X3 cost £5 per skirt, and selling expenses for the batch totalled £800. They were sold for £28 each.

What should the stock value be according to SSAP 9 Stocks and Long-term Contracts after considering the above items?

A   £281,200

B   £282,800

C   £329,200

D   None of these.

DOUBLE-ENTRY BOOKKEEPING AND ACCOUNTING SYSTEMS

24   **A sales ledger control account had a closing balance of £8,500. It contained a contra to the purchase ledger of £400, but this had been entered on the wrong side of the sales ledger control account.**

The correct balance on the control account should be:

£

25   **In a sales ledger control account, which of the following lists consists ONLY of items that would be recorded on the credit side of the account?**

A   Cash received from customers, sales returns, bad debts written off, contras against amounts due to suppliers in the purchases ledger.

B   Sales, cash refunds to customers, bad debts written off, discounts allowed.

C   Cash received from customers, discounts allowed, interest charged on overdue accounts, bad debts written off.

D   Sales, cash refunds to customers, interest charged on overdue accounts, contras against amounts due to suppliers in the purchases ledger.

26   **Y purchased some machinery on 1 January 20X3 for £38,000. The payment for the machinery was correctly entered in the cash book but was entered on the debit side of machinery repairs account.**

Y charges depreciation on machinery on a straight line basis at 20% per year, with a proportionate charge in the year of acquisition and assuming no scrap value at the end of the life of the asset.

How will Y's profit for the year ended 31 March 20X3 be affected by the error?

A   Understated by £30,400

B   Understated by £36,100

C   Understated by £38,000

D   Overstated by £1,900

27   **The trial balance of Z failed to agree. Total debit balances were £836,200 and total credit balances were £819,700. A suspense account was opened for the amount of the difference and the following errors were found and corrected:**

1   The totals of the cash discount columns in the cash book had not been posted to the discount accounts. The figures were Discount Allowed £3,900 and Discount Received £5,100.

2   A cheque for £19,000 received from a customer was correctly entered in the cash book but was posted to the customer's account as £9,100.

What will the remaining balance on the suspense account be after the correction of these errors?

A   £25,300 credit

B   £7,700 credit

C   £27,700 debit

D   £5,400 credit

28   The trial balance of C Limited did not agree, and a suspense account was opened for the difference. Checking in the bookkeeping system revealed a number of errors:

Error

1   £4,600 paid for motor van repairs was correctly treated in the cash book but was credited to motor vehicles asset account.

2   £360 received from Brown, a customer, was credited in error to the account of Green.

3   £9,500 paid for rent was debited to the rent account as £5,900.

4   The total of the discount allowed column in the cash book had been debited in error to the discounts received account.

5   No entries had been made to record a cash sale of £100.

Which of the errors above would require an entry to the suspense account as part of the process of correcting them?

A   Errors 3 and 4 only

B   Errors 1 and 3 only

C   Errors 2 and 5 only

D   Errors 2 and 3 only

29   The following attempt at a bank reconciliation statement has been prepared by Q Limited:

	£
Overdraft per bank statement	38,600
Add: deposits not credited	41,200
	79,800
Less: outstanding cheques	3,300
Overdraft per cash book	£76,500

Assuming the bank statement balance of £38,600 to be correct, what should the cash book balance be?

A   £76,500 overdrawn, as stated

B   £5,900 overdrawn

C   £700 overdrawn

D   £5,900 cash at bank

30   **After checking a business cash book against the bank statement, which of the following items could require an entry in the cash book?**

1   Bank charges

2   A cheque from a customer which was dishonoured

3   Cheque not presented

4   Deposits not credited

5   Credit transfer entered in bank statement

6   Standing order entered in bank statement.

A   Items 1, 2, 5 and 6 only

B   Items 3 and 4 only

C   Items 1, 3, 4 and 6 only

D   Items 3, 4, 5 and 6 only

31   **Drive Limited gives a cash discount of £40 to a customer. The discount is credited to the discounts allowed account.**

The effect of recording the discount in this way is that profit will be:

A   correct

B   overstated by £80

C   understated by £80

D   understated by £40.

32   **A business compiling its accounts for the year to 31 January each year, pays rent quarterly in advance on 1 January, 1 April, 1 July and 1 October each year. After remaining unchanged for some years, the rent was increased from £24,000 per year to £30,000 per year as from 1 July 20X3.**

Which of the following figures is the rent expense which should appear in the profit and loss account for the year ended 31 January 20X4?

A   £27,500

B   £29,500

C   £28,000

D   £29,000

33   **A company pays rent quarterly in arrears on 1 January, 1 April, 1 July and 1 October each year. The rent was increased from £90,000 per year to £120,000 per year as from 1 October 20X2.**

What rent expense and accrual should be included in the company's financial statements for the year ended 31 January 20X3?

	Rent expense £	Accrual £
A	100,000	20,000
B	100,000	10,000
C	97,500	10,000
D	97,500	20,000

34 A company receives rent from a large number of properties. The total received in the year ended 31 October 20X2 was £481,200.

The following are the amounts of rent in advance and in arrears at 31 October 20X1 and 20X2:

	31 October 20X1 £	31 October 20X2 £
Rent received in advance	28,700	31,200
Rent in arrears (all subsequently received)	21,200	18,400

What amount of rental income should appear in the company's profit and loss account for the year ended 31 October 20X2?

A £486,500

B £460,900

C £501,500

D £475,900

35 A company receives rent for subletting part of its office block.

Rent, receivable quarterly in advance, is received as follows:

Date of receipt	Period covered	£
1 October 20X1	3 months to 31 December 20X1	7,500
30 December 20X1	31 March 20X2	7,500
4 April 20X2	30 June 20X2	9,000
1 July 20X2	30 September 20X2	9,000
1 October 20X2	31 December 20X2	9,000

What figures, based on these receipts, should appear in the company's financial statements for the year ended 30 November 20X2?

	Profit and loss account	Balance sheet
A	£34,000 Debit	Prepayment (Dr) £3,000
B	£34,500 Credit	Accrual (Cr) £6,000
C	£34,000 Credit	Accrual (Cr) £3,000
D	£34,000 Credit	Prepayment (Dr) £3,000

Data for questions 36 and 37

The cash book of Lofty Ladders shows an overdraft balance of £4,360 as at 31st December 20X3. On comparing a bank statement with the cash book, it is found that the following items have not been recorded in the cash book.

1 Bank charges of £120 and bank overdraft interest of £90

2 A credit transfer from a customer of £2,500

3 A direct debit payment to a supplier of £1,700.

It is also noticed that the following items have been recorded in the cash book but do not appear in the bank statement.

1 Cheques received from customers £3,600

2 Cheques drawn in favour of suppliers £4,200

36   **What figure will be shown in the balance sheet as at 31st December 20X3 for 'bank overdraft'?**

£ [   ]

37   **What figure will be shown in the bank statement for the overdraft balance?**

£ [   ]

38   **The trial balance totals of Gamma at 30 September 20X3 are:**

Debit   £992,640

Credit   £1,026,480

Which TWO of the following possible errors could, when corrected, cause the trial balance to agree?

Error

1   An item in the cash book £6,160 for payment of rent has not been entered in the rent payable account.

2   The balance on the motor expenses account £27,680 has incorrectly been listed in the trial balance as a credit.

3   £6,160 proceeds from the sale of a motor vehicle have been posted to the debit of motor vehicles asset account.

4   The balance of £21,520 on the rent receivable account has been omitted from the trial balance.

A   Errors 1 and 2

B   Errors 2 and 3

C   Errors 2 and 4

D   Errors 3 and 4

39   **The trial balance of Delta Limited did not agree, and a suspense account was opened for the difference. The following errors were subsequently found:**

Error

1   A cash refund due to customer A was correctly treated in the cash book and then credited to the sales ledger account of customer B.

2   The sale of goods to a director for £300 was recorded by debiting sales revenue account and crediting the director's current account.

3   The total of the discount received column in the cash book had been credited in error to the discount allowed account.

4   Some of the cash received from customers had been used to pay sundry expenses before banking the money.

5   £5,800 paid for plant repairs was correctly treated in the cash book and then credited to plant and equipment asset account.

Which of the above errors would require an entry to the suspense account as part of the process of correcting them?

A   Errors 1, 3 and 5 only

B   Errors 1, 2 and 5 only

C   Errors 1 and 5 only

D   Errors 3 and 4 only

40 **Which of the following best explains the imprest system of petty cash control?**

    A   Weekly expenditure cannot exceed a set amount.

    B   The exact amount of expenditure is reimbursed at intervals to maintain a fixed float.

    C   All expenditure out of the petty cash must be properly authorised.

    D   Regular equal amounts of cash are transferred into petty cash at intervals.

41 **In reconciling a business cash book with the bank statement, which of the following items could require a subsequent entry in the cash book?**

Error

1   Cheques presented after the date of the bank statement
2   A cheque from a customer that has been dishonoured
3   An error by the bank
4   Bank charges
5   Deposits credited after the date of the bank statement
6   Standing order payment entered in the bank statement

    A   Items 2, 3, 4 and 6 only

    B   Items 1, 2, 5 and 6 only

    C   Items 2, 4 and 6 only

    D   Items 1, 3 and 5 only

42 **The following bank reconciliation statement has been prepared by a trainee accountant:**

Bank reconciliation 30 September 20X2

	£
Balance per bank statement (overdrawn)	36,840
add: Lodgements credited after date	51,240
	88,080
less: Outstanding cheques	43,620
Balance per cash book (credit)	44,460

Assuming the amounts stated for items other than the cash book balance are correct, what should the cash book balance be?

    A   £44,460 credit as stated

    B   £60,020 credit

    C   £29,220 debit

    D   £29,220 credit

43 **Listed below are some possible causes of difference between the cash book balance and the bank statement balance when preparing a bank reconciliation:**

    (1)   Cheque paid in, subsequently dishonoured

    (2)   Error by bank

    (3)   Bank charges

    (4)   Lodgements credited after date

    (5)   Outstanding cheques not yet presented.

Which of these items require an entry in the cash book?

A   (1) and (3) only

B   (1), (2), (3), (4) and (5)

C   (2), (4), and (5) only

D   (1), (2) and (3) only

44   **The following bank reconciliation statement has been prepared for Omega by a junior clerk:**

	£
Overdraft per bank statement	68,100
Add: Deposits not credited	141,200
	209,300
Less: outstanding cheques	41,800
Overdraft per cash book	167,500

Which of the following should be the correct balance per the cash book?

A   £31,300 cash at bank

B   £31,300 overdrawn

C   £114,900 overdrawn

D   £167,500 overdrawn, as stated

45   **Which ONE of the following is a book of prime entry AND part of the double-entry system?**

A   The journal

B   The petty cash book

C   The sales day book

D   The purchase ledger

46   **The sales day book of Darenth has been overcast by £800 and the purchase day book has been undercast by £1,100. Darenth maintains purchase and sales ledger control accounts as part of the double entry bookkeeping system.**

The effect of correcting these errors will be to make adjustments to the:

A   control accounts, with no effect on profit

B   control accounts, with a decrease in profit of £1,900

C   ledger balances of the individual debtors and creditors, with no effect on profit

D   ledger balances of the individual debtors and creditors, with a decrease in profit of £1,900.

47   **You are provided with the following information relating to a business:**

	£000
Creditors opening balance	540
Cash paid to creditors	1,470
Cash purchases	57
Credit purchases	1,590
Credit notes received from creditors	33
Discounts received from creditors	24

The creditors closing balance is:

£ _____

48 **Alpha received a statement of account from a supplier Beta, showing a balance to be paid of £8,950. Alpha's purchases ledger account for Beta shows a balance due to Beta of £4,140.**

Investigation reveals the following:

(1)   Cash paid to Beta £4,080 has not been allowed for by Beta.

(2)   Alpha's ledger account has not been adjusted for £40 of cash discount disallowed by Beta.

(3)   Goods returned by Alpha £380 have not been recorded by Beta.

What discrepancy remains between Alpha's and Beta's records after allowing for these items?

A   £9,310

B   £390

C   £310

D   £1,070

49 **Which of the following items could appear on the credit side of a sales ledger control account?**

(1)   Cash received from customers

(2)   Bad debts written off

(3)   Increase in provision for doubtful debts

(4)   Discounts allowed

(5)   Sales

(6)   Credits for goods returned by customers

(7)   Cash refunds to customers.

A   (1), (2), (4) and (6)

B   (1), (2), (4) and (7)

C   (3), (4), (5) and (6)

D   (5) and (7)

50 **A summary of the transactions of Ramsgate, who is registered for VAT at 17.5%, shows the following for the month of August 20X9.**

Outputs   £60,000 (exclusive of VAT)

Inputs   £40,286 (inclusive of VAT)

At the beginning of the period Ramsgate owed £3,400 to Customs & Excise, and during the period he has paid £2,600 to them.

At the end of the period the amount owing to Customs & Excise is:

A   £3,700

B   £3,930

C   £4,400

D   £5,300.

51 A trader who is not registered for VAT purposes buys goods on credit. These goods have a list price of £2,000 and the trader is given a trade discount of 20%. The goods carry VAT at 17.5%.

The correct ledger entries to record this purchase are to debit the Purchases account and to credit the Supplier's account with:

A   £1,600

B   £1,880

C   £2,000

D   £2,350.

52 Headington is owed £37,500 by its debtors at the start, and £39,000 at the end, of its year ended 31 December 20X8.

During the period, cash sales of £263,500 and credit sales of £357,500 were made, discounts allowed amounting to £15,750 and discounts received £21,400. Bad debts of £10,500 were written off and Headington wishes to retain its provision for bad debts at 5% of total debtors.

The cash received in the year totalled:

A   £329,750

B   £593,175

C   £593,250

D   £614,650.

53 The purchase day book of Arbroath has been undercast by £500, and the sales day book has been overcast by £700. Arbroath maintains purchase and sales ledger control accounts as part of the double entry bookkeeping system.

The effect of correcting these errors will be to:

A   make adjustments to the ledger balances of the individual debtors and creditors, with no effect on profit

B   make adjustments to the ledger balances of the individual debtors and creditors, with a decrease in profit of £1,200

C   make adjustments to the control accounts, with no effect on profit

D   make adjustments to the control accounts, with a decrease in profit of £1,200.

54 Stranraer Ltd provides you with the following details relating to wages paid:

Gross wages	£157,326
Employer's NI	£33,247
PAYE and NI deducted	£44,174

At the beginning of the year Stranraer Ltd owed £7,308 to the Inland Revenue.

The total charge for wages for the year will be:

A   £183,265

B   £190,573

C   £197,881

D   £234,747.

55 **A summary of the transactions of Witney plc, which is registered for VAT at 17.5%, shows the following for the month of November 20X4:**

Output   £122,610 (inclusive of VAT)

Inputs   £78,857 (exclusive of VAT)

At the beginning of the month Witney owed £7,200 to Customs and Excise and during November paid £6,800 to them. At 30 November 20X4 the amount owing to Customs and Excise is:

A   £4,461

B   £4,861

C   £9,000

D   £9,400.

56 **You are given the following figures relating to the purchases and trade creditors of a business:**

	£
Creditors at 1 November 20X6	76,104
Creditors at 31 October 20X7	80,643
Purchases	286,932
Cash paid to suppliers	271,845
Discounts received	5,698
Debit balances transferred to debtors ledger	107
Credit balances offset against debtors ledger debit balances	866
Sundry minor credit balances written off	82

The amount of purchases returned to suppliers during the year ending 31 October 20X7 was:

£ [ ]

57 **In reconciling the debtors ledger control account with the list of debtor ledger balances of Snooks Ltd, the following errors were found:**

1   The sales day book had been overcast by £370.

2   A total of £940 from the cash receipts book had been recorded in the debtors ledger control account as £490.

What adjustments must be made to correct the errors?

A   Credit debtors' control account £820. Decrease total of sales ledger balances by £820.

B   Credit debtors' control account £820. No change in total of sales ledger balances.

C   Debit debtors' control account £80. No change in total of sales ledger balances.

D   Debit debtors' control account £80. Increase total of sales ledger balances by £80.

58 **For the month of November 20X0 Figgins Ltd's purchases totalled £225,600 with VAT of £33,840. The total of £259,440 has been credited to the creditors' ledger control account as £254,940.**

Which of the following adjustments is correct?

	Control account	*List of creditors' balances*
A	£4,500 Cr	No adjustment
B	£4,500 Cr	Increase by £4,500
C	£29,340 Dr	No effect
D	£33,840 Dr	Increase by £4,500

59   **A supplier sends you a statement showing a balance outstanding of £14,350. Your own records show a balance outstanding of £14,500.**

The reason for this difference could be that:

A   the supplier sent an invoice for £150 which you have not yet received

B   the supplier has allowed you £150 cash discount which you had omitted to enter in your ledgers

C   you have paid the supplier £150 which he has not yet accounted for

D   you have returned goods worth £150 which the supplier has not yet accounted for.

60   **A trial balance includes a suspense account. Opening stock of £31,763 had been entered on the credit side of the trial balance as £31,673. The trial balance itself had been undercast on the debit side by £90.**

What net entry will be made in the suspense account to correct these errors?

A   £63,436 Dr

B   £63,436 Cr

C   £63,526 Dr

D   £63,526 Cr

61   **A suspense account was opened when a trial balance failed to agree. The following errors were later discovered:**

Error

1   A gas bill of £420 had been recorded in the Gas account as £240.

2   Discount of £50 given to a customer had been credited to Discounts Received.

3   Interest received of £70 had been entered in the bank account only.

The original balance on the suspense account was:

A   debit £210

B   credit £210

C   debit £160

D   credit £160.

62   **A trial balance has been extracted and a suspense account opened. One error relates to the misposting of an amount of £200, being discounts received from suppliers, to the wrong side of the discounts account.**

What will be the correcting journal entry?

A   Dr Discounts account £200, Cr Suspense account £200

B   Dr Suspense account £200, Cr Discounts account £200

C   Dr Discounts account £400, Cr Suspense account £400

D   Dr Suspense account £400, Cr Discounts account £400

63   **Which of the following will not cause an entry to be made in a suspense account?**

A   Drawings shown on the credit side of the trial balance

B   Discounts allowed shown on the debit side of the trial balance

C   Omission of a bad debt written off from the trial balance

D   The entry of cash in hand (£1,680) on the trial balance as £1,860

64 On extracting a trial balance a suspense account is opened with a credit balance on it. You discover that this is caused by a single error in the nominal ledger. Which of the following could therefore have caused the imbalance?

   A   The PAYE and National Insurance deductions for the current month have been entered twice in the deductions control account

   B   A debtors' ledger/creditors' ledger contra has been entered on the credit side of both control accounts

   C   The opening accrual for telephone charges has been brought forward at the beginning of the year on the wrong side of the ledger account

   D   The figure of closing stock has been entered on both sides of the trial balance

65 The book-keeper of High Hurdles was instructed to make a contra entry for £270 between the supplier account and the customer for Greyfold Limited. He recorded the transaction by debiting the customer account and crediting the supplier account with £270. The business accounts do not include control accounts.

   Which of the following statements is correct?

   A   Unless the error is corrected, profit will be over-stated by £540.

   B   Unless the error is corrected, net assets will be over-stated by £270.

   C   Unless the error is corrected, net assets will be over-stated by £540.

   D   The errors should be corrected, but neither the profit nor the net assets are over-stated.

66 Jones, a sole trader, has extracted a trial balance and needed to insert a suspense account to make it balance. He has discovered the following errors:

   Error

   1   Opening stock of £1,475 has been listed in the trial balance as a credit balance of £1,745.

   2   The sales for November (£5,390 inclusive of VAT) had been correctly entered in the control account and the sales account but no entry had been made in the VAT account. The amount entered in the sales account was £4,600.

   3   The opening accrual for telephone charges of £190 had been brought forward on the wrong side of the telephone expense account.

   What was the suspense account balance that Jones inserted into the trial balance?

   A   £2,050 Dr

   B   £2,050 Cr

   C   £2,840 Dr

   D   £2,840 Cr

67 An accountant is attempting to resolve a suspense account difference. One of the errors relates to the misposting of an amount of £3,079 of VAT on purchases to the wrong side of the VAT account.

   What will be the correcting entry?

   A   Debit VAT account £6,158, Credit Suspense account £6,158

   B   Debit Suspense account £6,158, Credit VAT account £6,158

   C   Debit VAT account £3,079, Credit Suspense account £3,079

   D   Debit Suspense account £3,079, Credit VAT account £3,079

68   **Net profit was calculated as being £10,200. It was later discovered that capital expenditure of £3,000 had been treated as revenue expenditure, and revenue receipts of £1,400 had been treated as capital receipts.**

The correct net profit should have been (ignoring depreciation):

£ [   ]

69   **A suspense account shows a credit balance of £130.**

This could be due to:

A   omitting a sale of £130 from the sales ledger

B   recording a purchase of £130 twice in the purchases account

C   failing to write off a bad debt of £130

D   recording an electricity bill paid of £65 by debiting the bank account and crediting the electricity account.

70   **The sales account is:**

A   credited with the total of sales made, including VAT

B   credited with the total of sales made, excluding VAT

C   debited with the total of sales made, including VAT

D   debited with the total of sales made, excluding VAT.

71   **Which of the following items appear on the same side of the trial balance?**

A   Drawings and accruals

B   Carriage outwards and prepayments

C   Carriage inwards and rental income

D   Opening stock and purchase returns

72   **A credit balance on a ledger account indicates:**

A   an asset or an expense

B   a liability or and expense

C   an amount owing to the organisation

D   a liability or a revenue.

73   **An inexperienced bookkeeper has drawn up the following sales ledger control account:**

Sales Ledger Control Account

	£		£
Opening balance	180,000	Credit sales	190,000
Cash from credit customers	228,000		
Sales returns	8,000	Bad debts written off	1,500
Cash refunds to credit customers	3,300	Contras against purchases	
Discount allowed	4,200	ledger amounts payable	2,400
		Closing balance (balancing figure)	229,600
	423,500		423,500

What should the closing balance be after correcting the errors made in preparing the account?

A   £130,600

B   £129,200

C   £142,400

D   £214,600

74   An error of principle would occur if:

A   plant and machinery purchased was credited to a Fixed Assets account

B   plant and machinery purchased was debited to the Purchases account

C   plant and machinery purchased was debited to the Equipment account

D   plant and machinery purchased was debited to the correct account but with the wrong amount.

75   Recording the purchase of computer stationery by debiting the Computer Equipment account at cost would result in:

A   an overstatement of profit and an overstatement of fixed assets

B   an understatement of profit and an overstatement of fixed assets

C   an overstatement of profit and an understatement of fixed assets

D   an understatement of profit and an understatement of fixed assets.

76   An organisation restores its petty cash balance to £500 at the end of each month. During January, the total column in the petty cash book was recorded as being £420, and hence the imprest was restored by this amount. The analysis columns, which had been posted to the nominal ledger, totalled only £400. This error would result in:

A   no imbalance in the trial balance

B   the trial balance being £20 higher on the debit side

C   the trial balance being £20 higher on the credit side

D   the petty cash balance being £20 lower than it should be.

77   The debit side of a trial balance totals £50 more than the credit side. This could be due to:

A   a purchase of goods for £50 being omitted from the creditors account

B   a sale of goods for £50 being omitted from the debtor's account

C   an invoice of £25 for electricity being credited to the electricity account

D   a receipt for £50 from a debtor being omitted from the cash book.

The following information is relevant for questions 78 and 79.

When Q's trial balance failed to agree, a suspense account was opened for the difference. The trial balance totals were:

Debit   £864,390
Credit   £860,930

The company does not have control accounts for its sales and purchases ledgers.

The following errors were found:

(1)   In recording an issue of shares at par, cash received of £333,000 was credited to the ordinary share capital account as £330,000.

(2)   Cash £2,800 paid for plant repairs was correctly accounted for in the cash book, but was credited to the plant and asset account.

(3)   The petty cash book balance £500 had been omitted from the trial balance.

(4)   A cheque for £78,400 paid for the purchase of a motor car was debited to the motor vehicles account as £87,400.

(5)   A contra between the sales ledger and the purchases ledger for £1,200 which should have been credited in the sales ledger and debited in the purchases ledger was actually debited in the sales ledger and credited in the purchases ledger.

78   **Which of these errors will require an entry to the suspense account to correct them?**

   A   All five items

   B   3 and 5 only

   C   2, 4 and 5 only

   D   1 2, 3 and 4 only

79   **What will the balance on the suspense account be after making the necessary entries to correct the errors affecting the suspense account?**

   A   £2,440 Debit

   B   £15,560 Credit

   C   £13,640 Debit

   D   £3,440 Debit

80   **The debit side of a trial balance totals £800 more than the credit side.**

   Which one of the following errors would fully account for the difference?

   A   £400 paid for plant maintenance has been correctly entered in the cash book and credited to the plant asset account.

   B   Discount received £400 has been debited to discount allowed account.

   C   A receipt of £800 for commission receivable has been omitted from the records.

   D   The petty cash balance of £800 has been omitted from the trial balance.

81   **The sales ledger control account at 1 May had balances of £32,750 debit and £1,275 credit. During May, sales of £125,000 were made on credit. Receipts from debtors amounted to £122,500 and cash discounts of £550 were allowed. Refunds of £1,300 were made to customers.**

   The closing balances at 31 May could be:

   A   £35,125 debit and £3,000 credit

   B   £35,675 debit and £2,500 credit

   C   £36,725 debit and £2,000 credit

   D   £36,725 debit and £1,000 credit.

82   If Sales (including VAT) amounted to £27,612.50, and Purchases (excluding VAT) amounted to £18,000, the balance on the VAT account, assuming all items are subject to VAT at 17.5%, would be:

   A   £962.50 debit

   B   £962.50 credit

   C   £1,682.10 debit

   D   £1,682.10 credit.

83   Andrea started a taxi business by transferring her car, worth £5,000, into the business. What are the accounting entries required to record this?

   A   Dr Capital £5,000, Cr Car £5,000

   B   Dr Car £5,000, Cr Drawings £5,000

   C   Dr Car £5,000, Cr Capital £5,000

   D   Dr Car £5,000, Credit Bank £5,000

84   A business sold goods that had a net value of £600 to Lucid plc. What entries are required to record this transaction if VAT is payable at 17.5%?

   A   Dr Lucid plc £600, Dr VAT £105, Cr Sales £705

   B   Dr Lucid plc £705, Cr VAT £105, Cr Sales £600

   C   Dr Lucid plc £600, Cr VAT £105, Cr Sales £600

   D   Dr Sales £600, Dr VAT £105, Cr Lucid plc £705

85   Laker Ltd returned goods that had a net value of £200. What entries are required to record this transaction if VAT is payable at 17.5%?

   A   Dr Returns inward £200, Dr VAT £35, Cr Laker Ltd £235

   B   Dr Returns inward £235, Cr VAT £35, Cr Laker Ltd £200

   C   Dr Purchases £200, Dr VAT £35, Cr Laker Ltd £235

   D   Dr Laker Ltd £235, Cr Returns inward £200, Cr VAT £35

86   How is closing stock recorded in the bookkeeping records?

   A   By a debit to stock and a credit to profit and loss

   B   By a debit to profit and loss and a credit to stock

   C   By a debit to stock and a credit to purchases

   D   By writing the figure in a note beneath the trial balance

87   Which of the following best describes the entries that are made using the sales day book totals at the end of each month?

   A   Debit sales with total net sales, credit sales ledger control with total gross sales and credit VAT with total VAT

   B   Debit sales with total gross sales, credit sales ledger control with total net sales and credit VAT with total VAT

   C   Debit sales ledger control with total net sales, debit VAT with total VAT and credit sales with total gross sales

   D   Debit sales ledger control with total gross sales, credit sales with total net sales and credit VAT with total VAT

88   Which of the following would NOT lead to a difference between the total of the balances on the sales ledger and the balance on the sales ledger control account?

   A   An error in totalling the sales day book

   B   An error in totalling the receipts column of the cash book

   C   An overstatement of an entry in a debtor's account

   D   An entry posted to the wrong debtor's account

89   Anthony receives goods from Brad on credit terms and Anthony subsequently pays by cheque. Anthony then discovers that the goods are faulty and cancels the cheque before it is cashed by Brad.

   How should Anthony record the cancellation of the cheque in his books?

   A   Debit creditors   Credit returns outwards

   B   Credit bank   Debit creditors

   C   Debit bank   Credit creditors

   D   Credit creditors   Debit returns outwards

90   On 1 May 20X3, Blister Ltd pays a rent bill of £1,800 for the period to 30 April 20X4. What are the charge to the profit and loss account and the entry in the balance sheet for the year ended 30 November 20X3?

   A   £1,050 charge to profit and loss account and prepayment of £750 in the balance sheet.

   B   £1,050 charge to profit and loss account and accrual of £750 in the balance sheet.

   C   £1,800 charge to profit and loss account and no entry in the balance sheet.

   D   £750 charge to profit and loss account and prepayment of £1,050 in the balance sheet.

91   A bank statement for Gorgon Trading shows a balance of £825 overdrawn. The bank statement includes bank charges of £50, which have not been entered in the cash book.

   There are unpresented cheques totalling £475 and deposits not yet credited of £800. The bank statement incorrectly shows a direct debit payment of £160, which belongs to another customer.

   The figure for the bank balance in the balance sheet should be overdrawn by:

   £ _____

92   Vase Ltd operates an imprest system for petty cash. At 1 September there was a float of £150, but it was decided to increase this to £200 from 1 October onwards. During September, the petty cashier received £25 from staff for using the photocopier and a cheque for £90 was cashed for an employee. In September, cheques were drawn for £500 for petty cash.

   How much cash was paid out as cash expenses by the petty cashier in September?

   A   £385

   B   £435

   C   £515

   D   £615

---

93   **A fixed asset register is:**

A   an alternative name for the fixed asset ledger account

B   a list of the physical fixed assets rather than their financial cost

C   a schedule of planned maintenance of fixed assets for use by the plant engineer

D   a schedule of the cost and other information about each individual fixed asset.

94   **At 30 June 20X3, an electricity expenses ledger account had an accrual of £300 and a credit balance was brought down at 1 July 20X3. During the financial year, electricity invoices totalling £4,000 were paid, including an invoice for £600 for the quarter ended 31 May 20X4.**

What is the profit and loss account charge for electricity payable for the year ended 30 June 20X4?

£ [   ]

95   **On 1 June, 20X2, H paid an insurance invoice of £2,400 for the year to 31 May 20X3. What is the charge to the profit and loss account and the entry in the balance sheet for the year ended 31 December 20X2?**

A   £1,000 profit and loss account and prepayment of £1,400

B   £1,400 profit and loss account and accrual of £1,000

C   £1,400 profit and loss account and prepayment of £1,000

D   £2,400 profit and loss account and no entry in the balance sheet.

96   **A Ltd's trial balance does not balance. Which ONE of the following errors may be the cause of this failure to balance?**

A   The purchase of a machine had been debited to the machine repairs account.

B   A cheque from a customer had been credited to the purchase ledger account of the customer.

C   Goods returned inwards had been debited to the sales ledger account of the customer.

D   The depreciation charge on machinery had been credited to the cost of machinery account.

97   **Which ONE of the following might explain a debit balance on a purchase ledger account?**

A   The company took a cash discount to which it was not entitled and paid less than the amount due.

B   The company mistakenly paid too much.

C   The book-keeper failed to enter a contra with the sales ledger.

D   The book-keeper failed to post a cheque paid to the account.

98   **The following information relates to a bank reconciliation.**

1   The bank balance in the cash book before taking the items below into account was £8,970 overdrawn.

2   Bank charges of £550 on the bank statement have not been entered in the cash book.

3   The bank has credited the account in error with £425 which belongs to another customer.

4   Cheque payments totalling £3,275 have been entered in the cash book but have not been presented for payment.

5   Cheques totalling £5,380 have been correctly entered on the debit side of the cash book but have not been paid in at the bank.

What was the balance as shown by the bank statement?

A   £8,970 overdrawn.

B   £11,200 overdrawn.

C   £12,050 overdrawn.

D   £17,750 overdrawn.

99   Stop plc's trial balance did not balance at 30 June 20X3. The following errors were discovered:

1   Insurance of £500 prepaid at 30 June 20X3 had not been brought down as an opening balance on the insurance account.

2   Wages of £5,000 had been incorrectly debited to the purchases account.

3   The book-keeper had failed to accrue £300 for the telephone invoice owing at 30 June 20X3.

What was the difference on the trial balance?

A   £500

B   £800

C   £5,500

D   £5,800

100   What is an audit trail in a computerised accounting system?

A   A list of all the transactions in a period.

B   A list of all the transactions in a ledger account in a period.

C   A list of all the items checked by the auditor.

D   A list of all the nominal ledger codes.

101   At 31 March 20X2 a company had oil in hand to be used for heating costing £8,200 and an unpaid heating oil bill for £3,600.

At 31 March 20X3 heating oil in hand was £9,300 and there was an outstanding heating oil bill of £3,200.

Payments made for heating oil during the year ended 31 March 20X3 totalled £34,600.

Based on these figures, what amount should be included in the company's profit and loss account for heating oil for the year?

A   £23,900

B   £36,100

C   £45,300

D   £33,100

102 The electricity expenses account for the year ended 30 June 20X3 was as follows:

	£
Opening balance for electricity accrued at 1 July 20X2	300
Payments made during the year:	
1 August 20X2 for three months to 31 July 20X2	600
1 November 20X2 for three months to 31 October 20X2	720
1 February 20X3 for three months to 31 January 20X3	900
30 June 20X3 for three months to 30 April 20X3	840

Which of the following is the appropriate entry for electricity?

	Accrued at June 20X3	*Charged to profit and loss account year ended 30 June 20X3*
A	£Nil	£3,060
B	£460	£3,320
C	£560	£3,320
D	£560	£3,420

103 The year end of Mud plc is 30 November 20X4. The company pays for its gas by a standing order of £600 per month. On 1 December 20X3, the statement from the gas supplier showed that Mud plc had overpaid by £200.

Mud plc received gas bills for the four quarters commencing on 1 December 20X3 and ending on 30 November 20X4 for £1,300, £1,400, £2,100 and £2,000 respectively.

Which of the following is the correct charge for gas in Mud plc's profit and loss account for the year ended 30 November 20X4?

A £6,800

B £7,000

C £7,200

D £7,400

104 A company has been notified that a debtor has been declared bankrupt. The company had previously provided for this doubtful debt. Which of the following is the correct double entry?

	Debit	*Credit*
A	Bad and doubtful debts account	The debtor
B	The debtor	Bad and doubtful debts account
C	Provision for doubtful debts	The debtor
D	The debtor	Provision for doubtful debts

105 A business has opening stock of £12,000 and closing stock of £18,000. Purchase returns were £5,000. The cost of goods sold was £111,000.

Purchases were:

£	

106   A business had a balance at the bank of £2,500 at the start of the month. During the following month, it paid for materials invoiced at £1,000 less trade discount of 20% and cash discount of 10% of the invoice amount.

It received a cheque from a debtor in respect of an invoice for £200, subject to cash discount of 5%.

The balance at the bank at the end of the month was:

£

107   After calculating your company's profit for 20X3, you discover that:

1   A fixed asset costing £50,000 has been included in the purchases account.

2   Stationery costing £10,000 has been included as closing stock of raw materials, instead of as stock of stationery.

These two errors have had the effect of:

A   understating gross profit by £40,000 and understating net profit by £50,000

B   understating both gross profit and net profit by £40,000

C   understating gross profit by £60,000 and understating net profit by £50,000

D   overstating both gross profit and net profit by £60,000.

108   A business commenced with capital in cash of £1,000. Stock costing £800 is purchased on credit, and half is sold for £1,000 plus VAT at 17.5%, the customer paying in cash at once.

The accounting equation after these transactions would show:

A   Assets £1,775 less Liabilities £175 equals Capital £1,600

B   Assets £2,175 less Liabilities £975 equals Capital £1,200

C   Assets £2,575 less Liabilities £800 equals Capital £1,775

D   Assets £2,575 less Liabilities £975 equals Capital £1,600.

109   A sole trader had opening capital of £10,000 and closing capital of £4,500. During the period, the owner introduced capital of £4,000 and withdrew £8,000 for her own use.

Her profit or loss during the period was:

A   £9,500 loss

B   £1,500 loss

C   £7,500 profit

D   £17,500 profit.

110   Diesel fuel in stock at 1 November 20X7 was £12,500 and there were invoices awaited for £1,700. During the year to 31 October 20X8, diesel fuel bills of £85,400 were paid, and a delivery worth £1,300 had yet to be invoiced.

At 31 October 20X8, the stock of diesel fuel was valued at £9,800. The diesel fuel to be charged to the profit and loss account for the year to 31 October 20X8 is:

A   £85,100

B   £87,700

C   £88,500

D   £91,100.

111 In preparing a company's bank reconciliation statement at March 20X3, the following items are causing the difference between the cash book balance and the bank statement balance:

(1) Bank charges £380

(2) Error by bank £1,000 (cheque incorrectly debited to the account)

(3) Lodgements not credited £4,580

(4) Outstanding cheques £1,475

(5) Direct debit £350

(6) Cheque paid in by the company and dishonoured £400

Which of these items will require an entry in the cash book?

A   2, 4 and 6

B   1, 5 and 6

C   3 and 4

D   3 and 5

112 The bank statement at 31 October 20X7 showed an overdraft of £800. On reconciling the bank statement, it was discovered that a cheque drawn by your company for £80 had not been presented for payment, and that a cheque for £130 from a customer had been dishonoured on 30 October 20X7, but that this had not yet been notified to you by the bank.

The correct bank balance to be shown in the balance sheet at 31 October 20X7 is a bank overdraft of:

£ _____

113 At 1 September, the motor expenses account showed four months' insurance prepaid of £96, and there is an unpaid petrol bill of £186. During September, the outstanding petrol bill is paid, plus further bills of £245. At 30 September there is a further outstanding petrol bill of £120, and there is a prepayment of £72 for car insurance.

The amount to be shown in the profit and loss account for motor expenses for September is:

£ _____

114 Your purchase ledger control account has a balance at 1 October 20X8 of £34,500 credit.

During October, credit purchases were £78,400, cash purchases were £2,400 and payments made to suppliers, excluding cash purchases, and after deducting cash discounts of £1,200, were £68,900. Purchase returns were £4,700.

The closing balance was:

A   £38,100

B   £40,500

C   £47,500

D   £49,900.

115 Your firm's bank statement at 31 October 20X8 shows a balance of £13,400. You subsequently discover that the bank has dishonoured a customer's cheque for £300 and has charged bank charges of £50, neither of which is recorded in your cash book.

There are unpresented cheques totalling £1,400. You further discover that an automatic receipt from a customer of £195 has been recorded as a credit in your cash book.

Your cash book balance, prior to correcting the errors and omissions, was:

A   £11,455

B   £11,960

C   £12,000

D   £12,155.

116   The petty cash imprest is restored to £100 at the end of each week. The following amounts are paid out of petty cash during week 23:

Stationery including VAT at 17.5%	£14.10
Travelling costs	£25.50
Office refreshments	£12.90
Sundry creditors	£24.00 plus VAT at 17.5%

The amount required to restore the imprest to £100 is:

A   £19.30

B   £25.60

C   £74.40

D   £80.70.

117   It is important to produce a trial balance prior to preparing the final accounts because:

A   it confirms the accuracy of the ledger accounts

B   it provides all the figures necessary to prepare the final accounts

C   it shows that the ledger accounts contain debit and credit entries of an equal value

D   it enables the accountant to calculate any adjustments required.

118   A computerised accounts package would be MOST useful in maintaining:

A   the ledger accounts

B   the books of prime entry

C   a register of fixed assets

D   the stock records.

119   The following sales ledger control account contains some inaccurate entries.

Sales ledger control account

	£		£
Opening debtors	14,500	Credit sales	53,500
Discounts allowed	350	Returns	1,400
Receipts from debtors	51,200	Contra to purchase ledger	50

The correct closing debtors figure should be:

£ _____

120   A sales ledger control account showed a debit balance of £37,642. The individual debtors' accounts in the sales ledger showed a total of £35,840. The difference could be due to:

A   undercasting the sales day book by £1,802

B   overcasting the sales returns day book by £1,802

C   entering a cash receipt of £1,802 on the debit side of a debtor's account

D   entering cash discount allowed of £901 on the debit side of the control account.

121 **A company's telephone bill consists of two elements. One is a quarterly rental charge, payable in advance; the other is a quarterly charge for calls made, payable in arrears.**

At 1 April 20X9, the previous bill dated 1 March 20X9 had included line rental of £90. Estimated call charges during March 20X9 were £80.

During the following 12 months, bills totalling £2,145 were received on 1 June, 1 September, 1 December and 1 March 20Y0, each containing rental of £90 as well as call charges. Estimated call charges during March 20Y0 were £120.

The amount to be charged to the profit and loss account for the year ended 31 March 20Y0 in respect of telephone costs is:

£ _____

122 **In the quarter ended 31 March 2002, C Ltd had VAT taxable outputs, net of VAT, of £90,000 and taxable inputs, net of VAT, of £72,000.**

If the rate of VAT is 10%, how much VAT is due?

A   £1,800 receivable

B   £2,000 receivable

C   £1,800 payable

D   £2,000 payable

123 **Which of the following are used in a coding system for accounting transactions?**

A   Department code

B   Nominal ledger code

C   Product code

D   All of the above

124 **At 31 March 20X3, accrued rent payable was £300. During the year ended 31 March 20X4, rent paid was £4,000, including an invoice for £1,200 for the quarter ended 30 April 20X4.**

What is the profit and loss account charge for rent payable for the year ended 31 March 20X4?

A   £3,300

B   £3,900

C   £4,100

D   £4,700

125 **The annual insurance premium for S Ltd for the period 1 July 20X3 to 30 June 20X4 is £13,200, which is 10% more than the previous year. Insurance premiums are paid on 1 July.**

What is the profit and loss account charge for insurance for the year ended 31 December 20X3?

A   £11,800

B   £12,540

C   £12,600

D   £13,200

126 **A bank reconciliation showed the following differences between the bank statement and the cash book:**

Unpresented cheque of	£750
Outstanding deposits of	£500
Bank charges of	£100

If the balance on the bank statement is £1,000 overdrawn, what is the balance in the cash book before any adjustments?

A   Debit £250

B   Credit £1,150

C   Credit £1,250

D   Credit £1,500

127 **The entries in a sales ledger control account are:**

Sales	£250,000
Bank	£225,000
Returns	£2,500
Bad debts	£3,000
Returned unpaid cheque	£3,500
Contra purchase ledger account	£4,000

What is the balance on the sales ledger control account?

A   £12,000

B   £19,000

C   £25,000

D   £27,000

ACCOUNTING TREATMENTS

128 **At the end of its financial year, a company has the following fixed assets:**

Land and buildings at cost	£10.4 million
Land and buildings: accumulated depreciation	£0.12 million

The company has decided to revalue its land and buildings at the year end to £15 million.

What will be the amount of the transfer to the revaluation reserve?

£	million

129 **Vox Limited acquired a lorry on 1 May 20X4 at a cost of £60,000. It has an estimated life of four years, at the end of which it should have a resale value of £12,000.**

Vox charges depreciation on a straight line basis, with a proportionate charge in the period of acquisition.

What will be the depreciation charge in the accounting period to 30 September 20X4?

£	

130 In times of rising prices, the FIFO method of stock valuation, when compared to the average cost method of stock valuation, will usually produce:

A   a higher profit and a lower closing stock value

B   a higher profit and a higher closing stock value

C   a lower profit and a lower closing stock value

D   a lower profit and a higher closing stock value.

131 The turnover in a company was £2 million and its debtors were 5% of turnover. The company wishes to have a provision for doubtful debts of 4% of debtors, which would make the provision one-third higher than the current provision.

How will the profit for the period be affected by the change in provision?

A   Profit will be reduced by £1,000

B   Profit will be increased by £1,000

C   Profit will be reduced by £1,333

D   Profit will be increased by £1,333

132 Which one of the following should be accounted for as capital expenditure?

A   The cost of painting a building

B   The replacement of windows in a building

C   The purchase of a car by a garage for re-sale

D   Legal fees incurred on the purchase of a building

133 Brunch Ltd exchanged stock for a delivery vehicle with Trip Ltd. The stock had cost Brunch Ltd £10,000 and the normal selling price was £12,000; the delivery vehicle had cost Trip Ltd £9,000 and the normal selling price was £13,000.

How should Brunch Ltd value the vehicle in its balance sheet?

A   £9,000

B   £10,000

C   £12,000

D   £13,000

134 A car was purchased for £12,000 on 1 April 20X1 and has been depreciated at 20% each year straight line, assuming no residual value.

The company policy is to charge a full year's depreciation in the year of purchase and no depreciation in the year of sale. The car was traded in for a replacement vehicle on 1 August 20X4 for an agreed figure of £5,000.

What was the profit or loss on the disposal of the vehicle for the year ended 31 December 20X4?

A   Loss £2,200

B   Loss £1,400

C   Loss £200

D   Profit £200

135 When valuing stock at cost, which of the following shows the correct method of arriving at cost?

	Include inward transport costs	*Include production overheads*
A	Yes	No
B	No	Yes
C	Yes	Yes
D	No	No

136 The provision for doubtful debts in the ledger of B Ltd at 31 October 20X1 was £9,000. During the year ended 31 October 20X2, bad debts of £5,000 were written off.

Debtor balances at 31 October 20X2 were £120,000 and the company policy is to have a general provision of 5%.

What is the charge for bad and doubtful debts in the profit and loss account for the year ended 31 October 20X2?

A £2,000

B £3,000

C £5,000

D £8,000

137 A company bought a machine on 1 October 20X2 for £52,000. The machine had an expected life of eight years and an estimated residual value of £4,000.

On 31 March 20X7, the machine was sold for £35,000. The company's year end is 31 December. The company uses the straight-line method for depreciation and it charges a full year's depreciation in the year of purchase and none in the year of sale.

What is the profit or loss on disposal of the machine?

A Loss £13,000

B Profit £7,000

C Profit £10,000

D Profit £13,000

138 Nick plc purchased a machine for £15,000. The transportation costs were £1,500 and installation costs were £750.

The machine broke down at the end of the first month in use and cost £400 to repair. Nick plc depreciates machinery at 10% each year on cost, assuming no residual value.

What is the net book value of the machine after one year, to the nearest pound?

£

139 In a period of inflation, which ONE of the following methods of charging stock issues to production will give the lowest profit figure?

A Average cost

B LIFO

C FIFO

D Replacement cost

140 SSAP 9 *Stocks and Long Term Contracts* defines the items that may be included in computing the value of a stock of finished goods manufactured by a business.

Which one of the following lists consists only of items which may be included in the balance sheet value of such stock, according to SSAP 9?

A   Foreman's wages, carriage inwards, carriage outwards, raw materials

B   Raw materials, carriage inwards, costs of storage of finished goods, plant depreciation

C   Plant depreciation, carriage inwards, raw materials, foreman's wages

D   Carriage outwards, raw materials, foreman's wages, plant depreciation

141 Best purchased some plant and equipment on 1 July 20X1 for £40,000. The estimated scrap value of the plant in ten years' time is estimated to be £4,000.

Best's policy is to charge depreciation on the straight line basis, with a proportionate charge in the period of acquisition.

What should the depreciation charge for the plant be in Best's accounting period of twelve months to 30 September 20X1?

£ _____

142 At 30 September 20X2, the following balances existed in the records of Lambda:

Plant and equipment:

Cost   £860,000

Accumulated depreciation   £397,000

During the year ended 30 September 20X3, plant with a written down value of £37,000 was sold for £49,000. The plant had originally cost £80,000. Plant purchased during the year cost £180,000. It is the company's policy to charge a full year's depreciation in the year of acquisition of an asset and none in the year of sale, using a rate of 10% on the straight line basis.

What net amount should appear in Lambda's balance sheet at 30 September 20X3 for plant and equipment?

A   £563,000

B   £467,000

C   £510,000

D   £606,000

143 A company's plant and machinery ledger account for the year ended 30 September 20X2 was as follows:

Plant and machinery – cost

20X1	£	20X2	£
1 October Balance	381,200	1 June Disposal account – cost of asset sold	36,000
1 December Cash – addition	18,000	30 September Balance	363,200
	399,200		399,200

The company's policy is to charge depreciation at 20% per year on the straight line basis, with proportionate depreciation in years of purchase and sale.

What is the depreciation charge for the year ended 30 September 20X2?

A   £74,440

B   £84,040

C   £72,640

D   £76,840

144   Which of these statements about research and development expenditure are correct?

Statement

1   If certain conditions are satisfied, applied research and development expenditure may be capitalised.

2   One of the conditions to be satisfied if development expenditure is to be capitalised is that the technical feasibility of the project is reasonably assured.

3   If capitalised, development expenditure must be amortised over a period not exceeding five years.

4   The amount of capitalised development expenditure for each project should be reviewed each year. If circumstances no longer justify the capitalisation, the balance should be written off over a period not exceeding five years.

5   Development expenditure may only be capitalised if it can be shown that adequate resources will be available to finance the completion of the project.

A   Statements 2 and 5 only

B   Statements 3, 4 and 5 only

C   Statements 2, 3 and 5 only

D   Statements 1, 2 and 3 only

145   The year-end stock of Hythe has been evaluated at £72,857. You discover that:

1   8,000 nails have been valued at £1 each, rather than £1 per hundred.

2   The running total of £6,872 on page 147 of the stock sheets has been carried forward as £8,726 on page 148.

3   200 units of component P have been included in stock at £250 each, their cost price. Their replacement cost is now £210 and the estimated net realisable value is £208, before allowing for selling expenses of £500 in total.

The correct year-end stock value should be:

£ [   ]

146   Percy Pilbeam is a book wholesaler. On each sale, commission of 4% is payable to the selling agent.

The following information is available in respect of total stocks of three of his most popular titles at his financial year-end:

	Cost £	Selling price £
Henry VII – Shakespeare	2,280	2,900
Dissuasion – Jane Armstrong-Siddeley	4,080	4,000
Pilgrim's Painful Progress – John Bunion	1,280	1,300

What is the total value of these stocks in Percy's balance sheet?

A £7,368

B £7,400

C £7,560

D £7,640

147 **Roberta Wickham decides to offer discounts on some of the slower-selling items in her music shop. These items are as follows at 31 March 20X0:**

Item	Cost	Estimated price	Discount (% of selling price)
	£	£	%
Liszt – To Port	50	70	20
Delius – Myth	70	55	10
Offenbach – Up the Wrong Tree	150	225	10
Bax – To the Wall	30	35	50

What is the total stock value of the above items at 31 March 20X0?

A £267.00

B £274.00

C £300.00

D £325.50

148 **Which of the following stock valuation methods is likely to lead to the lowest figure for closing stock at a time when prices are rising?**

A Average cost

B First in, first out (FIFO)

C Last in, first out (LIFO)

D Replacement cost

149 **Which of the following costs may be included when arriving at the cost of finished goods stock for inclusion in the financial statements of a manufacturing company?**

(1) Carriage inwards

(2) Carriage outwards

(3) Depreciation of factory plant

(4) Finished goods storage costs

(5) Factory supervisors' wages

A (1) and (5) only

B (2), (4) and (5) only

C (1), (3) and (5) only

D (1), (2), (3) and (4) only

150   **Depreciation is best described as:**

A   a means of spreading the payment for fixed assets over a period of years

B   a decline in the market value of the assets

C   a means of spreading the net cost of fixed assets over their estimated useful life

D   a means of estimating the amount of money needed to replace the assets.

151   **The plant account of a company is shown below:**

Plant – cost

20X3		£	20X3		£
1 Jan	Balance (plant purchased 20X0)	380,000	1 Oct	Transfer disposal account: cost of plant sold	30,000
1 April	Cash – plant purchased	51,000	31 Dec	Balance	401,000
		431,000			431,000

The company's policy is to charge depreciation on plant at 20% per year on the straight-line basis, with proportionate depreciation in years of purchase and sale.

What should the company's plant depreciation charge be for the year ended 31 December 20X3?

A   £82,150

B   £79,150

C   £77,050

D   £74,050

152   **An organisation's fixed asset register shows a net book value of £125,600. The fixed asset account in the nominal ledger shows a net book value of £135,600.**

The difference could be due to a disposed asset not having been deducted from the fixed asset ledger:

A   with disposal proceeds of £15,000 and a profit on disposal of £5,000

B   with disposal proceeds of £15,000 and a net book value of £5,000

C   with disposal proceeds of £15,000 and a loss on disposal of £5,000

D   with disposal proceeds of £5,000 and a net book value of £5,000.

153   **At 1 July 20X8 Herne Bay Ltd has a freehold property in its books at £380,000 (cost), £278,000 (net book value). Depreciation is charged at 2% straight line.**

At the end of its accounting year ended 30 June 20X9 Herne Bay wishes to include the property at a professional valuation of £411,000, the valuation being agreed at that date.

Assuming depreciation has already been charged for the year ended 30 June 20X9, Herne Bay should:

A	Dr	Freehold property – Valuation	£411,000
	Dr	Freehold property – Accumulated depreciation	£102,000
	Cr	Freehold property – Cost	£380,000
	Cr	Revaluation reserve	£133,000

B	Dr	Freehold property – Valuation	£411,000	
	Dr	Freehold property – Accumulated depreciation	£109,600	
	Cr	Freehold property – Cost		£380,000
	Cr	Revaluation reserve		£140,600
C	Dr	Freehold property – Valuation	£411,000	
	Dr	Freehold property – Accumulated depreciation	£278,000	
	Cr	Freehold property – Cost		£380,000
	Cr	Revaluation reserve		£309,000
D	Dr	Freehold property – Valuation	£411,000	
	Dr	Freehold property – Accumulated depreciation	£285,600	
	Cr	Freehold property – Cost		£380,000
	Cr	Revaluation reserve		£316,600

154 **A fixed asset register showed a net book value of £67,460. A fixed asset costing £15,000 had been sold for £4,000, making a loss on disposal of £1,250.**

No entries had been made in the fixed asset register for this disposal.

After amendment, the balance on the fixed asset register will be:

 £

155 **On 1 January 20X8 Wootton Ltd has a building in its books at cost £380,000, net book value £260,000.**

On 1 July 20X8 the asset is revalued at £450,000 and Wootton wishes to include that valuation in its books. Wootton's accounting policy is to depreciate buildings at 3% straight line.

The depreciation charge to profit and loss account is:

A £8,300

B £11,400

C £12,450

D £13,500.

156 **A business with a financial year-end 31 October buys a fixed asset on 1 July 20X3 for £126,000.**

Depreciation is charged at the rate of 15% per annum on the reducing balance basis. On 30 September 20X7 the asset was sold for £54,800. It is the policy of the business to charge a proportionate amount of depreciation in both the year of acquisition and the year of disposal.

What was the loss on sale of the asset (to the nearest £)?

A £19,792

B £8,603

C £7,674

D £1,106

157 **At 31 December 20X2 a company's debtors totalled £400,000 and a provision for doubtful debts of £50,000 had been brought forward from the year ended 31 December 20X1.**

It was decided to write off debts totalling £38,000 and to adjust the provision for doubtful debts to 10% of the debtors.

What charge for bad and doubtful debts should appear in the company's profit and loss account for the year ended 31 December 20X2?

A   £74,200

B   £51,800

C   £28,000

D   £24,200

158 **During the year ended 31 December 20X9 Follands' sales totalled £3,000,000, its debtors amounting to 4% of sales for the year.**

Follands wishes to maintain its bad debt provision at 3% of debtors, and discovers that the provision as a result is 25% higher than it was a year before.

During the year specific bad debts of £3,200 were written off and bad debts (written off three years previously) of £150 were recovered.

What is the net charge for bad and doubtful debts for the year ended 31 December 20X9?

A   £720

B   £900

C   £3,770

D   £3,950

159 **At the beginning of its accounting period a business has debtors of £13,720 after deducting a specific provision of £350 and a general provision against 2% of the remainder.**

At the year-end debtors before any provisions amount to £17,500. No specific provision is to be made but the general provision is to be increased to 3% of debtors.

What is the charge or credit in the profit and loss account in relation to bad debts for the year?

A   £525 Dr

B   £175 Dr

C   £105 Cr

D   £99 Cr

160 **A bad debt written off two years ago is unexpectedly recovered and entered in the sales ledger column in the cash book.**

What adjustment, if any, will be necessary – assuming that the receipt was treated as sales ledger cash?

	Debit	Credit
A	Bad debts account	Sales ledger control account
B	Sales ledger control account	Bad debts account
C	Suspense account	Bad debts account
D	No adjustment will be necessary	

161   **The opening balance on Jewel plc's bad debt provision was £1,000. Jewel plc wrote off £4,000 of bad debts during the year.**

The closing balance on the bad debt provision was £1,200. What is the total charge to Jewel plc's profit and loss account in respect of bad debts for the year?

£ [   ]

162   **A Ltd has an item in stock which cost £1,000 and can be sold for £1,200. However, before it can be sold, it will require to be modified at a cost of £150.**

The expected selling costs of the item are an additional £100.

How should this item be valued in stock?

£ [   ]

163   **Stan is a builder who has numerous small items of equipment. He calculates his depreciation using the revaluation method.**

At the beginning of his financial year he valued his equipment at £10,250; he bought equipment costing £3,450 and he sold equipment valued at £2,175. At the end of his financial year he valued his equipment at £8,000.

What is his depreciation charge on equipment for the year?

A   £2,250

B   £3,525

C   £5,700

D   £11,525

164   **Wand Ltd bought a new printing machine from abroad. The cost of the machine was £80,000.**

The installation costs were £5,000 and the employees received specific training on how to use this particular machine, at a cost of £2,000. Before using the machine to print customers' orders, a test was undertaken and the paper and ink at a cost of £1,000.

What should be the cost of the machine in the company's balance sheet?

A   £80,000

B   £85,000

C   £87,000

D   £88,000

165   **Suresh & Co sell three products — Basic, Super and Luxury. The following information was available at the year end:**

	Basic £ per unit	Super £ per unit	Luxury £ per unit
Original cost	6	9	18
Estimated selling price	9	12	15
Selling and distribution costs	1	4	5
	units	units	units
Units in stock	200	250	150

The value of stock at the year end should be:

A   £4,200

B   £4,700

C   £5,700

D   £6,150.

166   A car was purchased by a newsagent business in May 20X1 for:

	£
Cost	10,000
Road tax	150
Total	10,150

The business adopts a date of 31 December as its year end.

The car was traded in for a replacement vehicle in August 20X5 at an agreed value of £5,000.

It has been depreciated at 25 per cent per annum on the reducing balance method, charging a full year's depreciation in the year of purchase and none in the year of sale.

What was the profit or loss on disposal of the vehicle during the year ended December 20X5?

A   Profit: £718

B   Profit: £781

C   Profit: £1,788

D   Profit: £1,836

167   A stock record card shows the following details.

February:	1	50 units in stock at a cost of £40 per unit
	7	100 units purchased at a cost of £45 per unit
	14	80 units sold
	21	50 units purchased at a cost of £50 per unit
	28	60 units sold

What is the value of stock at 28 February using the FIFO method?

£ [   ]

168   A company values its stock using the first in, first out (FIFO) method. At 1 May 20X2 the company had 700 engines in stock, valued at £190 each.

During the year ended 30 April 20X3 the following transactions took place:

20X2			
1 July	Purchased 5	500 engines	at £220 each
1 November	Sold	400 engines	for £160,000
20X3			
1 February	Purchased	300 engines	at £230 each
15 April	Sold	250 engines	for £125,000

What is the value of the company's closing stock of engines at 30 April 20X3?

A   £188,500

B   £195,500

C   £166,000

D   None of these figures.

169   Which of the following statements about the valuation of stock are correct, according to SSAP 9 *Stocks and Long-term Contracts*?

(1)   Stock items are normally to be valued at the higher of cost and net realisable value.

(2)   The cost of stock manufactured by an enterprise will include materials and labour only. Overhead costs cannot be included.

(3)   LIFO (last in, first out) is not usually an appropriate method of stock valuation.

(4)   Selling price less estimated profit margin may be used to arrive at cost if this gives a reasonable approximation to actual cost.

A   1, 3 and 4 only

B   1 and 2 only

C   3 only

D   3 and 4 only

170   The net book value of a company's fixed assets was £200,000 at 1 August 20X2. During the year ended 31 July 20X3, the company sold fixed assets for £25,000 on which it made a loss of £5,000.

The depreciation charge for the year was £20,000. What was the net book value of fixed assets at 31 July 20X3?

A   £150,000

B   £155,000

C   £160,000

D   £180,000

171   Goodwill is most appropriately classed as:

A   a current asset

B   an intangible asset

C   a fictitious liability

D   a semi-fixed asset.

172   A business has made a profit of £8,000 but its bank balance has fallen by £5,000. This could be due to:

A   depreciation of £3,000 and an increase in stocks of £10,000

B   depreciation of £6,000 and the repayment of a loan of £7,000

C   depreciation of £12,000 and the purchase of new fixed assets for £25,000

D   the disposal of a fixed asset for £13,000 less than its book value.

173 A fixed asset costing £12,500 was sold at a book loss of £4,500. Depreciation had been provided using the reducing balance, at 20% per annum since its purchase.

Which of the following correctly describes the sale proceeds and length of time for which the asset had been owned?

	Sale proceeds	Length of ownership
A	Cannot be calculated	Cannot be calculated
B	Cannot be calculated	2 years
C	£8,000	Cannot be calculated
D	£8,000	2 years

174 Your company auditor insists that it is necessary to record items of plant separately and to depreciate them over several years, but that items of office equipment, such as hand-held stapling machines, can be grouped together and written off against profits immediately.

The main reason for this difference in treatment between the two items is because:

A treatment of the two items must be consistent with treatment in previous periods

B items of plant last for several years, whereas hand-held stapling machines last only for months

C hand-held stapling machines are not regarded as material items

D items of plant are revalued from time to time, whereas hand-held stapling machines are recorded at historical cost.

175 A fixed asset was purchased at the beginning of Year 1 for £2,400 and depreciated by 20% per annum by the reducing balance method. At the beginning of Year 4 it was sold for £1,200. The result of this was:

A a loss on disposal of £240.00

B a loss on disposal of £28.80

C a profit on disposal of £28.80

D a profit on disposal of £240.00.

176 You are given the following information for the year ended 31 October 20X7:

	£
Purchases of raw materials	112,000
Returns inwards	8,000
Decrease in stocks of raw materials	8,000
Direct wages	42,000
Carriage outwards	4,000
Carriage inwards	3,000
Production overheads	27,000
Increase in work-in-progress	10,000

The value of factory cost of goods completed is:

A £174,000

B £182,000

C £183,000

D £202,000.

177 **Your organisation uses the Weighted Average Cost method of valuing stocks. During August 20X7, the following stock details were recorded:**

Opening balance	30 units valued at £2 each
5 August	purchase of 50 units at £2.40 each
10 August	issue of 40 units
18 August	purchase of 60 units at £2.50 each
23 August	issue of 25 units

The value of the balance at 31 August 20X7 was:

A   £172.50

B   £176.25

C   £180.00

D   £187.50.

178 **A business incurs expenditure on the following research and development activities:**

£120,000 on pure research
£200,000 on applied research
£350,000 on product development

The amount which could be capitalised is:

A   nil

B   £350,000

C   £550,000

D   £670,000.

179 **Which of the following statements about research and development expenditure are correct?**

(1)   Research expenditure, other than capital expenditure on research facilities, should be recognised as an expense as incurred.

(2)   In deciding whether development expenditure qualifies to be recognised as an asset, it is necessary to consider whether there will be adequate finance available to complete the project.

(3)   Development expenditure recognised as an asset must be amortised over a period not exceeding five years.

A   (1), (2) and (3)

B   (1) and (2) only

C   (1) and (3) only

D   (2) and (3) only

180 **Which of the following statements about research and development expenditure are correct according to SSAP 13 *Accounting for Research and Development*?**

(1)   If certain conditions are met, development expenditure must be capitalised.

(2)   Research expenditure, other than capital expenditure on research facilities, must be written off as incurred.

(3)   Capitalised development expenditure must be amortised over a period not exceeding five years.

(4)   Capitalised development expenditure must be disclosed in the balance sheet under intangible fixed assets.

A   1, 2 and 4 only

B   1 and 3 only

C   2 and 4 only

D   3 and 4 only

181   Catch Limited provides the following note to fixed assets in its balance sheet.

Plant and machinery

	Cost	Depreciation	Net book value
	£000	£000	£000
Opening balance	453	143	310
Additions/charge	102	11	91
Disposals	(79)	(64)	(15)
Closing balance	476	90	386

The additional machinery was purchased for cash. The disposals were made at a loss of £6,000.

What was the net cash outflow on plant and machinery during the period?

£ [   ]

182   A machine cost £9,000. It has an expected useful life of 6 years, and an expected residual value of £1,000. It is to be depreciated at 30% per annum on the reducing balance basis.

A full year's depreciation is charged in the year of purchase, with none in the year of sale. During year 4, it is sold for £3,000.

The profit or loss on disposal is:

A   loss £87

B   loss £2,000

C   profit £256

D   profit £1,200.

183   An increase in the provision for doubtful debts results in:

A   a decrease in current liabilities

B   an increase in net profit

C   an increase in working capital

D   a decrease in working capital.

184   The draft balance sheet of Hocket Limited at 31 December 20X4 includes the following current assets.

Stock   £87,000

Debtors   £124,000

The figure for debtors includes goods sent out on a sale or return basis at a price of £6,000 (cost £4,500). These were still unsold at 31 December 20X4.

What should be the value of stock and debtors in the balance sheet of Hocket at 31 December 20X4?

		Stock	*Debtors*
	A	£87,000	£124,000
	B	£91,500	£118,000
	C	£91,500	£119,500
	D	£93,000	£118,000

185   A fixed asset was disposed of for £2,200 during the last accounting year.

It had been purchased exactly three years earlier for £5,000, with an expected residual value of £500, and had been depreciated on the reducing balance basis, at 20% per annum.

The profit or loss on disposal was:

A   £360 loss

B   £150 loss

C   £104 loss

D   £200 profit.

186   The reducing balance method of depreciating fixed assets is more appropriate than the straight-line method when:

A   there is no expected residual value for the asset

B   the expected life of the asset is not capable of being estimated

C   the asset is expected to be replaced in a short period of time

D   the asset decreases in value less in later years than in the early years of use.

187   A company started the year with total debtors of £87,000 and a provision for doubtful debts of £2,500.

During the year, two specific debts were written off, one for £800 and the other for £550. A debt of £350 that had been written off as bad in the previous year was paid during the year. At the year end, total debtors were £90,000 and the provision for doubtful debts was £2,300.

What is the charge to the profit and loss account for the year in respect of bad and doubtful debts?

A   £800

B   £1,000

C   £1,150

D   £1,550

FINANCIAL STATEMENTS

188   APM Ltd provides the following note to fixed assets in its balance sheet.

Plant and machinery

	Cost	*Depreciation*	*Net book value*
	£000	£000	£000
Opening balance	25	12	13
Additions/charge	15	4	11
Disposals	(10)	(8)	(2)
Closing balance	30	8	22

The additional machinery was purchased for cash. A machine was sold at a profit of £2,000.

What is the net cash outflow for plant and machinery?

A   £9,000

B   £11,000

C   £13,000

D   £15,000

189   The movement on the plant and machinery account for X Ltd is shown below:

	£
Cost b/fwd	10,000
Additions	2,000
Disposals	(3,000)
Cost c/fwd	9,000
Depreciation b/fwd	2,000
Charge for the year	1,000
Disposals	(1,500)
Depreciation c/fwd	1,500
Net book value b/fwd	8,000
Net book value c/fwd	7,500

The profit on the sale of the machine was £500. What figures would appear in the cash flow statement of X Ltd?

A   Movement on plant account £500 and profit on disposal of £500.

B   Movement on plant account £500 and proceeds on sale of plant £2,000.

C   Purchase of plant £2,000 and profit on disposal of £500.

D   Purchase of plant £2,000 and proceeds on sale of plant £2,000.

190   Extracts from the financial statements of CFS Ltd are set out below:

Profit and loss account for the year ended 31 December 20X1

	£000	£000
Turnover		300
Cost of sales		150
Gross profit		150
Profit on sale of fixed asset		75
		225
Expenses	15	
Depreciation	30	
		45
Net profit		180

	Balances at 31 December	
	20X0	20X1
	£000	£000
Stock, debtors, current liabilities (net)	40	50

What figure would appear for cash in the cash flow statement of CFS Ltd for the year ended 31 December 20X1 in respect of net cash flow from operating activities?

A   £125,000

B   £145,000

C   £215,000

D   £235,000

191   In the course of preparing a company's cash flow statement, the following figures are to be included in the reconciliation of operating profit to net cash inflow from operating activities.

	£
Depreciation charges	980,000
Profit on sale of fixed assets	40,000
Increase in stocks	130,000
Decrease in debtors	100,000
Increase in creditors	80,000

What will the net effect of these items be in the reconciliation?

		£
A	Addition to operating profit	890,000
B	Subtraction from operating profit	890,000
C	Addition to operating profit	1,070,000
D	Addition to operating profit	990,000

192   Which of the following items could appear in a company's cash flow statement?

(1)   Surplus on revaluation of fixed assets.

(2)   Proceeds of issue of shares.

(3)   Proposed dividend.

(4)   Bad debts written off.

(5)   Dividends received.

A   (1), (2) and (5) only

B   (2), (3), (4), (5) only

C   (2) and (5) only

D   (3) and (4) only

193   Part of the process of preparing a company's cash flow statement is the preparation of a reconciliation of operating profit to net cash inflow from operating activities.

Which of the following statements about that reconciliation are correct?

(1)   Loss on sale of operating fixed assets should be deducted from operating profits.

(2)   Increase in stocks should be deducted from operating profits.

(3)   Increase in creditors should be added to operating profits.

(4)   Depreciation charges should be added to operating profits.

A   (1), (2) and (3)

B   (1), (2) and (4)

C   (1), (3) and (4)

D   (2), (3) and (4)

194   In relation to cash flow statements, which, if any, of the following are correct?

Statement

1   The direct method of calculating net cash from operating activities leads to a different figure from that produced by the indirect method, but this is balanced elsewhere in the cash flow statement.

2   A company making high profits must necessarily have a net cash inflow from operating activities.

3   Profits and losses on disposals of fixed assets appear as items under capital expenditure in the cash flow statement or a note to it.

A   Statement 1 only

B   Statement 2 only

C   Statement 3 only

D   None of the statements

195   A cash flow statement prepared in accordance with FRS 1 *Cash Flow Statements* is accompanied by a note reconciling operating profit to net operating cash flow.

Which of the following lists of items consists only of items that would be ADDED to operating profit in that note?

A   Decrease in stock, depreciation, profit on sale of fixed assets.

B   Increase in creditors, decrease in debtors, profit on sale of fixed assets.

C   Loss on sale of fixed assets, depreciation, increase in debtors.

D   Decrease in debtors, increase in creditors, loss on sale of fixed assets.

196   Information about the fixed assets of Rabbit Limited is as follows.

	£000
Net book value at 1 January 20X4	2,400
Net book value at 31 December 20X4	6,000
Net book value of fixed assets disposed of during 20X4	500
Depreciation charge for the year ending 31 December 20X4	1,000
Loss arising on disposal of fixed assets during 20X4	150

What will be the figures for fixed asset disposals and fixed asset additions in the cash flow statement for the year to 31 December 20X4?

Disposals	£
Additions	£

197 **The following is an extract from the balance sheets of FRC plc for the years ended 31 July 20X1 and 31 July 20X2:**

	20X3	20X2
	£000	£000
Stock	50	80
Debtors	60	50
Creditors	35	30
Accruals	5	20

What figure would appear in the cash flow statement of FRC plc for the year ended 31 July 20X3 as part of the cash flow from operations?

A   £25,000 outflow

B   £10,000 outflow

C   £10,000 inflow

D   £25,000 inflow

198 **A company made a profit for the year of £18,750, after accounting for depreciation of £1,250.**

During the year, fixed assets were purchased for £8,000, debtors increased by £1,000, stocks decreased by £1,800 and creditors increased by £350.

The increase in cash and bank balances during the year was:

A   £10,650

B   £10,850

C   £12,450

D   £13,150.

199 **The profits of Gripe Limited were £63,400. This was after charging depreciation of £2,700.**

During the year, debtors decreased by £600, stocks increased by £2,500 and trade creditors increased by £900. Fixed asset purchases during the year amounted to £17,300 and there was a loss on disposal of fixed assets of £3,000.

What was the increase in cash balances during the year?

A   £40,800

B   £46,800

C   £50,800

D   £52,800

200 **Pat does not keep a full set of business records, but the following information is available for the month of June 20X9**

	£
Trade debtors, 1 June 20X9	800
Trade debtors, 30 June 20X9	550
Credit sales	6,800
Cash received from debtors	6,730
Bad debt written off	40
General provision for doubtful debts set up at 30 June 20X9	100

Assuming no other transactions, how much discount was allowed to customers during the month?

A   £240

B   £280

C   £340

D   £380

201   At 31 December 20X2 the following matters require inclusion in a company's financial statements:

(1)   On 1 January 20X2 the company made a loan of £12,000 to an employee, repayable on 30 April 20X3, charging her interest at 2% per year. On 30 April 20X3 she repaid the loan and paid the whole of the interest due on the loan to that date.

(2)   The company has paid insurance £9,000 in 20X2, covering the year ending 31 August 20X3.

(3)   In January 20X3 the company received rent from a tenant £4,000 covering the six months to 31 December 20X2.

For these items, what total figures should be included in the company's balance sheet at 31 December 20X2?

	Current assets	Current liabilities
	£	£
A	22,000	240
B	22,240	nil
C	10,240	nil
D	16,240	6,000

202   From the following information, calculate the value of purchases:

	£
Opening creditors	142,600
Cash paid to suppliers	542,300
Discounts received	13,200
Goods returned	27,500
Closing creditors	137,800

A   £302,600

B   £506,400

C   £523,200

D   £578,200

203   A business has compiled the following information for the year ended 31 October 20X2:

	£
Opening stock	386,200
Purchases	989,000
Closing stock	422,700

The gross profit as a percentage of sales is always 40%

Based on these figures, what is the sales revenue for the year?

A   £1,333,500

B   £1,587,500

C   £2,381,250

D   The sales revenue figure cannot be calculated from this information

204   A fire on 30 September 20X2 destroyed some of a company's stock and its stock records.

The following information is available:

	£
Stock 1 September 20X2	318,000
Sales for September 20X2	612,000
Purchases for September 20X2	412,000
Inventory in good condition at 30 September 20X2	214,000

Standard gross profit percentage on sales is 25%

Based on this information, what is the value of the stock lost?

A   £96,000

B   £271,000

C   £26,400

D   £57,000

205   A business commenced with a bank balance of £3,250; it subsequently purchased goods on credit for £10,000; gross profit mark-up is 120%; half the goods were sold for cash, less cash discount of 5%; all takings were banked.

The resulting net profit was:

A   £700

B   £3,700

C   £5,450

D   £5,700

206   The following information is relevant to the calculation of the sales figure for Alpha, a sole trader who does not keep proper accounting records:

	£
Opening debtors	29,100
Cash received from credit customers and paid into the bank	381,600
Expenses paid out of cash received from credit customers before banking	6,800
Bad debts written off	7,200
Refunds to credit customers	2,100
Discounts allowed to credit customers	9,400
Cash sales	112,900
Closing debtors	38,600

The figure which should appear in Alpha's trading account for sales is:

A   £525,300

B   £511,700

C   £529,500

D   £510,900

207 **A sole trader who does not keep full accounting records wishes to calculate her sales revenue for the year.**

The information available is:

1	Opening stock	£17,000
2	Closing stock	£24,000
3	Purchases	£91,000
4	Standard gross profit percentage on sales revenue :	40%

Which of the following is the sales figure for the year calculated from these figures?

A   £117,600

B   £108,000

C   £210,000

D   £140,000

208 **D, E and F are in partnership, sharing profits in the ratio 5:3:2 respectively, after charging salaries for E and F of £24,000 each per year.**

On 1 July 20X3 they agreed to change the profit-sharing ratio to 3:1:1 and to increase E's salary to £36,000 per year, F's salary continuing unchanged.

For the year ended 31 December 20X3 the partnership profit amounted to £480,000.

Which of the following correctly states the partners' total profit shares for the year?

	D	E	F
A	£234,000	£136,800	£109,200
B	£213,000	£157,800	£109,200
C	£186,000	£171,600	£122,400
D	£237,600	£132,000	£110,400

209 **X and Y are in partnership, sharing profits equally and preparing their accounts to 31 December each year.**

On 1 July 20X4, Z joined the partnership, and from that date profits are shared X 40%, Y 40% and Z 20%.

In the year ended 31 December 20X4, profits were:

	£
6 months to 31 June 20X4	200,000
6 months to 31 December 2000	300,000

It was agreed that X and Y only should bear equally the expense for a bad debt of £40,000 written off in the six months to 31 December 20X4 in arriving at the £300,000 profit.

How much is X's profit share for the year?

£

210 **P and Q are in partnership, sharing profits in the ratio 3:2 and compiling their accounts to 30 June each year.**

On 1 January 20X2 R joined the partnership, and from that date the profit-sharing ratio became P 50%, Q 25% and R 25%, after providing for salaries for Q and R as follows:

Q   £20,000 per year

R   £12,000 per year

The partnership profit for the year ended 30 June 20X2 was £480,000, accruing evenly over the year.

What are the partners' total profit shares for the year ended 30 June 20X2?

	P	Q	R
	£	£	£
A	256,000	162,000	62,000
B	248,000	168,000	64,000
C	264,000	166,000	66,000
D	264,000	156,000	60,000

211 **S and T are in partnership and prepare their accounts to 31 December each year. On 1 July 20X5, U joined the partnership.**

Profit sharing arrangements are:

		6 months to 30 June 20X5	6 months to 31 December 20X5
Salary	S	£15,000	£25,000
Share of balance of profit	S	60%	40%
	T	40%	40%
	U		20%

The partnership profit for the year ended 31 December 20X5 was £350,000 accruing evenly over the year.

What are the partners' total profit shares for the year ended 31 December 20X5?

	S	T	U
	£000	£000	£000
A	196	124	30
B	217	108	25
C	155	130	65
D	175	145	35

212 **At 30 September 20X4, Z Ltd had a provision for doubtful debts of £37,000.**

During the year ended 30 September 20X5 the company wrote off debts totalling £18,000, and at the end of the year it is decided that the provision for doubtful debts should be £20,000.

What should be included in the profit and loss account for bad and doubtful debts?

A   £35,000 debit

B   £1,000 debit

C   £38,000 debit

D   £1,000 credit

213 On 31 December 20X3 the stock of V Limited was completely destroyed by fire.

The following information is available:

1	Stock at 1 December 20X3 at cost	£28,400
2	Purchases for December 20X3	£49,600
3	Sales for December 20X3	£64,800
4	Standard gross profit percentage on sales revenue	30%

Based on this information, which of the following is the amount of stock destroyed?

£ _____

214 Drab Limited made a profit of £63,200 for the year, after deducting depreciation charges of £15,900 and allowing for a profit of £7,000 on disposal of a fixed asset.

Fixed asset purchases in the period were £18,000. Debtors increased by £4,000, stocks increased by £3,500 and trade creditors decreased by £1,600.

What was the increase in cash balances during the year?

A £45,000

B £48,200

C £59,000

D £63,200

215 Paolo is a sole proprietor whose accounting records are incomplete. All the sales are cash sales and during the month £50,000 was banked, including £5,000 from the sale of a business car.

He paid £12,000 wages in cash from the till and withdrew £2,000 as drawings. The cash in the till at the beginning and end of the month was £300 and £400 respectively. There were no other payments.

What were the sales for the month?

A £58,900

B £59,100

C £63,900

D £64,100

216 There is £100 in the cash till at the year end at F Ltd, but the accountant has discovered that some cash has been stolen.

At the beginning of the year there was £50 in the cash till and debtors were £2,000. Total sales in the year were £230,000. Debtors at the end of the year were £3,000. Cheques banked from credit sales were £160,000 and cash sales of £50,000 have been banked.

How much cash was stolen during the year?

£ _____

217 During September, your organisation had sales of £148,000, which made a gross profit of £40,000. Purchases amounted to £100,000 and opening stock was £34,000.

The value of closing stock was:

A £24,000

B £26,000

C £42,000

D £54,000

218 **The following totals appear in the day books for March 20X8:**

	Goods excluding VAT	VAT
	£	£
Sales day book	40,000	7,000
Purchases day book	20,000	3,500
Returns inwards day book	2,000	350
Returns outwards day book	4,000	700

The balance of stock, debtors and trade creditors were the same at the end of the month as at the beginning of the month. The gross profit for March 20X8 is:

A £18,000

B £21,150

C £22,000

D £25,850

219 **The bank balance of a business increased by £750,000 during its last financial year.**

During the same period it issued shares of £1 million and repaid a debenture of £750,000. It purchased fixed assets for £200,000 and charged depreciation of £100,000. Working capital (other than the bank balance) increased by £575,000.

Its profit for the year was:

A £1,175,000

B £1,275,000

C £1,325,000

D £1,375,000

220 **At 31 December 20X1 the capital structure of a company was as follows:**

	£
Ordinary share capital	
100,000 shares of 50p each	50,000
Share premium account	180,000

During 20X2 the company made a bonus issue of one share for every two held, using the share premium account for the purpose, and later issued for cash another 60,000 shares at 80p per share.

What is the company's capital structure at 31 December 20X2?

	Ordinary share capital	Share premium account
	£	£
A	130,000	173,000
B	105,000	173,000
C	130,000	137,000
D	105,000	137,000

221 **The issued share capital of Alpha Limited is as follows:**

	£
Ordinary shares of 10p each	1,000,000
8% Preference shares of 50p each	500,000

In the year ended 31 October 20X2, the company has paid the preference dividend for the year and an interim dividend of 2p per share on the ordinary shares. A final ordinary dividend of 3p per share is proposed.

What is the total amount of dividends relating to the year ended 31 October 20X2?

A £580,000

B £90,000

C £130,000

D £540,000

222 **A company made an issue for cash of 1,000,000 50p shares at a premium of 30p per share.**

Which of the following journal entries correctly records the issue?

		Debit	Credit
		£	£
A	Share capital	500,000	
	Share premium	300,000	
	Bank		800,000
B	Bank	800,000	
	Share capital		500,000
	Share premium		300,000
C	Bank	1,300,000	
	Share capital		1,000,000
	Share premium		300,000
D	Share capital	1,000,000	
	Share premium	300,000	
	Bank		1,300,000

223 **At 1 January 20X3 the capital structure of Q Limited was as follows:**

	£
Issued share capital 1,000,000 ordinary shares of 50p each	500,000
Share premium account	300,000

On 1 April 20X3 the company made an issue of 200,000 50p shares at £1.30 each, and on 1 July the company made a bonus (capitalisation) issue of one share for every four in issue at the time, using the share premium account for the purpose.

Which of the following correctly states the company's share capital and share premium account at 31 December 20X3?

	Share capital	Share premium account
A	£750,000	£230,000
B	£875,000	£285,000
C	£750,000	£310,000
D	£750,000	£610,000

224 **At 1 July 20X3 the share capital and share premium account of a company were as follows:**

	£
Share capital – 300,000 ordinary shares of 25p each	75,000
Share premium account	200,000

During the year ended 30 June 20X4 the following events took place:

1   On 1 January 20X4 the company made a rights issue of one share for every five held, at £1.20 per share.

2   On 1 April 20X4 the company made a bonus (capitalisation) issue of one share for every three in issue at that time, using the share premium account to do so.

What are the correct balances on the company's share capital and share premium accounts at 30 June 20X4?

	Share capital	*Share premium account*
A	£460,000	£287,000
B	£480,000	£137,000
C	£120,000	£137,000
D	£120,000	£227,000

225 **At 1 January 20X3, the share capital and share premium account of Flood Limited were as follows:**

Share capital: 600,000 ordinary shares of 25p each	£150,000
Share premium account	£480,000

During the year to 31 December 20X3, the following events took place:

1   On 1 July 20X3, the company made a rights issue of one new share for every five held, at £1.10 per share.

2   On 1 November 20X3, the company made a bonus issue (capitalization issue) of one share for every three held, using the share premium account to do so.

The balance on the share capital account and the share premium account at 30 June 20X4 is:

Share capital   £ _____

Share premium   £ _____

226 **Which of the following would cause a company's net profit to increase?**

A   Issue of 100,000 ordinary shares at a premium of 2%

B   Revaluation of a freehold property from £70,000 to £100,000

C   Disposal of a fork lift truck which originally cost £15,000 and has a net book value of £9,250 for £8,500

D   Receipt of £25 from a debtor previously written off as bad

227 **Which of the following is not a permitted use of the share premium account?**

A   Financing the issue of partly-paid bonus shares

B   Writing off preliminary expenses on the formation of a company

C   Providing the premium payable on the redemption of debentures

D   Writing off expenses of share issues

228 **The following information is available for Ropley plc:**

	Authorised share capital £	Issued share capital £
25p ordinary shares	2,000,000	1,000,000
6% 50p preference shares	500,000	250,000

In addition to providing for the preference dividend for a financial year, an ordinary dividend of 2p per share is to be paid. What is the total amount of dividends for the year?

A   £35,000

B   £95,000

C   £110,000

D   £190,000

229 **Revenue reserves are:**

A   accumulated and undistributed profits of a company

B   amounts which cannot be distributed as dividends

C   amounts set aside out of profits to replace revenue items

D   amounts set aside out of profits for a specific purpose.

230 **The purchase of a business for more than the aggregate of the fair value of its separable identifiable assets results in the creation of a:**

A   share premium account

B   reserve account

C   suspense account

D   goodwill account.

231 **A company has £100,000 of ordinary shares at a par value of 10 pence each and 100,000 5% preference shares at a par value of 50 pence each.**

The directors decide to declare a dividend of 5p per ordinary share.

The total amount to be paid out in dividends amounts to:

A   £5,000

B   £7,500

C   £52,500

D   £55,000.

232 **The correct ledger entries needed to record the issue of 200,000 £1 shares at a premium of 30p, and paid for by cheque, in full, would be:**

A	Debit share capital account	£200,000
	Credit share premium account	£60,000
	Credit bank account	£140,000
B	Debit bank account	£260,000
	Credit share capital account	£200,000
	Credit share premium account	£60,000

	C	Debit share capital account	£200,000
		Debit share premium account	£60,000
		Credit bank account	£260,000
	D	Debit bank account	£200,000
		Debit share premium account	£60,000
		Credit share capital account	£260,000

233 **A draft balance sheet has been prepared for Z Ltd. It is now discovered that a loan due for repayment by Z Ltd fourteen months after the balance sheet date has been included in trade creditors.**

The necessary adjustment will:

A   have no effect on net current assets

B   increase net current assets

C   reduce net current assets

D   increase current assets but reduce net current assets.

234 **Listed below are some items that may appear in a company's profit and loss account, either separately disclosed or included in another figure.**

(1)   Profit or loss on discontinued operations

(2)   Profit or loss on the sale of part of the enterprise.

(3)   Extraordinary items

(4)   Writing off a bad debt.

According to FRS3 Reporting Financial Performance, which of these items must always be shown separately on the face of the profit and loss account if material?

A   1, 2 and 3

B   1, 3 and 4

C   2, 3 and 4

D   1, 2 and 4

235 **What is the correct treatment of extraordinary items in a company's profit and loss account, according to FRS 3 *Reporting Financial Performance*?**

A   Add to or subtract from profit after tax.

B   Include in calculating operating profit with an explanatory note.

C   Show separately in the profit and loss account as part of operating profit with an explanatory note.

D   Exclude from profit and loss account and disclose by note.

236 **Which of the following are included in a company's profit and loss account?**

(1)   Profit from discontinued operations.

(2)   Profit on disposal of discontinued operations.

(3)   Gain on revaluation of fixed assets.

(4)   Interest on debt.

A   (1), (3) and (4) only

B   (1), (2) and (4) only

C   (1) and (2) only

D   (3) and (4) only

237 **Which ONE of the following is an appropriation by a limited company?**

A   Directors' salaries.

B   Dividends.

C   Donation to a charity.

D   Loan interest.

238 **A company has authorised capital of 50,000 5% preference shares of £2 each and 500,000 ordinary shares with a par value of 20p each.**

All of the preference shares have been issued, and 400,000 ordinary shares have been issued at a premium of 30p each. Interim dividends of 5p per ordinary share plus half the preference dividend have been paid during the current year. A final dividend of 15p per ordinary share is declared.

The total of dividend payable for the year is:

£

239 **A business can make a profit and yet have a reduction in its bank balance. Which ONE of the following might cause this to happen?**

A   The sale of fixed assets at a loss.

B   The charging of depreciation in the profit and loss account.

C   The lengthening of the period of credit given to customers.

D   The lengthening of the period of credit taken from suppliers.

240 **Which ONE of the following does NOT form part of the equity capital of a limited company?**

A   Preference share capital.

B   Share premium.

C   Revaluation reserve.

D   Ordinary share capital

241 **A company's working capital was £43,200. Subsequently, the following transactions occurred:**

•   Creditors were paid £3,000 by cheque.

•   A bad debt of £250 was written off.

•   Stock valued at £100 was sold for £230 on credit.

Working capital is now:

£

242 A company has an authorised share capital of 1,000,000 ordinary shares of £1 each, of which 800,000 have been issued at a premium of 50p each, thereby raising capital of £1,200,000. The directors are considering allocating £120,000 for dividend payments this year.

This amounts to a dividend of:

A   12p per share

B   10p per share

C   15p per share

D   12%.

243 Which one of the following would you expect to find in the appropriation account of a limited company, for the current year?

A   Preference dividend proposed during the previous year, but paid in the current year.

B   Preference dividend proposed during the current year, but paid in the following year.

C   Directors' fees.

D   Auditors' fees.

244 The current liabilities of CFS Ltd include the following:

	20X1	20X0
Dividends payable	£30,000	£25,000

The cash flow statement for the year ended in 20X1 shows dividends paid of £27,000.

What were the dividends in the profit and loss account for the year ended 20X1?

A   £22,000

B   £27,000

C   £28,000

D   £32,000

The following information is relevant for questions 245 to 247

On 1 January 20X0 Alpha Limited purchased 80,000 £1 ordinary shares in Beta Limited for £180,000. At that date Beta's retained profits amounted to £90,000 and the fair values of the net assets of Beta at acquisition were equal to their book values.

Three years later, on 31 December 20X2, the balance sheets of the two companies were:

	Alpha	Beta
	£	£
Sundry net assets	230,000	260,000
Shares in Beta	180,000	–
	410,000	260,000
Share capital		
Ordinary shares of £1 each	200,000	100,000
Profit and loss account	210,000	160,000
	410,000	260,000

The share capital of Beta has remained unchanged since 1 January 20X0.

Goodwill on consolidation is being amortised over four years.

245 **What amount should appear in the group's consolidated balance sheet at 31 December 20X2 for goodwill?**

A   £25,000

B   £28,000

C   £7,000

D   £14,000

246 **What amount should appear in the group's consolidated balance sheet at 31 December 20X2 for minority interest?**

A   £52,000

B   £20,000

C   £34,000

D   £32,000

247 **What amount should appear in the group's consolidated balance sheet at 31 December 20X2 for profit and loss account?**

A   £266,000

B   £338,000

C   £370,000

D   £245,000

248 **At 1 January 20X5 H Limited acquired 80% of the share capital of S for £160,000.**

At that date the share capital of S consisted of 100,000 ordinary shares of £1 each and its reserves totalled £40,000. Goodwill on acquisition of subsidiaries is amortised on the straight line basis over five years.

In the consolidated balance sheet of H and its subsidiary S at 31 December 20X7 the amount appearing for goodwill should be:

A   £16,000

B   £19,200

C   £28,800

D   £4,000

249 **At 1 January 20X2 H acquired 75% of the share capital of S for £220,000. At that date the share capital of S consisted of 200,000 shares of 50p each. The reserves of H and S are stated below:**

	At 1 January 20X2 £	At 31 December 20X4 £
H	280,000	360,000
S	60,000	200,000

The share capital of S has remained unchanged since 1 January 20X2. In the consolidated balance sheet of H and its subsidiary S at 31 December 20X4, what figure should appear for the minority interest in S?

A   £40,000

B   £50,000

C   £60,000

D   £75,000

250 At 1 January 20X1 H Limited acquired 60% of the share capital of S for £180,000. At that date the share capital of S consisted of 200,000 shares of 50p each. The reserves of H and S are stated below:

	At 1 January 20X1 £	At 31 December 20X4 £
H	280,000	340,000
S	250,000	180,000

In the consolidated balance sheet of H and its subsidiary S, what amount should appear for the minority interest in S?

A £92,000

B £280,000

C £152,000

D £112,000

251 H Limited acquired 75% of the share capital of S for £280,000 on 1 January 20X1.

Goodwill arising on consolidation has been fully amortised.

Details of the share capital and reserves of S are as follows:

	At 1 January 20X1 £	At 31 December 20X7 £
Share capital	200,000	200,000
Profit and loss account reserve	120,000	180,000

At 31 December 20X7 the profit and loss account reserve of H amounted to £480,000.

What figure should appear in the consolidated balance sheet of H and S for the profit and loss account reserve at 31 December 20X7?

A £530,000

B £525,000

C £485,000

D £575,000

252 Which of the following items may appear as current liabilities in a company's balance sheet?

(1) Minority interests in subsidiaries.

(2) Loan due for repayment within one year.

(3) Taxation.

(4) Preference dividend payable.

A (1), (2) and (3)

B (1), (2) and (4)

C (1), (3) and (4)

D (2), (3) and (4)

INTERPRETATION

253   The formula for calculating the rate of stock turnover is:

A   average stock at cost divided by cost of goods sold

B   sales divided by average stock at cost

C   sales divided by average stock at selling price

D   cost of goods sold divided by average stock at cost.

254   A company has the following current assets and liabilities at 31 October 20X8:

		£000
Current assets:	stock	970
	debtors	380
	bank	40
		1,390
Current liabilities:	creditors	420

When measured against accepted 'norms', the company can be said to have:

A   a high current ratio and an ideal acid test ratio

B   an ideal current ratio and a low acid test ratio

C   a high current ratio and a low acid test ratio

D   ideal current and acid test ratios.

255   A business has the following capital and long-term liabilities:

	31.10.X8	31.10.X9
	£m	£m
12% debentures	20	40
Issued share capital	15	30
Share premium	3	18
Retained profits	22	12

At 31 October 20X9, its gearing ratio, compared to that at 31 October 20X8, has:

A   risen, resulting in greater risk for shareholders

B   risen, resulting in greater security for shareholders

C   fallen, resulting in greater security for shareholders

D   remained the same.

256   An analysis of its financial statements revealed that the debtor collection period of R Limited was 100 days, when 60 days is a reasonable figure.

Which one of the following could NOT account for the high level of 100 days?

A   Poor performance in R's credit control department

B   A large credit sale made just before the balance sheet date

C   R's trade is seasonal

D   A downturn in R's trade in the last quarter of the year

257 The analysis of a company's financial statements revealed that the number of days' sales in stock was 80 days. The average for companies in the same industry was 35 days.

Which of the following is LEAST likely to account for the high level of 80 days?

A   The company's trade is seasonal

B   Poor stock control

C   A large purchase was made just before the balance sheet date

D   An increase in the company's sales in the three months before the balance sheet date

258 Which of the following correctly defines working capital?

A   Fixed assets plus current assets minus current liabilities

B   Current assets minus current liabilities

C   Fixed assets plus current assets

D   Share capital plus reserves

The following data relates to Questions 259 and 260.

Extracts from a company's financial statements for the year ended 30 September 20X1 are given below.

Balance sheet		Profit and loss account	
	£000		£000
Issued share capital	500	Operating profit	300
Share premium	200	Interest payable	100
Profit and loss account	800	Profit before tax	200
Non-current liabilities:			
10% debentures	1,000		

259 What is the return on shareholders' equity as a percentage, based on these figures?

A   40%

B   20%

C   13.3%

D   12%

260 What is the return on total capital employed as a percentage, based on these figures?

A   12%

B   8%

C   13.3%

D   20%

261 You are given the following extract from a company's profit and loss account:

	£000
Turnover	15,000
Opening stock at cost	1,750
Purchases	10,200
Closing stock at cost	1,950

Assuming continuity in the rate of turnover, how many days' worth of sales does the business have in stock at the year-end (to the nearest day)?

A   47 days

B   68 days

C   70 days

D   71 days

262   **Mr Worthing expects that his business will have net current liabilities at the financial year-end. The raising of extra funds on a short term loan at the balance sheet date would:**

A   improve the current ratio

B   worsen the current ratio

C   have no effect on the current ratio

D   either improve or worsen the current ratio depending upon the balances involved and the extra funds raised.

263   **George Bentley discovers that his business has made a loss during the financial year just ended, but that it has more cash at the end of the year than it did at the beginning.**

Which of the following could be a reason for this?

A   George drew more out of the business this year than last

B   Some fixed assets were sold during the year

C   Debtors took longer to pay this year than last

D   Prepayments were higher at the end of this year

264   **The rate of stock turnover is 6 times where:**

A   sales are £120,000 and average stock at selling price is £20,000

B   purchases are £240,000 and average stock at cost is £40,000

C   cost of goods sold is £180,000 and average stock at cost is £30,000

D   net purchases are £90,000 and closing stock at cost is £15,000.

265   **The formula for calculating the rate of stock turnover is:**

A   average stock at cost divided by cost of goods sold

B   sales divided by average stock at cost

C   sales divided by average stock at selling price

D   cost of goods sold divided by average stock at cost.

266   **The net profit percentage in a company is 12% and the asset turnover ratio is 2.**

What is the return on capital employed?

A   6%

B   10%

C   14%

D   24%

267   Which **ONE** of the following formulae correctly expresses the relationship between the return on capital employed (ROCE), net profit margin (NPM) and asset turnover (AT)?

A $ROCE = NPM \div AT$

B $ROCE = NPM + AT$

C $ROCE = NPM \times AT$

D $ROCE = NPM - AT$

268   A summary of the balance sheet of M Ltd at 31 March 20X2 was as follows:

	£000
Total assets less current liabilities	120
Ordinary share capital	40
Share premium account	10
Profit and loss account	10
5% debentures 2010	60
	120

If the operating profit for the year ended 31 March 20X2 was £15,000, what is the return on capital employed?

A   12.5 per cent

B   25 per cent

C   30 per cent

D   37.5 per cent

269   The annual sales of a company are £235,000 including VAT at 17.5 per cent. Half of the sales are on credit terms; half are cash sales. The debtors in the balance sheet are £23,500.

What are the debtor days (to the nearest day)?

A   37 days

B   43 days

C   73 days

D   86 days

270   The draft balance sheet of B Ltd at 31 March 20X3 is set out below.

	£	£
Fixed assets		450
Current assets		
Stock	65	
Debtors	110	
Prepayments	30	
	205	
Current liabilities		
Creditors	30	
Bank overdraft (Note 1)	50	
	80	
		125
		575

Long-term liability:
Loan (75)

500

Ordinary share capital 400
Profit and loss account 100

500

Note 1: The bank overdraft first occurred on 30 September 20X2.

What is the gearing of the company?

A   13 per cent

B   16 per cent

C   20 per cent

D   24 per cent

271   An increase in stock of £250, a decrease in the bank balance of £400 and an increase in creditors of £1,200 result in:

A   a decrease in working capital of £1,350

B   an increase in working capital of £1,350

C   a decrease in working capital of £1,050

D   an increase in working capital of £1,050.

272   Working capital will reduce by £500 if:

A   goods costing £3,000 are sold for £3,500 on credit

B   goods costing £3,000 are sold for £3,500 cash

C   fixed assets costing £500 are purchased on credit

D   fixed assets with a net book value of £750 are sold for £250 cash.

273   From the following information regarding the year to 31 August 20X6, what is the creditors' payment period?

	£
Sales	43,000
Cost of sales	32,500
Opening stock	6,000
Closing stock	3,800
Creditors at 31 August 20X6	4,750

A   40 days

B   50 days

C   53 days

D   57 days

274 During the year ended 31 October 20X7, your organisation made a gross profit of £60,000, which represented a mark-up of 50%. Opening stock was £12,000 and closing stock was £18,000.

The rate of stock turnover was:

A   4 times

B   6.7 times

C   7.3 times

D   8 times.

275 A business operates on a gross profit margin of $33\frac{1}{3}$%. Gross profit on a sale was £800, and expenses were £680.

The net profit percentage is:

A   3.75%

B   5%

C   11.25%

D   22.67%.

276 A company's gross profit as a percentage of sales increased from 24% in the year ended 31 December 20X1 to 27% in the year ended 31 December 20X2.

Which of the following events is most likely to have caused the increase?

A   An increase in sales volume

B   Goods received in December 20X1 mistakenly being recorded as a purchase in January 20X2

C   Overstatement of the closing stock at 31 December 20X1

D   Understatement of the closing stock at 31 December 20X1

277 A company's capital structure at 31 December 20X2 is as follows:

	£m
Ordinary share capital	380
Profit and loss account	120
	500
8% Debentures	100
	600

The company's profit and loss account shows the following for the year ended 31 December 20X2:

	£m
Operating profit	40
Interest paid	(8)
	32
Taxation	(10)
	22
Dividends paid and proposed	(10)
Retained profit for year	12

What is the return on equity shareholders' capital employed, using closing capital figures?

A   4.4%

B   2.4%

C   3.7%

D   5.8%

278   **A business has the following trading account for the year ending 31 May 20X8:**

	£	£
Sales turnover		45,000
Opening stock	4,000	
Purchases	26,500	
	30,500	
Less: Closing stock	6,000	
		24,500
Gross profit		20,500

Its rate of stock turnover for the year is:

A   4.9 times

B   5.3 times

C   7.5 times

D   9 times.

279   **A company's gearing ratio would rise if:**

A   a decrease in long-term loans is LESS than a decrease in shareholders' funds

B   a decrease in long-term loans is MORE than a decrease in shareholders' funds

C   interest rates rose

D   dividends were paid.

280   **When a company makes a rights issue of equity shares which of the following effects will the issue have?**

(1)   Working capital is increased.

(2)   Gearing ratio is increased.

(3)   Share premium account is reduced.

(4)   Investments are increased.

A   (1) only

B   (1) and (2)

C   (3) only

D   (1) and (4)

281 **Which one of the following would help a company with high gearing to reduce its gearing ratio?**

A   Making a rights issue of equity shares.

B   Issuing further long-term loan stock.

C   Making a bonus issue of shares.

D   Paying dividends on its equity shares.

282 **Which one of the following would cause a company's gross profit percentage on sales to fall?**

A   Sales volume has declined.

B   Closing stock is lower than opening stock.

C   Some closing stock items were included at less than cost.

D   Selling and distribution costs have risen.

283 **A company has the following details extracted from its balance sheet:**

	£'000
Stocks	1,900
Debtors	1,000
Bank overdraft	100
Creditors	1,000

Its liquidity position could be said to be:

A   very well-controlled because its current assets far outweigh its current liabilities

B   poorly-controlled because its quick assets are less than its current liabilities

C   poorly-controlled because its current ratio is significantly higher than the industry norm of 1.8

D   poorly-controlled because it has a bank overdraft.

284 **The gross profit mark-up is 40% where:**

A   sales are £120,000 and gross profit is £48,000

B   sales are £120,000 and cost of sales is £72,000

C   sales are £100,800 and cost of sales is £72,000

D   sales are £100,800 and cost of sales is £60,480.

285 **A company has the following current assets and liabilities at 31 October 20X8:**

		£000
Current assets:	stock	1,740
	debtors	863
	bank	95
		2,698
Current liabilities:	creditors	1,349

When measured against accepted 'norms', the company can be said to have:

A   a high current ratio and an ideal acid test ratio

B   an ideal current ratio and a low acid test ratio

C   a high current ratio and a low acid test ratio

D   ideal current and acid test ratios.

286   Your company's profit and loss account for the year ended 30 September 20X8 showed the following:

	£000
Net profit before interest and tax	1,200
Interest	200
	1,000
Corporation tax	400
Retained profit for the year	600

Its balance sheet at 30 September 20X7 showed the following capital:

	£000
Share capital	8,000
Profit and loss account balance	1,200
	9,200
10% debenture	2,000
	11,200

Return on average capital employed for the year ended 30 September 20X8 is:

A   5.88%

B   10.17%

C   10.43%

D   none of these.

287   An increase in both debtors' and creditors' payment periods will result in:

A   an increase in working capital

B   a decrease in working capital

C   an increase in current assets and current liabilities

D   a decrease in current assets and current liabilities.

288   The gearing ratio is often calculated as:

A   long-term loans as a percentage of total shareholders' funds

B   current and long-term debt as a percentage of total net assets

C   long-term loans and preference shares as a percentage of total shareholders' funds

D   preference shares as a percentage of equity capital.

289 An increase in the gross profit margin of a business is most likely to be due to which ONE of the following combinations:

	Selling price per unit	Quantity sold	Cost per unit
A	increased	no change	increased
B	no change	increased	no change
C	no change	no change	decreased
D	decreased	increased	increased

290 A business has the following capital and long-term liabilities:

	31.10.X3 £million	31.10.X4 £million
8% Debentures	15	50
Issued share capital	20	30
Share premium	10	20
Retained profits	43	36

At 31 October 20X4, its gearing ratio, compared to that at 31 October 20X3, has:

A risen, resulting in greater risk for shareholders

B risen, resulting in greater security for shareholders

C fallen, resulting in greater security for shareholders

D remained the same.

291 A business has the following trading accounts:

	Year ended 31 October 20X8		Year ended 31 October 20X9	
	£000	£000	£000	£000
Sales		2,000		2,650
Less: Cost of sales				
Opening stock	75		85	
Purchases	1,260		1,330	
	1,335		1,415	
Less: Closing stock	85		115	
		1,250		1,300
Gross profit		750		1,350

During the year ended 31 October 20X9, its rate of stock turnover, compared with that for the year ended 31 October 20X8, has:

A decreased, with a possible beneficial effect on liquidity

B decreased, with a possible detrimental effect on liquidity

C increased, with a possible detrimental effect on liquidity

D increased, with a possible beneficial effect on liquidity.

292   A company had the following gross profit calculation in its last accounting period:

	£
Sales	130,000
Cost of sales	60,000
Gross profit	70,000

Average stock during that period was £7,500.

In the next accounting period, sales are expected to increase by 40% and the rate of stock turnover is expected to double. If average stock remains at £7,500 the gross profit mark-up percentage will be:

A   30.0%

B   34.1%

C   51.7%

D   65.9%.

293   In 20X3, a company's current ratio was 2.5 : 1 and its acid test ratio was 0.8 : 1. By the end of 20X4, the ratios are expected to be 3 : 1 and 0.6 : 1 respectively.

These changes are most likely to be due to which ONE of the following?

A   Increased bank balances.

B   Decreased bank balances.

C   Increased stocks.

D   Increased debtors and creditors.

Section 2

PRACTICE QUESTIONS

GENERAL FRAMEWORK; ACCOUNTING CONCEPTS AND PRINCIPLES

1   STANDARD-SETTING PROCEDURE

The existing procedures for setting accounting standards in the UK were established in 1990.

Required:

(a)   Explain the roles of the following in relation to accounting standards:

    (i)   Financial Reporting Council (FRC)

    (ii)   Accounting Standards Board (ASB)

    (iii)   Financial Reporting Review Panel (FRRP)

    (iv)   Urgent Issues Task Force (UITF).   **(10 marks)**

(b)   Explain how the standard setting authority approaches the task of producing a standard, with particular reference to the ways in which comment or feedback from interested parties is obtained.   **(5 marks)**

(c)   It is possible that there could be a difference between the requirements of Financial Reporting Standards and those of the Companies Acts in preparing financial statements. How may such a difference be resolved?   **(5 marks)**

(Total: 20 marks)

2   SOLE TRADER V LIMITED LIABILITY COMPANY

The owner of a business may choose to run it as a sole trader or as a limited liability company.

Briefly explain eight differences between the two methods of operation.   **(12 marks)**

3   DEFINITIONS

Define the following accounting concepts and give for each one an example of its application:

(a)   accruals   **(3 marks)**

(b)   money measurement   **(3 marks)**

(c)   substance over form   **(3 marks)**

(d)   consistency (see note below)   **(4 marks)**

(e)   duality   **(3 marks)**

(f)   prudence.   **(4 marks)**

Note: Your answer to (d) should include a brief explanation of the circumstances in which the consistency concept should not be applied.   **(Total: 20 marks)**

4   ASB STATEMENT OF PRINCIPLES

The Accounting Standards Board's Statement of Principles for Financial Reporting (the Statement) sets out, among other things, the qualitative characteristics of financial information, and states that information provided by financial statements needs to be relevant and reliable.

Required:

(a)   Explain what is meant by materiality in relation to financial statements, and state two factors affecting the assessment of materiality   **(4 marks)**

(b)   Explain what makes information in financial statements relevant to users.   **(5 marks)**

(c)   Two characteristics contributing to reliability are 'neutrality' and 'prudence'.

(i)   Explain the meaning of these two terms;

(ii)   Explain how a possible conflict between them could arise, and indicate how that conflict should be resolved.   **(5 marks)**

(d)   One of the requirements of the Statement is that financial statements should be free from material error. Suggest *three* safeguards which may exist, inside or outside a company, to ensure that the financial statements are in fact free from material error.

(6 marks)

(Total: 20 marks)

5   ACCOUNTING CONCEPTS

Financial statements must be prepared according to established accounting concepts, many of which may be found in the ASB's Statement of Principles for the preparation and presentation of financial statements.

Define and explain the relevance of the following accounting concepts:

(a)   Going concern   **(3 marks)**

(b)   Accruals   **(2 marks)**

(c)   Substance over form   **(3 marks)**

(d)   Historical cost   **(2 marks)**

(Total: 10 marks)

6   CHARACTERISTICS AND CONCEPTS

If the information in financial statements is to be useful, regard must be had to the following:

(a)   comparability

(b)   objectivity

(c)   consistency.

Required:

Explain the meaning of each of these factors as they apply to financial accounting, including in your explanations one example of the application of each of them. **(12 marks)**

7 HISTORICAL COST ACCOUNTING

Historical cost accounting has been the normal method of accounting in most countries for many years.

Required:

(a) Explain four respects in which the use of historical cost accounting may distort financial statements or their interpretation **(12 marks)**

(b) Give four reasons why historical cost accounting continues in use despite its limitations. **(8 marks)**

(Total: 20 marks)

8 EXPLAIN

The ASB's Statement of Principles for Financial Reporting presents concepts important in the preparation of financial statements including materiality, prudence and comparability.

Required:

(a) Explain the meaning of the following terms, giving one example of the application of each of them:

(i) Materiality

(ii) Prudence. **(6 marks)**

(b) Explain how accounting standards and the Statement of Principles promote comparability. **(4 marks)**

(Total: 10 marks)

DOUBLE-ENTRY BOOKKEEPING AND ACCOUNTING SYSTEMS

9 SUSPENSE ACCOUNT

A trial balance has an excess of debits over credits of £14,000 and a suspense account has been opened to make it balance. It is later discovered that:

(1) the discounts allowed balance of £3,000 and the discounts received balance of £7,000 have both been entered on the wrong side of the trial balance

(2) the creditors control account balance of £233,786 had been included in the trial balance as £237,386

(3) an item of £500 had been omitted from the sales records (i.e., from the sales day book)

(4) the balance on the current account with the senior partner's wife had been omitted from the trial balance. This item when corrected removes the suspense account altogether.

Required:

Open the suspense account and record the necessary corrections in it. Show in the account the double entry for each item entered. **(8 marks)**

10 REASONS FOR CONTROL ACCOUNTS

(a) Why are many accounting systems designed with a purchase ledger (creditors ledger) control account, as well as with a purchase ledger (creditors ledger)? **(4 marks)**

(b) The following errors have been discovered:

(i) An invoice for £654 has been entered in the purchase day book as £456

(ii) A prompt payment discount of £100 from a creditor had been completely omitted from the accounting records

(iii) Purchases of £250 had been entered on the wrong side of a supplier's account in the purchase ledger

(iv) No entry had been made to record an agreement to contra an amount owed to X of £600 against an amount owed by X of £400

(v) A credit note for £60 had been entered as if it was an invoice.

State the numerical effect on the purchase ledger control account balance of correcting each of these items (treating each item separately). **(8 marks)**

(c) Information technology and computerised systems are rapidly increasing in importance in data recording.

Do you consider that this trend will eventually remove the need for control accounts to be incorporated in the design of accounting systems? Explain your answer briefly.

(4 marks)

(Total: 16 marks)

11 RHEA LIMITED

The trial balance of Rhea Limited at 30 June 20X2 failed to agree and a suspense account was opened with a debit balance of £386,400 pending further action to find the difference.

Subsequent checking revealed the following errors:

(1) The balance of £48,900 on the carriage outwards account was omitted from the trial balance.

(2) Discount columns in the cash book had been misposted:

– Discount allowed £38,880 had been credited to discount received account.

– Discount received £68,200 had been debited to discount allowed account.

(3) An issue of 100,000 £1 ordinary shares in exchange for an asset with an agreed value of £400,000 had been recorded by crediting the ordinary share capital account with £400,000 and debiting the fixed asset account with £400,000.

Required:

(a) Prepare journal entries with narratives to correct these errors.

(b) Write up the suspense account and bring down the balance of difference not yet found.

(9 marks)

12   OTTER LIMITED

Otter Limited operates a computerised accounting system for its sales and purchases ledgers. The control accounts for the month of September 20X9 are in balance and incorporate the following totals:

		£
Sales ledger:		
Balances at 1 September 20X9:	Debit	386,430
	Credit	190
Sales revenue		163,194
Cash received		158,288
Discounts allowed		2,160
Sales returns inwards		590
Credit balances at 30 September 20X9		370
Purchases ledger:		
Balances at 1 September 20X9:	Credit	184,740
	Debit	520
Purchases		98,192
Cash payments		103,040
Discounts received		990
Purchases returns outwards		1,370
Debit balances at 30 September 20X9		520

Although the control accounts agree with the underlying ledgers, a number of errors have been found, and there are also several adjustments to be made. These errors and adjustments are detailed below:

(1)   Four sales invoices totalling £1,386 have been omitted from the records.

(2)   A cash refund of £350 paid to a customer, A Smith, was mistakenly treated as a payment to a supplier, A Smith Limited.

(3)   A contra settlement offsetting a balance of £870 due to a supplier against the sales ledger account for the same company is to be made.

(4)   Bad debts totalling £1,360 are to be written off.

(5)   During the month, settlement was reached with a supplier over a disputed account. As a result, the supplier issued a credit note for £2,000 on 26 September. No entry has yet been made for this.

(6)   A purchases invoice for £1,395 was keyed in as £1,359.

(7)   A payment of £2,130 to a supplier, B Jones, was mistakenly entered to the account of R Jones.

(8)   A debit balance of £420 existed in the purchases ledger at the end of August 20X9. The supplier concerned cannot now be traced and it has been decided to write off this balance.

Required:

Prepare the sales ledger and purchases ledger control accounts as they should appear after allowing, where necessary, for the errors and adjustments listed.   (16 marks)

13   ANDROMEDA LIMITED

The trial balance of Andromeda Limited at 31 December 20X0 did not balance. On investigation the following errors and omissions were found. When all were corrected, the trial balance agreed.

(1)   A loan of £20,000 from Jason, one of the directors of the company, had been correctly entered in the cash book but posted to the wrong side of the loan account.

(2)   The purchase of a motor vehicle on credit for £28,600 had been recorded by debiting the supplier's account and crediting motor expenses account.

(3)   A cheque for £800 received from A Smith, a customer to whom goods are regularly supplied on credit, was correctly entered into the cash book but was posted to the credit of bad debts recovered account in the mistaken belief that it was a receipt from B Smith, a customer whose debt had been written off some time earlier.

(4)   In reconciling the company's cash book with the bank statement it was found that bank charges of £380 had not been entered in the company's records.

(5)   The totals of the cash discount columns in the cash book for December 20X0 had not been posted to the discount accounts.

The figures were:

Discount allowed	£1,840
Discount received	£3,970

(6)   The company had purchased some plant on 1 January 20X0 for £16,000. The payment was correctly entered in the cash book but was debited to plant repairs account. The depreciation rate for such plant is 20% per year on the straight-line basis.

Required:

Prepare journal entries with narratives to correct the errors, write up the suspense account and hence derive the opening balance on the suspense account representing the original difference.   **(16 marks)**

14   WHOLESALERS

On 1 January 20X1 the accounting records of Wholesalers plc included the following balances. All figures are in £000.

			£000
Sales ledger control account			50
Provision for doubtful debts			2
Individual sales ledger memorandum balances	– positive	A	10
	"	B	20
	"	C	8
	"	D	9
	"	E	6
	– negative	F	2
	"	G	1

The following unaudited information is presented to you concerning the year 20X1.

Sales day book		Cash book receipts		
Customer	Amount	Customer	Amount	Discount
	£000		£000	£000
A	30	A	35	2
B	35	B	30	
D	18	C	5	
E	9	D	20	
F	8	E	12	
G	7	F	5	1
		G	4	
	___		___	___
	107		111	3
	___		___	___

Sales returns book		Bad debts written off	
Customer	Amount	Customer	Amount
	£000		£000
A	2	C	2
F	3		
	___		___
	5		2
	___		___

Contras with creditors ledger	
Customer	Amount
	£000
E	2
G	4
	___
	6
	___

The closing balance on the provision for doubtful debts account is required to be 4% of remaining debtors.

You are required to prepare sales ledger control account, provision for doubtful debts account, and memorandum sales ledger accounts for each customer, for the year 20X1. Carry down year-end balances and prove that the sales ledger control balance reconciles with the memorandum balances. The ledger accounts may be presented in any summarised form you find convenient provided all entries are clear.   **(18 marks)**

15   DEBTORS CONTROL

A company maintains a debtors control account in the nominal ledger, and includes the balance on this account in its trial balance. It also maintains a memorandum individual debtors ledger.

The following errors relating to debtors have been discovered.

(a)   A credit note for £90 had been entered as if it were an invoice.

(b)   Sales of £400 had been entered on the wrong side of a customer's account in the individual debtors ledger.

(c)   A prompt payment discount of £70 had been completely omitted from the records.

(d)   An invoice of £123 had been entered in the sales day book as £321.

(e)   No entry had been made to record an agreement to contra an amount owed to P of £600 against an amount owed by P of £700.

(f)   Bad debts of £160 had been omitted from the individual debtors accounts, though otherwise correctly treated.

Required:

Prepare journal entries to correct each of the errors described in (a) to (f) above. Accounts should be fully named, but narrative descriptions are not required.   **(12 marks)**

16   UPRIGHT

The draft final accounts of Upright for the year ended 31 October 20X5 show a net profit of £48,200.

The trial balance still has a difference for which a suspense account has been opened. The suspense account appears in Upright's balance sheet as a debit balance of £1,175.

In the course of subsequent checking, the following errors and omissions were found:

(i)   At 1 November 20X4 insurance of £1,305 has been prepaid, but the figure had not been brought down on the insurance account as an opening balance.

(ii)   A vehicle held as a fixed asset, which had originally cost £22,000, was sold for £6,000. At 1 November 20X4, depreciation of £17,600 had been charged on the vehicle. The £6,000 proceeds of sale had been credited to sales account, and no other entries had been made.

(iii)   Depreciation on vehicles had been calculated at 20% (straight line basis) on the balance on the vehicles cost account. The charge for the year now needs to be adjusted for the effect of item (ii) above.

(iv)   At 31 October 20X5, insurance of £1,500 paid in advance had not been allowed for in the insurance account.

(v)   The credit side of the rent receivable account had been undercast by £400.

(vi)   A credit purchase of £360 had been correctly entered into the purchases day book (list of purchase invoices) but had been entered as £630 on the credit side of the supplier's account in the creditors' ledger. Upright does not maintain a creditors' ledger control account in the nominal ledger.

When these errors had been corrected, the suspense account balanced.

Required:

(a)   Prepare a statement showing the effect on Upright's profit of the correction of these errors.   **(12 marks)**

(b)   Show the suspense account as it would appear in Upright's records.   **(6 marks)**

(Total: 18 marks)

17   TURNER

The bookkeeping system of Turner Limited is not computerised, and at 30 September 20X8 the bookkeeper was unable to balance the accounts.

The trial balance totals were:

Debit	£1,796,100
Credit	£1,852,817

He nevertheless proceeded to prepare draft financial statements, inserting the difference as a balancing figure in the balance sheet. The draft profit and loss account showed a profit of £141,280 for the year ended 30 September 20X8.

He then opened a suspense account for the difference and began to check through the accounting records to find the difference. He found the following errors and omissions:

(i)   £8,980, the total of the sales returns book for September 20X8, had been credited to purchases returns account.

(ii) £9,600 paid for an item of plant purchased on 1 April 20X8 had been debited to plant repairs account. The company depreciates its plant at 20% per annum on the straight line basis, with proportional depreciation in the year of purchase.

(iii) The cash discount totals for the month of September 20X8 had not been posted to the nominal ledger accounts. The figures were:

Discount allowed   £836
Discount received   £919

(iv) £580 insurance prepaid at 30 September 20X7 had not been brought down as an opening balance.

(v)   The balance of £38,260 on the telephone expense account had been omitted from the trial balance.

(vi) A car held as a fixed asset had been sold during the year for £4,800. The proceeds of sale were entered in the cash book but had been credited to sales account in the nominal ledger. The original cost of the car £12,000, and the accumulated depreciation to date £8,000, were included in the motor vehicles account and the accumulated depreciation account. The company depreciates motor vehicles at 25% per annum on the straight line basis with proportionate depreciation in the year of purchase but none in the year of sale.

Required:

(a) Open a suspense account for the difference between the trial balance totals. Prepare the journal entries necessary to correct the errors and eliminate the balance on the suspense account. Narratives are not required.   **(10 marks)**

(b) Draw up a statement showing the revised profit after correcting the above errors.

(6 marks)

(Total: 16 marks)

18   USE OF COMPUTERS

Over the past few decades, routine bookkeeping and accountancy work has been transformed by the extensive use of computers to perform that work.

Required:

(a) List and briefly explain two types of error which could occur in a manual sales ledger system which could not occur in a computerised system.   **(4 marks)**

(b) List and briefly explain two types of error which could occur in a manual sales ledger system which could also occur in a computerised system.   **(4 marks)**

(c) Explain the main advantages and disadvantages of computerised accounting systems compared with manual systems.   **(12 marks)**

(Total: 20 marks)

19   GEORGE

George had completed his financial statements for the year ended 31 March 20X9, which showed a profit of £81,208, when he realised that no bank reconciliation statement had been prepared at that date.

When checking the cash book against the bank statement and carrying out other checks, he found the following:

(1)   A cheque for £1,000 had been entered in the cash book but had not yet been presented.

(2)   Cheques from customers totalling £2,890 entered in the cash book on 31 March 20X9 were credited by the bank on 1 April 20X9.

(3)   Bank charges of £320 appear in the bank statement on 30 March 20X9 but have not been recorded by George.

(4)   A cheque for £12,900 drawn by George to pay for a new item of plant had been mistakenly entered in the cash book and the plant account as £2,900. Depreciation of £290 had been charged in the profit and loss account for this plant.

(5)   A cheque for £980 from a credit customer paid in on 26 March was dishonoured after 31 March 20X9 and George decided that the debt would have to be written off as the customer was now untraceable.

(6)   A cheque for £2,400 in payment for some motor repairs had mistakenly been entered in the cash book as a debit and posted to the credit of motor vehicles account. Depreciation at 25% per annum (straight line) is charged on motor vehicles, with a full year's charge calculated on the balance at the end of each year.

(7)   The total of the payments side of the cash book had been understated by £1,000. On further investigation it was found that the debit side of the purchases account had also been understated by £1,000.

(8)   George had instructed his bank to credit the interest of £160 on the deposit account maintained for surplus business funds to the current account. This the bank had done on 28 March. George had made an entry on the payments side of the cash book for this £160 and had posted it to the debit of interest payable account.

(9)   George had mistakenly paid an account for £870 for repairs to his house with a cheque drawn on the business account. The entry in the cash book had been debited to repairs to premises account.

(10)   George had also mistakenly paid £540 to Paul, a trade supplier, to clear his account in the purchases ledger, using a cheque drawn on George's personal bank account. No entries have yet been made for this transaction.

The cash book showed a debit balance of £4,890 before any correcting entries had been made. The balance in the bank statement is to be derived in your answer.

Required:

(a)   Prepare an adjusted cash book showing the revised balance which should appear in George's balance sheet at 31 March 20X9.   **(6 marks)**

(b)   Prepare a bank reconciliation statement as at 31 March 20X9.   **(2 marks)**

(c)   Draw up a statement for George showing the effect on his profit of the adjustments necessary to correct the errors found.   **(8 marks)**

(d)   Prepare journal entries to correct items (9) and (10). Narratives *are* required.**(4 marks)**

                                                                (Total: 20 marks)

ACCOUNTING TREATMENTS

20 DEPRECIATION / AMORTISATION

Explain the extent, if any, to which the following assets should be depreciated/amortised.

(a)   Land and buildings that have been revalued upwards since acquisition.   **(3 marks)**

(b)   Capitalised development expenditure on a project expected to begin commercial
production in two years' time.   **(3 marks)**

(c)   A holding of quoted equity shares.   **(2 marks)**

(Total: 8 marks)

21 DIAMOND

Diamond plc is a trading company making up its accounts regularly to 31 December each
year.

At 1 January 20X5 the following balances existed in the records of Diamond plc.

	£000
Freehold land – cost	1,000
Freehold buildings – cost	500
Aggregate depreciation provided on buildings to 31.12.X4	210
Office equipment – cost	40
Aggregate depreciation provided on office equipment to 31.12.X4	24

The company's depreciation policies are as follows:

Freehold land – no depreciation.

Freehold buildings – depreciation provided at 2% per annum on cost on the straight-line
basis.

Office equipment – depreciation provided at 12½% per annum on the straight-line basis.

A full year's depreciation is charged in the year of acquisition of all assets and none in the
year of disposal.

During the two years to 31 December 20X6 the following transactions took place:

(1)   Year ended 31 December 20X5:

    (a)   10 June: Office equipment purchased for £16,000. This equipment was to
replace some old items which were given in part exchange. Their agreed part
exchange value was £4,000. They had originally cost £8,000 and their book
value was £1,000. The company paid the balance of £12,000 in cash.

    (b)   8 October: An extension was made to the building at a cost of £50,000.

(2)   Year ended 31 December 20X6:

    1 March: Office equipment which had cost £8,000 and with a written-down value of
£2,000 was sold for £3,000.

    In preparing the financial statements at 31 December 20X6 it was decided to revalue
the land upwards by £200,000 to reflect a recent survey.

Required:

(a)   Write up the necessary ledger accounts to record these transactions for the *two* years ended 31 December 20X6. (Separate cost (or valuation) and aggregate depreciation accounts are required – you should *not* combine cost and depreciation in a single account.)   **(11 marks)**

(b)   Explain the purpose of depreciation according to FRS 15, *Tangible fixed assets*, and the factors which need to be taken into account in assessing the amount of depreciation required each year.   **(5 marks)**

(Total: 16 marks)

22   AGATHA LTD

Agatha Limited made up its financial statements to 31 December each year until 31 December 20X7, when the company changed its accounting date by making up its next financial statements for the *fifteen months* to 31 March 20X9.

The company's depreciation policy is to charge proportionate depreciation in the periods of purchase and sale of its fixed assets, charging depreciation as from the first day of the month in which assets are acquired, and up to the last day of the month before the month of any disposal. Annual rates of depreciation taken are:

Plant and machinery: 15 per cent straight line

Motor vehicles: 25 per cent straight line

At 1 January 20X8 the following balances existed in the company's accounting records:

		£
Plant and machinery:	cost	819,000
	accumulated depreciation	360,000
Motor vehicles:	cost	148,000
	accumulated depreciation	60,000

During the fifteen months ended 31 March 20X9 the following transactions took place:

(1)   10 January 20X8

An item of plant was purchased. The cost was made up as follows:

	£
Cost ex factory	41,200
Delivery	300
Installation costs	800
Construction of foundations	3,600
Spare parts for repairs	4,000
Cost of one year maintenance agreement	2,000
	51,900

(2)   18 April 20X8

A new motor vehicle was purchased for £18,000. An existing vehicle which had cost £12,000, and which had a book value at 1 January 20X8 of £6,000, was given in part exchange at an agreed value of £5,000. The balance of £13,000 was paid in cash.

Required:

(a)   Prepare the ledger accounts to show the balances at 1 January 20X8 and to record the fixed asset transactions as stated.   **(11 marks)**

(b)   Prepare the schedule of figures detailing the movements in fixed assets and depreciation for the company's financial statements for publication for the period ended 31 March 20X9.

(Figures may be rounded to the nearest £100 for part (b)).   **(5 marks)**

(Total: 16 marks)

23   ROOK

The following transactions of Rook Limited took place in the year ended 31 March 20X0:

(a)   The clearance of a difference in the trial balance for which a suspense account had been opened. The difference was found to be caused by a £2,000 understatement of the debit side of the salaries account in the nominal ledger.   **(2 marks)**

(b)   The acceptance of a car worth £6,000 in settlement of a sales ledger debt of £7,500 due from Wren Limited. No other money will be received from Wren Limited. The car is to be used by one of the sales representatives of Rook Limited.   **(2 marks)**

(c)   The construction of an extension to Rook's factory using materials from stock and the company's own labour force. The costs were:

Materials taken from stock	£27,600
Labour	£18,500

(3 marks)

(d)   Rook Limited purchased a number of assets from Crow Limited. It was agreed that the total purchase price was not to be paid immediately but was to remain as a loan to be repaid by Rook over several years. The assets purchased were:

	£
Motor vehicles	18,000
Plant and machinery	33,000
Goods for resale in the normal course of Rook's business	20,000
	———
	71,000
	———

(3 marks)

(e)   The purchase of a car from Car Dealer on 18 March 20X0 for £20,000. On that date, Rook Limited gave in part exchange a vehicle which had cost £18,000 and which had a written down value £12,000. The agreed part exchange value of this vehicle was its written down value of £12,000. The balance of £8,000 is to be paid on 30 April 20X0.

(6 marks)

Required:

Show journals entries, with narrations, to record these transactions. Note that entries to ledger control accounts are not required for item (b).   **(Total: 16 marks)**

24 PENTLAND

Pentland Limited compiles its financial statements for the year to 30 June each year. At 1 July 20X0 the company's balance sheet included the following figures:

	Cost £000	Accumulated depreciation £000	Net book value £000
Land	4,000	Nil	4,000
Buildings	2,200	800	1,400
Plant and machinery	1,600	600	1,000
Motor vehicles	600	200	400

Depreciation is charged at the following annual rates (all straight line):

Land	Nil
Buildings	2%
Plant and machinery	15%
Motor vehicles	20%

A proportionate depreciation charge is made in the year of purchase, sale or revaluation of an asset.

During the year ended 30 June 20X1 the following transactions took place:

(1)   1 January 20X1: The company decided to adopt a policy of revaluing its buildings, and they were revalued to £3.4m.

(2)   1 January 20X1: Plant which had cost £300,000 was sold for £50,000. Accumulated depreciation on this plant at 30 June 20X0 amounted to £230,000. New plant was purchased at a cost of £400,000.

(3)   1 April 20X1: A new motor vehicle was purchased for £30,000. Part of the purchase price was settled by part exchanging another motor vehicle, which had cost £20,000, at an agreed value of £12,000. The balance of £18,000 was paid in cash.

The motor vehicle given in part-exchange had a net book value (cost less depreciation) at 30 June 20X0 of £10,000.

Required:

Prepare ledger accounts to record these transactions in the records of Pentland Limited.

(16 marks)

25 RUBENS

Rubens plc is a company in the pharmaceuticals industry which spends heavily on research and development each year. The company's policy is to capitalise development expenditure meeting the conditions in SSAP 13 Research and Development and to amortise it over five years on the straight line basis beginning when sales revenue is first generated from the developed product. Amortisation is apportioned on a time basis in the first year of amortisation.

The company's finance director has asked you to compute the amounts for research and development to be included in the financial statements for the year ended 30 September 20X8 in accordance with the company's accounting policy. The company's profit is expected to be about £8m.

The company's ledger accounts for development expenditure and research expenditure, before amortisation and other adjustments for the year ended 30 September 20X8, showed the following details:

Development expenditure

Project	Balance at 30.9.X7 £000	Expenditure year ended 30.9.X8 £000	Balance at 30.9.X8 £000
A	600		
B	2,400		
C	3,600	400	4,000
D	1,200	300	1,500
E		800	800
F		400	400

Notes

A   Project A was completed in 20X5 at a total cost of £1,000,000 and is being amortised in accordance with the company's policy.

B   Project B was completed in June 20X7. Sales revenue began on 1 November 20X7.

C   Project C is not yet complete and development is proceeding. It continues to meet the criteria for capitalisation in SSAP 13.

D   Project D was abandoned during the year ended 30 September 20X8 when a competitor launched a superior product.

E   Project E is a new development project commenced in 20X7/X8. It meets the criteria for capitalisation in SSAP 13.

F   Project F was commenced and completed during 20X7/X8. Sales revenue is expected to begin in 20X9.

Research expenditure

The balance on the research expenditure account was £1,800,000, representing payments made during the year ended 30 September 20X8.

Required:

(a)   State the criteria which must be met under SSAP 13 *Research and Development* if development expenditure is to be capitalised.   **(6 marks)**

(b)   Compute the amounts to be included in the profit and loss account for research and development expenditure and in the balance sheet for deferred development expenditure, and state the heading under which they should be included or disclosed.

(6 marks)

(c)   Prepare notes to the financial statements of Rubens plc giving the supporting information required by SSAP 13 *Research and Development* and FRS 3 *Reporting Financial Performance* regarding research and development.   **(8 marks)**

(Total: 20 marks)

26   LOMOND

Lomond plc is engaged in a number of research and development projects. Its accounting policy as regards research and development is to capitalise expenditure as far as allowed by SSAP 13 *Accounting for Research and Development*. At 30 June 20X3, the following balances existed in the company's accounting records:

Project A   Development completed 30 June 20X1. Total expenditure £200,000. Being amortised over five years on the straight line basis. Balance at 30 June 20X3: £120,000.

Project B   A development project commenced 1 July 20X1. Total expenditure in the years ended 30 June 20X2 and 30 June 20X3 totalled £175,000. During the year ended 30 June 20X4, it became clear that a competitor had launched a superior product and the project was abandoned. Further development expenditure in the year ended 30 June 20X4 amounted to £55,000.

Project C   Development commenced 1 October 19X2. Expenditure to date:

Year ended	30 June 19X3	£85,000
Year ended	30 June 20X4	£170,000

All expenditure on Project C meets the criteria for capitalisation in SSAP 13.

Project D   In addition, research project D commenced on 1 July 20X3. Expenditure to date (all on research):

Year ended	30 June 20X4	£80,000

Required:

(a)   State the conditions which must be met if development expenditure is to be capitalised.   **(6 marks)**

(b)   On the basis that Lomond capitalises development expenditure to the maximum allowed by SSAP 13, calculate the amounts which should appear in the company's profit and loss account and balance sheet for research and development for the year ended 30 June 20X4.   **(7 marks)**

(c)   Show the notes which SSAP 13 requires in the financial statements for the year giving supporting figures for the items in the profit and loss account and balance sheet.

(7 marks)

(Total: 20 marks)

27   SAMPI

(a)   SSAP 9 *Stocks and Long-term Contracts* requires stocks of raw materials and finished goods to be valued in financial statements at the lower of cost and net realisable value.

Required:

(i)   Appendix 1 to SSAP 9 states that in arriving at the cost of stock methods such as last in, first out (LIFO) are not usually appropriate. Explain how LIFO is applied.   **(2 marks)**

(ii)   Describe three methods of arriving at cost of stock which are acceptable under SSAP 9 and explain why they are regarded as acceptable, and LIFO is not.

(5 marks)

(iii)   Explain how the cost of a stock of finished goods held by the manufacturer would normally be arrived at when obtaining the figure for the financial statements.   **(3 marks)**

(b)   Sampi is a manufacturer of garden furniture. The company has consistently used FIFO (first in, first out) in valuing stock, but it is interested to know the effect on its stock valuation of using LIFO (last in, first out) and weighted average cost instead of FIFO.

At 28 February 20X8 the company had a stock of 4,000 standard plastic tables, and has computed its value on each of the three bases as:

Basis	Unit cost £	Total value £
FIFO	16	64,000
LIFO	12	48,000
Weighted average	13	52,000

During March 20X8 the movements on the stock of tables were as follows:

Received from factory

Date	Number of units	Production cost per unit £
8 March	3,800	15
22 March	6,000	18

Sales

Date	Number of units
12 March	5,000
18 March	2,000
24 March	3,000
28 March	2,000

On a FIFO basis the stock at 31 March 20X8 was £32,400.

Required:

Compute what the value of the stock at 31 March 20X8 would be using:

(i) LIFO   **(5 marks)**

(ii) Weighted average cost.   **(5 marks)**

In arriving at the total stock values you should make calculations to two decimal places (where necessary) and deal with each stock movement in date order.

(Total: 20 marks)

28 LAMORGAN

You are preparing a trading and profit and loss account and balance sheet for Lamorgan, a sole trader who does not keep adequate accounting records.

The following information is available to you to compute the figures for inclusion in the accounts for sales, purchases and closing stock for the year ended 30 June 20X1:

(a) **Sales**

	£
Cash received from credit customers	218,500
Cash sales receipts paid into bank	114,700
Expenses paid out of cash sales before banking	9,600
Trade debtors: 30 June 20X0	41,600
Trade creditors: 30 June 20X1	44,200
Refunds to customers	800
Discounts allowed	2,600
Bad debts written off	1,500
Amount due from credit customer deducted by Lamorgan in paying supplier's account	700

Required:

Compute the sales figures from this information. **(5 marks)**

(b) **Purchases**

	£
Payments to suppliers	114,400
Trade creditors: 30 June 20X0	22,900
Trade creditors: 30 June 20X1	24,800
Cost of items taken from stock by Lamorgan for personal use	400
Amount due from credit customer deducted by Lamorgan in setting Supplier's account	700

Required:

Compute the purchases figure from this information. **(3 marks)**

(c) Closing stock

	£
Cost of stock obtained from physical count on 30 June 20X1	77,700

This figures does NOT include any amounts for the two items below.

(i) A stock line which had cost £1,800 was found to be damaged. Remedial work costing £300 is needed to enable the items to be sold for £1,700. Selling expenses of £100 would also be incurred in selling these items.

(ii) Goods sent to a customer on approval in May 20X1 were not included in the stock. The sale price of the goods was £4,000 and the cost £3,000. The customer notified his acceptance of the goods in July 20X1.

Note: No adjustment to the sales figure in (a) above is required for this item.

Required:

Compute the adjusted closing stock figure from this information. **(2 marks)**

(Total: 10 marks)

29   PERSEUS LIMITED

The trial balance of Perseus Limited contains the following items at 31 December 20X0:

	Dr	Cr
	£	£
Opening stock	3,850,000	
Sales ledger balances	2,980,000	1,970
Purchases ledger balances	14,300	1,210,400
Prepayments	770,000	
Cash at bank A	940,000	
Overdraft at bank B		360,000

The closing stock amounted to £4,190,000, before allowing for the adjustments required by items (2) and (3) below.

In the course of preparing the financial statements at 31 December 20X0, the need for a number of adjustments emerged, as detailed below:

(1) The *opening stock* was found to have been overstated by £418,000 as a result of errors in calculations of values in the stock sheets.

(2)   Some items included in closing stock at cost of £16,000 were found to be defective and were sold after the balance sheet date for £10,400. Selling costs amounted to £600.

(3)   Goods with a sales value of £88,000 were in the hands of customers at 31 December 20X0 on a sale or return basis. The goods had been treated as sold in the records and the full sales value of £88,000 had been included in trade debtors. After the balance sheet date, the goods were returned in good condition. The cost of the goods was £66,000.

(4)   Debtor balances amounting to £92,000 are to be written off.

(5)   An allowance for doubtful debts is to be set up for 5% of the debtors total.

(6)   The manager of the main selling outlet of Perseus is entitled, from 1 January 20X0, to a commission of 2% of the company's profit *after* charging that commission. The profit amounted to £1,101,600 *before* including the commission, and after adjusting for items (1) to (5) above. The manager has already received £25,000 on account of the commission due during the year ended 31 December 20X0.

Required:

(a)   (i)   Explain how adjustment should be made for the error in the opening stock. (Assume that it constitutes a material and fundamental amount).

         (ii)   State *two* disclosures which should be made in the financial statements at 31 December 20X0 for the adjustment in (i) above.   **(6 marks)**

(b)   Show how the final figures for current assets should be presented in the balance sheet at 31 December 20X0.   **(14 marks)**

(Total: 20 marks)

30   THETA

At 31 December 20X7 the totals of the personal ledger balances of Theta Limited were as follows:

		£
Sales ledger –	debit	384,600
	credit	2,900
Purchases ledger –	debit	1,860
	credit	222,230

After reviewing these balances in preparing the financial statements for the year ended 31 December 20X7, a number of adjustments are necessary:

(i)   A contra settlement had been agreed during the year offsetting an amount due from Zeta Limited in the sales ledger of £1,080 against the balance due to that company in the purchases ledger. No entry had been made for this contra.

(ii)   The following debts due from sales ledger customers are to be written off:

Customer	£
P	840
Q	120
R	360
S	2,090
T	180

(iii)   The provision for doubtful debts, which stood at £3,060 after the debts in (ii) above had been written off, is to be increased to £5,200.

(iv)   During the year £200 cash received from Tau Limited had mistakenly been entered into the account of Vau Limited in the sales ledger.

Further information:

The purchases ledger balances included £56,000 relating to a purchase in September 20X7 on extended credit terms.

The £56,000 balance is due to be cleared by payments in four equal instalments at six-monthly intervals as follows:

	£
31 March 20X8	14,000
30 September 20X8	14,000
31 March 20X9	14,000
30 September 20X9	14,000

No ledger control accounts are kept by Theta Limited.

Required:

(a)   Prepare journal entries to give effect to adjustments (i) to (iv).   **(4 marks)**

(b)   Calculate the amounts which should appear under the various headings in the company's published balance sheet as at 31 December 20X7 for debtors and creditors, assuming that there are no other items for inclusion apart from those stated above.

(6 marks)

(c)   Define and explain the difference between a provision and a reserve, giving one example of each (other than a provision for doubtful debts).   **(6 marks)**

(Total: 16 marks)

31   DOUBTFUL DEBTS

You are given the following balances at 1 January 20X1:

Debtors	£10,000
Bank overdraft	£5,000
Provision for doubtful debts	£400

You ascertain the following information:

	£
Sales for the year 20X1 (all on credit)	100,000
Sales returns for the year 20X1	1,000
Receipts from customers during 20X1	90,000
Bad debts written off during 20X1	500
Discounts allowed during 20X1	400

At the end of 20X1 the provision for doubtful debts is required to be 5% of debtors, after making a specific provision for a debt of £200 from a customer who has gone bankrupt.

	£
Sales for the year 20X2 (90% on credit)	100,000
Sales returns for the year 20X2 (90% relating to credit customers)	2,000
Receipts from credit customers during 20X2	95,000
Debtor balances settled by contra against creditor balances during 20X2	3,000

Bad debts written off during 20X2 (including 50%
of the debt due from the customer who had
gone bankrupt, the other 50% having been received
in cash during 20X2)   1,500
Discounts allowed during 20X2   500

At the end of 20X2 the provision for doubtful debts is still required to be 5% of debtors.

You are required to write up the debtors and provision for doubtful debts accounts for 20X1 and 20X2, bringing down the balances at the end of each year and showing in those accounts the double entry for each item.   **(14 marks)**

32   PROVISION FOR DOUBTFUL DEBTS

The following transactions are to be recorded. At the beginning of year 1 the provision for doubtful debts account shows a provision of 2% against debtors of £50,000. During the year bad debts of £2,345 are to be charged to the provision account. At the end of year 1 the bad debt provision is required to be 2% against debtors of £60,000.

In year 2 bad debts of £37 are to be charged against the account. At the end of year 2 a provision of 1% against debtors of £70,000 is required.

You are required to prepare a provision for doubtful debts account for the two years. Show in the account the double entry for each item, and carry down the balance at the end of each year.   **(9 marks)**

33   JURIEN

The directors of Jurien Limited are considering the draft financial statements for the year ended 31 March 20X1.

Matters under discussion are:

(a)   After a party in February 20X0, eighteen people died as a result of food poisoning from eating food manufactured by Jurien. At 31 March 20X1 the company was advised that there was probably no liability and the matter was disclosed as a contingent liability at that date. As the result of developments in the case, which is still not settled, the company was advised that it is now probable, as at 31 March 20X1, that the company will be found liable.

Some directors consider that the matter should remain a contingent liability until the court case decides the matter, while others consider that provision should be made for it in the financial statements for the year ended 31 March 20X1.   **(3 marks)**

(b)   No provision has yet been made for a trade debtor of £560,000 outstanding at 31 March 20X1. In June 20X1 the directors of Jurien became aware that the debtor was in financial difficulties. Directors are divided as to whether a provision should be made or not.   **(3 marks)**

(c)   The company's closing stock of finished goods is valued by taking the cost of labour and materials plus an allocation of overheads. One director has queried the basis on which overheads are added and has asked for clarification of the relevant rules, with two examples of overheads which must be excluded.   **(4 marks)**

Required:

Write a memorandum to the directors advising them on the three points raised, explaining the authority for your advice in each case.   **(Total: 10 marks)**

34   ACCOUNTING TREATMENTS

The directors of a company are reviewing the company's most recent draft financial statements and the following points have been raised for discussion:

(a)   **Research and development**

This year the company has begun a substantial programme of research and development. To spread the cost fairly over the years, the draft financial statements have been prepared on the basis that all such costs are to be capitalised and written off on the straight-line basis over three years, beginning in the year in which the expenditure is incurred.   **(8 marks)**

(b)   **Post balance sheet events**

Shortly after the balance sheet date a major debtor of the company went into liquidation because of heavy trading losses and it is expected that little or nothing will be recoverable for the debt.

In the financial statements the debt has been written off, but one of the directors has pointed out that, as a post balance sheet event, the debt should not in fact be written off but disclosure should be made by note to this year's financial statements, and the debt written off next year.   **(6 marks)**

(c)   **Contingency**

An ex-director of the company has commenced an action against the company claiming substantial damages for wrongful dismissal. The company's solicitors have advised that the ex-director is unlikely to succeed with his claim. The solicitors' estimates of the company's potential liabilities are:

	£
– legal costs (to be incurred whether the claim is successful or not)	50,000
– settlement of claim if successful	500,000
	550,000

(6 marks)

Required:

State with reasons whether you consider the accounting treatments in the draft financial statements, as described above, are acceptable. Include in your answer, where appropriate, an explanation of the relevant provisions of accounting standards.   **(Total: 20 marks)**

35   OCHIL

The draft financial statements of Ochil Limited for the year ended 31 March 20X1 are currently under consideration by the directors. The profit for the year is shown as £350,000.

Since 31 March 20X1 the following events have occurred, but have not been reflected in any way in the draft financial statements to that date:

(1)   A substantial quantity of slow-moving stock was sold for £160,000. The stock had cost £300,000 and had been valued for the accounts at 31 March at its estimated net realisable value of £200,000.

(2)   A trade debtor paid the amount owing of £65,000 in full. At 31 March there were doubts as to whether it would be paid and a specific provision for the full amount had been made in the accounts.

(3)   A senior manager who was dismissed in December 20X0 commenced an action against the company alleging wrongful dismissal and claiming damages of £50,000. The company's solicitors estimate that the manager has a 25% chance of success in her claim. Irrecoverable legal costs of £10,000 will be incurred by Ochil regardless of the result of the action.

(4)   Some years previously, Ochil Limited guaranteed the overdraft of an associated company, Sidlaw Limited, up to a limit of £100,000. Shortly after Ochil's balance sheet date, it was announced that Sidlaw was in financial difficulties, and it is now probable that Ochil will have to meet the guarantee in full.

(5)   In May 20X1 plans to merge Ochil with Cairngorm Limited were announced.

(6)   It was discovered that an error was made in arriving at the stock figure at 31 March 20X1. Stock which had cost £30,000, with a net realisable value of £40,000, had been omitted.

Required:

(a)   Briefly explain the required accounting treatment of post balance sheet events and contingent liabilities according to SSAP 17 *Accounting for Post Balance Sheet Events* and FRS 12 *Provisions, Contingent Liabilities and Contingent Assets.*   **(5 marks)**

(b)   Apply the treatment you have stated in (a) to the six events (1) to (6) listed above in relation to the company's financial statements for the year ended 31 March 20X1.

(12 marks)

(c)   Prepare a statement showing the effect on the profit for the year of the adjustments required.   **(3 marks)**

(Total: 20 marks)

36   GERMAINE LTD

(a)   The financial position of an enterprise as revealed by its financial statements may be seriously affected by events occurring after the balance sheet date and contingencies. For this reason SSAP 17 *Post Balance Sheet Events* and FRS 12 *Provisions, Contingent Liabilities and Contingent Assets* lay down rules to ensure that such events and contingencies are properly reflected in financial statements.

Required:

(i)   What factors determine whether post balance sheet events require adjustment to the financial statements, according to SSAP 17 *Post Balance Sheet Events*?

(3 marks)

(ii)   Explain the meaning of the term 'contingent liability'.   **(2 marks)**

(iii)   Explain the different accounting treatments required for contingent liabilities *and* contingent assets depending on their degree of probability.   **(4 marks)**

(iv)   Up to what date would it normally be necessary to adjust for or disclose post balance sheet events or to disclose contingent liabilities and contingent assets?

(2 marks)

(b)   Germaine Limited prepared its draft financial statements for the year ended 31 March 20X9 shortly after the balance sheet date. They showed a profit of £980,000. After they were prepared and before the directors formally approved them, the following events took place:

(i) A customer commenced an action against the company to recover £120,000 of losses incurred as a result of Germaine's alleged supply of faulty components in February 20X9. Germaine Limited intends to defend the case vigorously. The company's legal advisers consider it has a 70% chance of successfully defending the action. If the customer's action is successful, damages and costs are expected to amount to £180,000. If Germaine successfully defends the action, non-recoverable legal costs of £30,000 will be incurred. **(6 marks)**

(ii) A trade debtor, for whose balance a full specific provision had been made at 31 March 20X9, paid the account of £84,000 in full. **(3 marks)**

Required:

Advise the directors of Germaine Limited as to the correct accounting treatment of these items, giving your reasons. If you consider that the financial statements require adjustment, draft journal entries with narrations to give effect to the adjustment. If you consider that a note to the financial statements is required, draft a suitable disclosure note. **(Total: 20 marks)**

FINANCIAL STATEMENTS

OBJECTIVES OF FINANCIAL STATEMENTS AND USERS OF FINANCIAL STATEMENTS

37 FRS 3 AND USERS

The Accounting Standards Board's draft Statement of Principles for Financial Reporting states that the objective of financial statements is to provide information about the financial position, performance and financial adaptability of an enterprise that is useful to a wide range of users.

Required:

(a) List five potential users of company financial statements, and briefly explain for each why they need information about the company. **(10 marks)**

(b) State the main provisions of FRS 3 *Reporting Financial Performance* and briefly explain how they benefit users of financial statements. Your answer should include reference to the provisions relating to the profit and loss account and to the additional statements or notes required by FRS 3. **(10 marks)**

(Total: 20 marks)

SOLE TRADERS AND INCOMPLETE RECORDS

38 ALTESE

(a) The net assets of Altese, a trader, at 1 January 20X2 amounted to £128,000.

During the year to 31 December 20X2 Altese introduced a further £50,000 of capital and made drawings of £48,000.

At 31 December 20X2 Altese's net assets totalled £184,000.

Required:

Using this information compute Altese's total profit for the year ended 31 December 20X2.

(3 marks)

(b)   Senji does not keep proper accounting records, and it is necessary to calculate her total purchases for the year ended 31 January 20X3 from the following information:

	£
Trade creditors 31 January 20X2	130,400
31 January 20X3	171,250
Payments to suppliers	888,400
Cost of goods taken from stock by Senji for her personal use	1,000
Refunds received from suppliers	2,400
Discounts received	11,200

Required:

Compute the figure for purchases for inclusion in Senji's financial statements.

(3 marks)

(c)   Aluki fixes prices to make a standard gross profit percentage on sales of 33 1 /3% The following information for the year ended 31 January 20X3 is available to compute her sales total for the year.

	£
Stock: 1 February 20X2	243,000
31 January 20X3	261,700
Purchases	595,400
Purchases returns	41,200

Required:

Calculate the sales figure for the year ended 31 January 20X3.   **(3 marks)**

(Total: 9 marks)

39   GOSHAWK

Goshawk owns a shop selling men's and women's clothing. He purchased the shop on 1 April 20X0 paying £200,000 for a forty year lease.

Most of Goshawk's sales are for cash, but he has a contract to supply uniforms to a small local security firm to which sales are on monthly credit terms.

At 31 March 20X1 his assets and liabilities were:

	£	Assets £	Liabilities £
Shop		195,000	
Shop fittings: cost	28,000		
Less: accumulated depreciation	4,200		
		23,800	
Stock of goods for sale		28,500	
Trade debtors		1,380	
Prepaid insurance		800	
Cash at bank		3,600	
Loan repayable in 20X7 and carrying interest at 10% per year			100,000
Trade creditors			39,000
Miscellaneous accrued shop expenses			1,800

During the year ended 31 March 20X2, Goshawk's receipts and payments were:

	£
Receipts banked	
Sales (cash and credit customers)	299,580
(Before banking the sales revenue, cash totalling £1,300 was taken out to pay miscellaneous shop expenses)	
Payments by cheque	
Cash paid to suppliers for clothes for sale	211,830
Staff wages	25,870
Insurance	2,000
Miscellaneous shop expenses	2,180
Shop fittings purchased	8,400
Drawings by Goshawk	30,000
Refunds to cash customers for goods returned	960
Loan interest for six months to 30 September 20X1	5,000

The following further information is available:

(1)   Goshawk's assets and liabilities at 31 March 20X2 included the following, in addition to the shop itself and the shop fittings:

	Assets £	Liabilities £
Stock	37,100	
Trade debtors	1,460	
Prepaid insurance	1,000	
Balance at bank	To be calculated	
Loan		100,000
Trade creditors		48,000
Miscellaneous accrued shop expenses		2,100

(2)   Appropriate amounts are to be allowed for amortisation of the lease and for depreciation of the shop fittings, consistent with previous policy, using the straight line method. A full year's depreciation is taken in the year of acquisition of fixed assets.

Required:

(a)   Prepare Goshawk's trading and profit and loss account for the year ended 31 March 20X2, and his balance sheet as at that date.   **(20 marks)**

(b)   Goshawk suspects that one of this staff has been stealing items from stock.

Prepare a statement showing the possible cost of the items stolen, using the information that all the sales are at a standard mark-up of 50% on costs, except for:

	Sales value £
Security uniform rates at a mark-up of 40% on costs	14,000
Sales at a reduced mark-up of 25% on cost	34,000

(4 marks)

(Total: 24 marks)

40 CYGNUS

Cygnus is a sole trader selling antiques from a rented shop. He has not kept proper accounting records for the year ended 31 January 20X1, in spite of his accountant's advice after the preparation of his accounts for the year ended 31 January 20X0.

His assets and liabilities at 31 January 20X0 and 31 January 20X1 were as follows:

	Reference to notes		31 January	
			20X0	20X1
		£	£	£
Assets				
Shop equipment				
Cost		14,800		
Less Depreciation	2	6,900	7,900	To be calculated
Stock			146,400	128,700
Trade debtors			14,400	15,700
Rent in advance	3		1,000	To be calculated
Cash at bank			–	4,850
Cash in hand			800	900
Liabilities				
Loan – Draco	4		24,000	12,000
Trade creditors			12,100	14,200
Accrued expenses	5		2,300	To be calculated
Bank overdraft			2,600	See summary below

The following summary shows bank receipts and payments by Cygnus.

Receipts			Cash Book Summary		Payments
	Notes	£		Notes	£
Sales revenue banked		131,600	Opening balance		2,600
Proceeds of sale of shop equipment	2	300	Payments for purchases	3	81,400
			Rent paid		8,250
			Purchase of shop equipment	2	1,800
			Sundry expenses	5	18,600
			Interest on loan	4	2,400
			Repayment of loan	4	12,000
			Closing balance		4,850
		131,900			131,900

Before banking the shop takings, Cygnus took various amounts as drawings.

Notes

(1) Cygnus fixes his selling prices by doubling the cost of all items purchased.

(2) During the year, Cygnus sold for £300 equipment that had cost £800, and had a written down value at 1 February 20X0 of £200. He purchased further equipment on 1 August 20X0 for £1,800.

Depreciation is charged at 10% per year on the straight-line basis, with no depreciation in the year of sale and proportionable depreciation in the year of purchase.

(3) Rent is payable quarterly in advance on 1 January, 1 April, 1 July and 1 October each year. On 1 July 20X0, the annual rent was increased from £6,000 to £9,000.

(4) The loan from Draco carries interest at 10% per year payable annually on 31 December. On 31 December 20X0, Cygnus repaid £12,000 of the loan. The balance is repayable on 31 December 20X4.

(5) The accrued expenses at 31 January 20X0 consist of the £200 interest accrued on Draco's loan (see Note 4) and sundry expenses of £2,100. At 31 January 20X1, accruals for sundry expenses amounted to £3,300.

Required:

(a) Prepare for Cygnus a trading and profit and loss account for the year ended 31 January 20X1 and a balance sheet as at that date. **(20 marks)**

(b) The use of incomplete records techniques is likely to lead to inaccuracies in the financial statements produced.

State *two* incomplete records techniques which could cause inaccuracies and briefly explain the likely inaccuracies that could result from their use.

Note: Your answer to part (b) need *not* be confined to the effects of techniques used in answering part (a). **(4 marks)**

(Total: 24 marks)

41 HALBERD

Halberd runs a fish shop. He buys supplies daily from the wholesale market paying immediately by cheque. Most of his sales are for cash, except for sales to three local restaurants, which are supplied on monthly credit terms.

Halberd keeps only partial accounting records, and he has asked for your help in preparing his financial statements for the year ended 30 June 20X7. In previous years, he has been assisted by a friend who is now ill and unable to continue or give any information.

Halberd's balance sheet at 30 June 20X6 was as follows:

	Reference to notes	Cost £	Aggregate depreciation £	Net book value £
Fixed assets				
Refrigeration equipment		8,400	2,520	5,880
Shop fittings		3,720	2,090	1,630
Van		9,200	4,600	4,600
		21,320	9,210	12,110
Current assets				
Stock			680	
Trade debtors			4,270	
Prepayments	(1)		1,150	
Cash at bank			3,240	
Cash in till			100	
			9,440	

Less current liabilities:				
Accrued expenses	(2)		440	
Net current assets				9,000
				21,110
Capital 30 June 20X6				21,110
				21,110

Notes

(1) Prepayments at 30 June 20X6:

	£
Insurance: paid in advance to 30 September 20X6	300
Business rates: paid in advance to 31 March 20X7	850
	1,150

(2) Accrued expenses owing at 30 June 20X6:

Van expenses	320
Miscellaneous expenses	120
	440

Halberd has prepared an analysis of his bank transactions for the year to 30 June 20X7 and this is summarised below:

	£	£
Balance per balance sheet 30 June 20X6		3,240
Receipts		
Cash sales banked	108,600	
Receipts from credit customers (the restaurants)	28,440	
Loan received 1 January 20X7 carrying interest at 10% per annum and repayable in 20X9	10,000	
		147,040
		150,280
Payments		
Purchases of fish for sale	81,470	
Rent and rates of shop	8,600	
Staff wages	21,400	
Drawings	20,600	
Insurance	1,400	
Van expenses	3,270	
Miscellaneous expenses	3,600	
Purchase of new shop fittings	1,570	
		141,910
Balance at 30 June 20X7		8,370

The following further information is available:

(1) Depreciation is to be provided as follows:

Refrigeration equipment:10% on cost (straight line)

Shop fittings: 15% (reducing balance)

Van: 25% on cost (straight line)

A full year's depreciation is to be taken for the shop fittings purchased during the year.

(2) At 30 June 20X7 the following assets and liabilities existed:

	Assets £	Liabilities £
Stock of fish for sale	810	
Trade debtors (see note (3))	6,190	
Prepayments: Insurance	350	
Business rates	1,000	
Amounts owing for miscellaneous expenses		200

(3) Halberd is worried about the amount owing by one of the restaurants. The account is three months in arrears and a provision for the full amount due of £1,860 is to be made.

(4) In addition to the drawings of £20,600 shown in the bank statement summary, Halberd always takes £300 per week (£15,600 for the year) out of the takings before banking them. He also estimates that he has had fish costing £400 from stock for his own use during the year.

(5) Halberd had a balance of cash in his till of £150 at 30 June 20X7.

Required:

Prepare Halberd's trading and profit and loss account for the year ended 30 June 20X7 and a balance sheet as at that date. Ignore VAT. **(24 marks)**

42 ERNIE

Ernie is a building contractor, doing repair work for local householders. His wife keeps some accounting records but not on a double-entry basis.

The assets and liabilities of the business at 30 June 20X7 were as follows:

	£
Assets	
Plant and equipment: cost	12,600
depreciation to date	5,800
Motor van: cost	9,000
depreciation to date	6,500
Stock of materials	14,160
Debtors	9,490
Rent of premises paid in advance to 30 September 20X7	750
Insurance paid in advance to 31 December 20X7	700
Bank balance	1,860
Cash in hand	230
Liabilities	
Creditors for supplies	3,460
Telephone bill owing	210
Electricity owing	180

His cash and bank transactions for the year from 1 July 20X7 to 30 June 20X8 are as follows:

Cash and Bank summary

Receipts	Cash £	Bank £	Payments	Cash £	Bank £
Opening balances	230	1,860	Suppliers		83,990
Receipts from customers	52,640	150,880	Rent of premises		3,600
Loan received		10,000	Insurance (to 31.12.X8)		1,600
Proceeds of sale of vehicle held at beginning of year		3,000	Purchase of plant and equipment		8,400
			Purchase of new vehicle		12,800
Cash paid into bank		24,040	Telephone		860
Cash withdrawn from bank	48,260		Electricity		890
Closing balance		2,100	Wages of repair staff	68,200	
			Miscellaneous expenses		1,280
			Drawings by Ernie	8,000	29,800
			Refund to customer		400
			Cash paid into bank	24,040	
			Cash withdrawn from bank		48,260
			Closing balance	890	
	101,130	191,880		101,130	191,880

The following further information is available:

(1) Plant and equipment is to be depreciated at 25% per annum on the reducing balance with a full year's charge in the year of purchase.

(2) The new motor vehicle was purchased on 1 January 20X8. Ernie's depreciation policy is to charge depreciation at 25% per annum on the straight line basis, with a proportionate charge in the year of purchase, but none in the year of sale.

(3) The rent of the premises was increased by 20% from 1 October 20X7.

(4) The loan of £10,000 was obtained from Ernie's brother on 1 April 20X8. It carries interest at 10% per annum, payable on 30 September and 31 March.

(5) At 30 June 20X8, Ernie owed the following amounts:

	£
Suppliers	4,090
Telephone	240
Electricity	220
Miscellaneous expenses	490

(6) At 30 June 20X8, amounts due from customers totalled £10,860. Of this amount, Ernie considered that debts totalling £1,280 were bad and should be written off.

(7) Stock of materials at 30 June was £12,170.

(8) Ernie agreed to pay his wife £5,000 for her assistance with his office work during the year. This amount was actually paid in August 20X8.

Required:

Prepare Ernie's trading and profit and loss account for the year ended 30 June 20X8 and his balance sheet as at that date. **(24 marks)**

PARTNERSHIP ACCOUNTS

43 ALAMUTE AND BRADOR

Alamute and Brador have been in partnership for several years, compiling their financial statements for the year ending 31 March and sharing profits in the ratio 60:40 after allowing for interest on capital account balances at 5% per year.

Extracts from their trial balance at 31 March 20X3 are given below:

		Reference to notes	£	
Capital accounts:	Alamute		50,000	
	Brador		50,000	
Current accounts:	Alamute		3,800	Credit
	Brador		2,600	Debit
Drawings:	Alamute		48,400	
	Brador		36,900	
Office equipment:	cost	1	48,300	
accumulated depreciation, 1 April 20X2			12,800	
Stock, 1 April 20X2		2	15,600	
Trade debtors		3	68,400	
Provision for doubtful debts, 1 April 20X2		3	3,800	
Sales revenue			448,700	
Purchases			184,600	
Rent paid		4	30,000	
Salaries			88,000	
Insurance		5	4,000	
Sundry expenses			39,400	

Notes:

(1) Office equipment should be depreciated at 20% per year on the reducing balance basis.

(2) Closing stock amounted to £21,400.

(3) Debts of £2,400 are to be written off, and the provision for doubtful debts is to be adjusted to 5% of trade debtors.

(4) Rent paid £30,000 is the amount for the nine months to 31 December 20X2. From that date the rent was increased by 10%.

(5) Insurance paid in advance amounted to £1,500.

Required:

(a) Prepare the partnership's trading and profit and loss account and appropriation account for the year ended 31 March 20X3. **(9 marks)**

(b) Write up the partners' current accounts for the year ended 31 March 20X3. **(3 marks)**

(Total: 12 marks)

44   WEASEL AND STOAT

Weasel and Stoat are in partnership. Their capital and current account balances at 1 January 20X0 were as follows:

	Weasel £	Stoat £
Capital accounts	180,000	120,000
Current accounts	3,000 Credit	2,700 Debit

On 30 September 20X0 Stoat introduced an additional £60,000 of capital. The net profit of the partnership for the year to 31 December 20X0 was £316,500.

Their profit sharing arrangements are as follows:

Annual salaries	Weasel	£20,000
	Stoat	£15,000
Interest on capital account		10%
Share of balance of profits	Weasel	60%
	Stoat	40%
Drawings during the year were:	Weasel	£186,000
	Stoat	£129,000

Required:

Prepare the partnership appropriation account for the year and the partners' capital and current accounts for the year ended 31 December 20X0.   **(10 marks)**

LIMITED COMPANY ACCOUNTS

45   CRONOS LIMITED

The following items have been extracted from the trial balance of Cronos Limited as at 30 September 20X2:

	Reference to notes	£	£
Opening stock		186,400	
Purchases		1,748,200	
Carriage inwards		38,100	
Carriage outwards	2	47,250	
Sales			3,210,000
Trade debtors		318,000	
Wages and salaries	2 and 3	694,200	
Sundry administrative expenses	2	381,000	
Provision for doubtful debts as at 1 October 20X1	4		18,200
Bad debts written off during the year	4	14,680	
Office equipment as at October 20X1:			
Cost	5	214,000	
Accumulated depreciation	5		88,700
Office equipment: additions during year	5	48,000	
proceeds of sale of items during year	5		12,600
Interest paid	2	30,000	

Notes

1   Closing stock amounted to £219,600

2   Prepayments and accruals

	Prepayments	*Accruals*
	£	*£*
Carriage outwards		1,250
Wages and salaries		5,800
Sundry administrative expenses	4,900	13,600
Interest payable		30,000

3   Wages and salaries cost is to be allocated:

       –   cost of sales   10%

       –   distribution costs   20%

       –   administrative expenses   70%

4   Further bad debts totalling £8,000 are to be written off, and the closing provision for doubtful debts is to be equal to 5% of the final trade debtors figure.

      The bad and doubtful debt expense is to be included in administrative expenses.

5   Office equipment:

      Depreciation is to be provided at 20% per annum on the straight line basis, with a full year's charge in the year of purchase and none in the year of sale.

      During the year equipment which had cost £40,000, with accumulated depreciation of £26,800, was sold for £12,600.

Required:

Prepare the company's profit and loss account for publication, in accordance with the Companies Act 1985, using the headings in Format 1.

Notes to the profit and loss account are not required.   **(12 marks)**

46   RESERVES

(a)   The term 'reserves' is frequently found in company balance sheets.

      Required:

      (i)   Explain the meaning of 'reserves' in this context.

      (ii)   Give two examples of reserves and explain how each of your examples comes into existence.   **(6 marks)**

(b)   A company's issued share capital may be increased by a bonus (capitalisation) issue or by a rights issue.

      Required:

      Define 'bonus issue' and 'rights issue' and explain the fundamental difference between these two types of share issue.   **(5 marks)**

                                (Total: 11 marks)

47 DRAFT FINANCIAL STATEMENTS

The directors of a company are considering the company's draft financial statements for the year ended 30 September 20X2.

The following material points are unresolved:

(a) One of the company's buildings was destroyed in a flood in October 20X2. The estimated value of the building was £4m, but it was insured for only £3m. The company's going concern status is not jeopardised. The directors are unsure what adjustment or disclosure, if any, should be made. **(2 marks)**

(b) The company gives warranties on its products at the time of sale, undertaking to repair or replace any defective item free of charge. Some directors believe that a provision should be made for estimated warranty liabilities at 30 September 20X2 based on sales to that date, and other directors argue that the expense of warranty work should be borne in the period in which it is incurred. **(2 marks)**

(c) Some stock which had cost £120,000, and which was included in closing stock at 30 September 20X2 at that figure, was subsequently sold for £80,000 after it was found to have deteriorated while held in stock. The directors are unsure whether to adjust the stock figure downwards by £40,000 or allow the loss to fall in the period when the deterioration was discovered. **(2 marks)**

(d) The company had supplied £100,000 worth of goods to a customer on a sale or return basis in September 20X2. The transaction was included as a credit sale in the accounting records, and as a result a profit of £20,000 was taken. In October 20X2 the customer returned all of the items in good condition. **(4 marks)**

Required:

Advise the board of directors as to the correct treatment of each of these items, quoting the authority for your advice in each case and stating the effect, if any, on the profit and loss account and balance sheet. **(Total: 10 marks)**

48 ALPACA LIMITED

The following information is available about the balances and transactions of Alpaca Limited:

Balances at 30 April 20X1	£
Fixed assets – cost	1,000,000
Fixed assets – accumulated depreciation	230,000
Stocks	410, 000
Debtors	380,000
Cash at bank	87,000
Creditors	219,000
Issued share capital – ordinary shares of £1 each	400,000
Profit and loss account	818,000
10% Debentures	200,000
Debenture interest owing	10,000

Transactions during year ended 30 April 20X2:	£
Sales revenue	4,006,000
Purchases	2,120,000
Expenses	1,640,000
Interest on debentures paid during year	20,000
Issue of 100,000 £1 ordinary shares at a premium of 50p per share	

There were no purchases or sales of fixed assets during the year.

Adjustments at 30 April 20X2

(1)   Depreciation of £100,000 is to be provided for.

(2)   Debts totalling £20,000 are to be written off.

Balances at 30 April 20X2	£
(1) Stocks	450,000
(2) Debtors (before writing off debts shown above)	690,000
(3) Cash at bank	114,000
(4) Trade creditors	180,000

Required:

Prepare the balance sheet of Alpaca Limited as at 30 April 20X2 using the format in the Companies Act 1985 as far as the information available allows.

Note: No formal profit and loss account is required, but your answer should include a working showing your computation of the profit and loss account figure in the balance sheet. This working carries 4 of the 11 marks available in all. **(11 marks)**

49   ATOK LIMITED

Atok Limited compiles its financial statements to 30 June annually. At 30 June 20X9, the company's trial balance was as follows:

		£000	£000
Sales revenue			14,800
Purchases		8,280	
Stock at 1 July 20X8		1,390	
Distribution costs		1,080	
Administrative expenses		1,460	
Land at valuation		10,500	
Buildings:	cost	8,000	
	accumulated depreciation at 1 July 20X8		2,130
Plant and equipment:	cost	12,800	
	accumulated depreciation at 1 July 20X8		2,480
Trade debtors and creditors		4,120	2,240
Cash at bank		160	
Ordinary shares of 50p each:	as at 1 July 20X8		10,000
	issued during year		4,000
Share premium account:	as at 1 July 20X8		2,000
	arising on shares issued during year		2,000
Revaluation reserve as at 1 July 20X8			3,000
Profit and loss account			3,140
10% debentures (redeemable 20Y8)			
(issued 1 April 20X9 with interest payable 31 March and 30 September each year)			2,000
		47,790	47,790

The following matters remain to be adjusted for in preparing the financial statements for the year ended 30 June 20X9:

(1)   Stock at 30 June 20X9 amounted to £1,560,000 at cost. A review of stock items revealed the need for some adjustments for two stock lines:

    (i)   Items which had cost £80,000 and which would normally sell for £120,000 were found to have deteriorated. Remedial work costing £20,000 would be needed to enable the items to be sold for £90,000.

    (ii)   Some items sent to customers on sale or return terms had been omitted from stock and included as sales in June 20X9. The cost of these items was £16,000 and they were included in sales at £24,000. In July 20X9, the items were returned in good condition by the customers.

(2)   Depreciation is to be provided as follows:

    Buildings: 2% per year on cost.

    Plant and equipment: 20% per year on cost.

    80% of the depreciation is to be charged in cost of sales, and 10% each in distribution costs and administrative expenses.

(3)   The land is to be revalued to £12,000,000. No change was required to the value of the buildings.

(4)   Accruals and prepayments were:

	Accruals £000	Prepayments £000
Distribution costs	190	120
Administrative expenses	70	60

(5)   A dividend of 2½ pence per share is proposed. All shares in issue at 30 June 20X9 qualify for this dividend.

Required:

(a)   Prepare the company's profit and loss account for the year ended 30 June 20X9 and balance sheet as at that date for publication, complying as far as possible with the provisions of the Companies Acts and accounting standards.   **(20 marks)**

(b)   Prepare a statement detailing all reserve movements during the year. Other notes to the financial statements are *not* required.   **(4 marks)**

(Total: 24 marks)

50   MOORFOOT

Moorfoot Limited operates a chain of wholesale grocery outlets. Its trial balance at 30 June 20X1 was as follows:

	£000	£000
Sales revenue		13,600
Purchases	8,100	
Stock 1 July 20X0	1,530	
Distribution costs	1,460	
Administrative expenses	1,590	
Interest on debentures	50	
Interim dividend paid	360	
Freehold land at cost	1,510	

Buildings		
– Cost	8,300	
– Accumulated depreciation at 30 June 20X0		1,020
Warehouse and office equipment		
– Cost	1,800	
– Accumulated depreciation at 30 June 20X0		290
Motor vehicles		
– Cost	1,680	
– Accumulated depreciation at 30 June 20X0		620
Trade debtors	810	
Provision for doubtful debts		18
Cash at bank	140	
Trade creditors		820
10% debentures (issued five years ago and to be redeemed 20Y1)		1,000
Called up share capital – Ordinary shares of 25p each		1,200
Share premium account		2,470
Profit and loss account 30 June 20X0		6,292
	27,330	27,330

The following additional information is available:

(1)   Closing stock was £1,660,000.

(2)   Trade debts totalling £6,000 are to be written off and the provision for doubtful debts increased to £30,000. It is the company's practice to include the charge for bad and doubtful debts in administrative expenses in the profit and loss account.

(3)   Accruals and prepayments:

	Prepayments	Accruals
	£000	£000
Distribution costs	60	120
Administrative expenses	70	190
Interest on debentures		50

(4)   In early July 20X1 the company received invoices for credit purchases totalling £18,000 for goods delivered before 30 June. These invoices have not been included in the purchases ledger at 30 June 20X1.

It was also found that credit sales invoices totalling £7,000 for goods delivered to customers before 30 June 20X1 had mistakenly been dated in July 20X1 and thus excluded from sales for the year and from debtors at the year end.

The goods received had been included in the year end stock figure given at (1) above, and the goods sold had been excluded from it. No adjustment to the stock figure is therefore required.

(5)   Depreciation should be provided as follows:

Land	Nil
Buildings	2 per cent per year on cost
Warehouse and office equipment	15 per cent per year on cost
Motor vehicles	25 per cent per year on cost

All depreciation is to be divided equally between distribution costs and administrative expenses.

(6)   A final dividend of 10p per share is proposed.

Required:

Prepare the company's profit and loss account for the year ended 30 June 20X1, and balance sheet as at that date, complying as far as possible with the requirements of the Companies Act 1985. Ignore taxation. Notes to the financial statements are not required. **(24 marks)**

51 PRIDE

The following extracts have been taken from the trial balance of Pride Limited at 31 March 20X1:

	£000	£000
Issued share capital:		
500,000 ordinary shares of 50p each		250
Share premium account 1 April 20X0		180
Profit and loss account 31 March 20X1		34
Land at cost	210	
Buildings		
– cost 1 April 20X0	200	
– accumulated depreciation at 1 April 20X0		120
– cost	318	
– accumulated depreciation at 1 April 20X0		88
Debtors	146	
Cash at bank	50	
Creditors		94
10% debentures issued six years ago		100
Allowance for doubtful debts		10
Suspense account		166

Notes

(1) The profit and loss account balance of £34,000 shown above is the final balance of retained profit for the year and may be incorporated into your answer as such.

(2) The balance on the suspense account is made up as follows:

	£000
Receipt of cash on 8 January 20X1 on the issue of 200,000 ordinary shares of 50p each at a premium of 30p per share.	160
Proceeds of sale of plant*	6
	166

* This plant had originally cost £18,000 and had been written down to £6,000 at 31 March 20X0.

The company's policy is to provide depreciation for a full year in the year of acquisition of assets and none in the year of sale.

(3) Depreciation is to be provided for on the straight line basis at the following annual rates:

Land	Nil
Buildings	2 per cent
Plant and equipment	20 per cent

(4) The provision for doubtful debts is to be increased to £12,000.

(5) Prepayments and accruals at 31 March 20X1 were:

	£000
Prepayments	8,000
Accruals	4,000

(6)   The closing stock was £180,000.

Required:

Prepare the balance sheet of Pride Limited as at 31 March 20X1 for publication, complying as far as possible with the provisions of the Companies Acts.   **(10 marks)**

52   TAFFORD LIMITED

The following is an extract from the trial balance of Tafford Limited, at 30 September 20X2:

	£000	£000
Warehouse machinery:		
Cost	3,000	
Accumulated depreciation at 1 October 20X1		1,700
Motor vehicles:		
Cost	1,180	
Accumulated depreciation at 1 October 20X1		500
Stock at 1 October 20X1	13,000	
Sales		41,600
Purchases	22,600	
Distribution costs	6,000	
Administrative expenses	5,000	
Provision for doubtful debts, 1 October 20X1		1,300
Bad debts written off	600	
10% Debentures (issued 20X0)		10,00
Interest paid on debentures	500	
Suspense account		100

Notes

(1)   Closing stock at 30 September 20X2 was £15,600,000.

(2)   Bad debts written off and the movement on the provision for doubtful debts are to be included in administrative costs. The provision for doubtful debts is to be reduced to £500,000.

(3)   The balance on the suspense account is the proceeds of sale of motor vehicles, entered to the suspense account pending correct treatment in the records.

The vehicles sold had cost £180,000 and had a written down value at 1 October 20X2 of £60,000. It is the company's policy to provide for a full year's depreciation in the year of purchase of vehicles and none in the year of sale. The vehicles sold were all used in the distribution of the company's sales.

(4)   Depreciation is to be provided for on the straight line basis as follows:

Warehouse machinery	10 per cent
Motor vehicles	25 per cent

Depreciation of motor vehicles is to be divided equally between distribution costs and administrative expenses, and depreciation of warehouse machinery charged wholly to distribution costs.

(5)   Prepayments and accruals at 30 September 20X2 were:

	Prepayments	Accruals
	£000	£000
Distribution costs	200	100
Administrative expenses	100	60

(6)   The estimated tax liability for the year is £3,000,000.

Required:

Prepare Tafford's profit and loss account in a form suitable for publication, complying as far as possible with the requirements of the Companies Acts. **(10 marks)**

53 HARMONICA

The trial balance of Harmonica Limited at 31 December 20X5 is given below.

Trial Balance 31 December 20X5

	Dr £000	Cr £000
Purchases and sales	18,000	28,600
Stock at 1 January 20X5	4,500	
Warehouse wages	850	
Salespersons' salaries and commission	1,850	
Administrative salaries	3,070	
General administrative expenses	580	
General distribution expenses	490	
Directors remuneration	870	
Debenture interest paid	100	
Dividends – interim dividend paid	40	
Fixed assets – cost	18,000	
– aggregate depreciation, 1 January 20X5		3,900
Trade debtors and creditors	6,900	3,800
Provision for doubtful debts at 1 January 20X5		200
Balance at bank		2,080
10% Debentures (repayable 20X9)		1,000
Called up share capital (£1 ordinary shares)		4,000
Share premium account		1,300
Profit and loss account, 1 January 20X5		8,720
Suspense account (see Note 3 below)		1,650
	55,250	55,250

The following further information should be allowed for:

(1) Closing stock amounted to £5m.

(2) A review of the trade debtors total of £6.9m showed that it was necessary to write off debts totalling £0.4m, and that the provision for doubtful debts should be adjusted to 2% of the remaining trade debtors.

(3) Two transactions have been entered in the company's cash record and transferred to the suspense account shown in the trial balance.

They are:

(a) The receipt of £1.5m from the issue of 500,000 £1 ordinary shares at a premium of £2 per share.

(b) The sale of some surplus plant. The plant had cost £1m and had a written down value of £100,000. The sale proceeds of £150,000 have been credited to the suspense account but no other entries have been made.

(4) Depreciation should be charged at 10% per annum on cost at the end of the year and allocated 70% to distribution costs and 30% to administration.

(5)   The directors propose a final dividend of 4 pence per share on the shares in issue at the end of the year.

(6)   Accruals and prepayments still to be accounted for are:

	Prepayments £000	Accruals £000
General administrative expenses	70	140
General distribution expenses	40	90
	110	230

(7)   Directors' remuneration is to be analysed between distribution costs and administrative expenses as follows:

	£000
– distribution	300
– administration	570
	870

(8)   Ignore taxation

Required:

(a)   Prepare the company's profit and loss account for the year ended 31 December 20X5 and balance sheet as at 31 December 20X5 in a form suitable for publication. Notes to the accounts are not required.   **(16 marks)**

(b)   Explain the differences between the following pairs of terms or items which may be found in company accounting:

   (i)   authorised share capital and called up share capital

   (ii)   a capital reserve and a revenue reserve
          (Give one example of each type of reserve)

   (iii) a rights issue and a bonus issue.   **(6 marks)**

                                                                  (Total: 22 marks)

54   ARBALEST

The summarised balance sheet of Arbalest Limited at 30 September 20X6 was as follows:

	Cost £000	Aggregate depreciation £000	Net book value £000
Fixed assets			
Land	2,000	nil	2,000
Buildings	1,500	450	1,050
Plant and machinery	2,800	1,000	1,800
	6,300	1,450	4,850
Current assets		3,180	
Less: Current liabilities		2,070	1,110
			5,960

Capital and reserves	
Called-up share capital	
3,000,000 ordinary shares of 50p each	1,500
Share premium account	400
Profit and loss account	4,060
	5,960

During the year ended 30 September 20X7 the company had the following transactions:

(1)   1 November 20X6:

A rights issue of one share for every three held at a price of £1.50 per share. All the rights issue shares were taken up.

(2)   1 December 20X6:

Sale for £70,000 of plant and machinery which had cost £1,000,000 and had a book value of £200,000.

(3)   1 March 20X7:

A bonus (capitalisation) issue of one share for every one held at that date using the share premium account as far as possible for the purpose.

(4)   1 June 20X7:

Purchased a new factory block for £3,000,000 (including land £600,000).

(5)   1 July 20X7:

Purchased plant and machinery for £1,600,000.

(6)   30 September 20X7:

The company decided to revalue the freehold land held at 30 September 20X6 from £2,000,000 to £2,500,000.

The company depreciation policies are:

Land	no depreciation
Buildings	2% per annum on cost, straight-line basis
Plant and machinery	10% per annum on cost, straight-line basis

Proportionate depreciation is provided in the year of purchase of an asset, with none in the year of disposal. The retained profit for the year was £370,000.

Required:

(a)   Prepare the notes required for the company's balance sheet for publication at 30 September 20X7 detailing:

(i)   movements on reserves

(ii)   movements on fixed assets.

Ledger accounts for the transactions are *not* required.   **(16 marks)**

(b)   Neither the share premium account nor the revaluation reserve is distributable by way of dividend. Explain why it would be contrary to generally accepted accounting principles if these balances were to be distributable as dividend.   **(4 marks)**

(Total: 20 marks)

55 HELIOS LIMITED

Helios Limited acquired 80% of the ordinary share capital of Luna Limited for £700,000 on 1 July 20X0, when the retained profits of Luna amounted to £60,000. There have been no movements on Luna's share capital or share premium account since that date.

At 30 June 20X3 the balance sheets of the two companies were as follows:

	Helios £	Luna £
Tangible fixed assets	280,000	490,000
Investment in Luna Limited	700,000	–
Net current assets	130,000	260,000
	1,110,000	750,000
Share capital	600,000	400,000
Share premium account	350,000	200,000
Profit and loss account	160,000	150,000
	1,110,000	750,000

The policy of Helios Limited is to amortise goodwill arising on consolidation over five years on the straight line basis.

Required:

Prepare the consolidated balance sheet of Helios Limited and its subsidiary as at 30 June 20X3.

(11 marks)

56 KOPPA

The following balances existed in the accounting records of Koppa Limited at 31 December 20X7:

		£000
Development costs capitalised, 1 January 20X7		180
Freehold land as revalued 31 December 20X7		2,200
Buildings	– cost	900
	– aggregate depreciation at 1 January 20X7	100
Office equipment	– cost	260
	– aggregate depreciation at 1 January 20X7	60
Motor vehicles	– cost	200
	– aggregate depreciation at 1 January 20X7	90
Trade debtors		1,360
Cash at bank		90
Trade creditors		820
12% debentures (issued 20X0 and redeemable 20X9)		1,000
Called up share capital – ordinary shares of 50p each		1,000
Share premium account		500
Revaluation reserve		200
Profit and loss account 1 January 20X7		1,272
Sales		8,650
Purchases		5,010
Research and development expenditure for the year		162
Stock 1 January 20X7		990
Distribution costs		460
Administrative expenses		1,560
Debenture interest		120
Interim dividend paid		200

In preparing the company's profit and loss account and balance sheet at 31 December 20X7 the following further information is relevant:

(1)   Stock at 31 December 20X7 was £880,000.

(2)   Depreciation is to be provided for as follows:

Land	nil
Buildings	2% per annum on cost
Office equipment	20% per annum, reducing balance basis
Motor vehicles	25% per annum on cost

Depreciation on buildings and office equipment is all charged to administrative expenses. Depreciation on motor vehicles is to be split equally between distribution costs and administrative expenses.

(3)   The £180,000 total for development costs as at 1 January 20X7 relates to two projects:

	£000
Project 836: completed project:	82
(balance being amortised over the period expected to benefit from it. Amount to be amortised in 20X7: £20,000)	
Project 910: in progress:	98
	180

(4)   The research and development expenditure for the year is made up of:

	£000
Research expenditure	103
Development costs on Project 910 which continues to satisfy the requirements in SSAP 13 for capitalisation	59
	162

(5)   The freehold land had originally cost £2,000,000 and was revalued on 31 December 20X7.

(6)   Prepayments and accruals at 31 December 20X7 were:

	Prepayments £000	Accruals £000
Administrative expenses	40	11
Sundry distribution costs		4

(7)   The share premium account balance arose as a result of the issue during 20X7 of 1,000,000 50p ordinary shares at £1.00 each. All shares qualify for the proposed final dividend to be provided for (see note below).

(8)   A final dividend of 20p per share is proposed.

Required:

Prepare the company's profit and loss account for the year ended 31 December 20X7 and balance sheet as at that date, in a form suitable for publication as far as the information provided permits. The note detailing reserve movements for the year should be given, but no other notes are required. Ignore taxation.   **(24 marks)**

GROUPS OF COMPANIES

57   HANSON

Five years ago, Hanson Ltd acquired the following shares in Pickford Ltd:

	£
75,000 Ordinary shares of £1 – cost	93,100
15,000 6% Preference shares of £1 – cost	16,050
	109,150

At the date of acquisition, the accumulated profits of Pickford Ltd amounted to £11,000. The summarised balance sheets of the two companies at 31.12.X8 were as follows:

	Hanson Ltd £	Pickford Ltd £
Ordinary shares of £1	350,000	100,000
6% preference shares of £1	–	60,000
Profit and loss account	348,420	132,700
Sundry creditors	93,400	51,150
	791,820	343,850

	£	£
Fixed assets	431,100	219,350
Investments	109,150	–
Stock	143,070	71,120
Debtors	89,200	36,230
Cash at bank	19,300	17,150
	791,820	343,850

Goodwill should be amortised over a period of ten years.

You are required to prepare the consolidated balance sheet of Hanson Ltd as at 31 December 20X8. **(20 marks)**

58   PIXIE AND DIXIE

Ten years ago, Pixie Ltd acquired the following shareholdings in Dixie Ltd. At the date of both acquisitions, the accumulated profits of Dixie Ltd amounted to £20,000.

	Number of shares	Cost of investment £
£1 Ordinary shares	37,500	58,000
£1 Preference shares	16,000	15,000
		73,000

The balance sheets of the two companies at 31 December 20X9 were as follows:

	Pixie Ltd £	Dixie Ltd £
Ordinary share capital	200,000	50,000
7% Preference share capital	–	40,000
Profit and loss account	120,000	38,000
Sundry creditors	76,100	26,000
	396,100	154,000

Fixed assets	210,000	110,600
Current assets	113,100	43,400
Investment in Dixie Ltd	73,000	–
	396,100	154,000

You further ascertain that the group amortises goodwill over a period of ten years.

You are required to prepare the consolidated balance sheet of Pixie Ltd and its subsidiary as at 31 December 20X9. **(20 marks)**

59 EVON AND ORSET

On 1 April 20X0, Evon Limited acquired 75% of the ordinary share capital of Orset Limited for £180,000. At that date the balance sheet of Orset Limited was as follows:

	£
Sundry net assets	160,000
Share capital	
100,000 Ordinary shares of £1 each	100,000
Profit and loss account	60,000
	160,000

At 31 March 20X3, the balance sheets of the two companies were as follows:

	Evon Ltd	Orset Ltd
	£	£
Sundry net assets	560,000	230,000
Investment in Orset	180,000	
	740,000	230,000
Share capital		
Shares of £1 each	500,000	100,000
Profit and loss account	240,000	130,000
	740,000	230,000

Goodwill arising on consolidation is to be amortised over five years.

Required:

Prepare the consolidated balance sheet of Evon Limited and its subsidiary as at 31 March 20X3. **(10 marks)**

PROFIT AND LOSS ACCOUNTS: FRS 3

60 TOPAZ

Topaz Limited makes up its accounts regularly to 31 December each year. The company has operated for some years with four divisions A, B, C and D, but on 30 June 20X6 Division B was sold for £8m, realising a profit of £2.5m. During 20X6 there was a fundamental reorganisation of Division C, the costs of which were £1.8m.

The trial balance of the company at 31 December 20X6 included the following balances:

	Division B		Divisions A, C and D Combined	
	Dr	Cr	Dr	Cr
	£m	£m	£m	£m
Sales		13		68
Costs of sales	8		41	
Distribution costs (including a bad debt of £1.9m – Division D)	1		6	
Administrative expenses	2		4	
Profit on sale of Division B		2.5		
Reorganisation costs, Division C			1.8	
Interest on £10m 10% debenture stock issued in 20X1			1	
Taxation			4.8	
Interim dividend paid			2	
Revaluation reserve				10

A final dividend of £4m is proposed.

The balance on the revaluation reserve relates to the company's freehold property and arose as follows:

	£m
Balance at 1.1.X6	6
Revaluation during 20X6	4
	—
Balance at 31.12.X6 per trial balance	10
	—

Required:

(a)   (i)   Prepare the profit and loss account of Topaz Limited for the year ended 31 December 20X6, complying as far as possible with the provisions of the Companies Act 1985 and FRS 3 *Reporting Financial Performance.*

       (ii)   Prepare the statement of total recognised gains and losses for the year as required by FRS 3.   **(16 marks)**

(b)   Explain why the changes to the profit and loss account introduced by FRS 3 improve the quality of information available to users of the financial statements.   **(4 marks)**

(Total: 20 marks)

61   LARK

An extract from the trial balance of Lark Limited for the year ended 31 March 20X0 is given below:

	£000	£000
Sales		20,000
Cost of sales	12,300	
Distribution costs	2,100	
Administrative expenses	3,600	
Interest receivable		1,200
Interest payable	800	

The taxation charge for the year is estimated to be £480,000.

During the year the company sold trading division B.

The extracts from the company's trial balance shown above include the following items for division B:

	£000	£000
Sales		6,000
Cost of sales	4,800	
Distribution costs	840	
Administrative expenses (excluding the loss on disposal £400,000 shown below)	700	

The total of £3,600,000 for administrative expenses is currently made up as follows:

	£000
General administrative expenses:	
Continuing activities	1,930
Discontinued activities as shown above	700
Bad debt arising from the insolvency of a major customer in continuing activities	360
Cost of a fundamental reorganisation of continuing activities	210
Loss on disposal of trading division B	400
	3,600

Required:

(a)   Prepare the company's profit and loss account for publication for the year ended 31 March 20X0 in accordance with the Companies Act 1985 and FRS 3 *Reporting Financial Performance*. Include any note you consider necessary.   **(16 marks)**

(b)   FRS 3 requires companies to produce several other statements or notes in addition to the profit and loss account and balance sheet. Name and briefly describe the contents of *any two* of these statements or notes.   **(4 marks)**

(Total: 20 marks)

CASH FLOW STATEMENTS: FRS 1

62   PANIEL LTD

The balance sheets of Paniel Limited at 31 March 20X2 and 20X3 were as follows:

	Reference to notes	31 March 20X2	20X3
		£	£
Fixed assets	2	2,140,000	3,060,000
Less: Accumulated depreciation		(580,000)	(840,000)
		1,560,000	2,220,000
Net current assets	3	1,520,000	1,570,000
		3,080,000	3,790,000
6% Debentures	4	(800,000)	(1,200,000)
		2,280,000	2,590,000
Ordinary share capital		1,000,000	1,100,000
Share premium account		800,000	900,000
Profit and loss account		480,000	590,000
		2,280,000	2,590,000

Notes

1   The net cash inflow from operating activities for the year is £746,000.

2   During the year the company sold fixed assets which had cost £480,000 for £280,000.

3   The net current asset figures include cash at bank:

31 March 20X2   £14,000

31 March 20X3   £18,000

All other movements in net current assets have already been allowed for in computing the net cash inflow from operating activities given in Note 1 above. There were no proposed dividends at 31 March 20X2 or at 31 March 20X3.

4   The debenture issue during the year took place on 1 April 20X2 and all interest for the year ended 31 March 20X3 was paid in the year.

5   The profit for the year ended 31 March 20X3 before allowing for dividends paid was £260,000. As noted in 3 above there were no proposed dividends at 31 March 2002 or 31 March 20X3.

6   Ignore taxation.

Required:

Prepare the company's cash flow statement for the year ended 31 March 20X3, beginning with the net cash inflow from operating activities given in Note 1 above.

The reconciliation of net cash flow to net debt is *not* required.   **(9 marks)**

63   MARMOT LIMITED

The following information is available about the transactions of Marmot Limited for the year ended 31 December 20X1.

	£000
Depreciation	880
Cash paid for expenses	2,270
Increase in stocks	370
Cash paid to employees	2,820
Decrease in debtors	280
Cash paid to suppliers	4,940
Decrease in creditors	390
Cash received from customers	12,800
Operating profit before taxation	2,370

Required:

Compute Marmot's net cash flow from operating activities for the company's cash flow statement for the year ended 31 December 20X1 using:

(a)   the direct method;

(b)   the indirect method.   **(10 marks)**

64   ADDAX LIMITED

The following balances appeared in the balance sheet of Addax Limited at 31 March 20X1.

	£
Plant and equipment – cost	840,000
Accumulated depreciation	370,000

In the year ended 31 March 20X2 the following transactions took place:

(1)   Plant which had cost £100,000 with a written down value of £40,000 was sold for £45,000 on 10 December.

(2)   New plant was purchased for £180,000 on 1 October 20X1.

It is the policy of the company to charge depreciation at 10% per year on the straight line basis with a proportionate charge in the year of acquisition and no charge in the year of sale. None of the plant was over ten years old at 31 March 20X1.

Required:

(a)   Prepare ledger accounts recording the above transactions. A cash account is NOT required.   **(5 marks)**

(b)   List the items which should appear in Addax's cash flow statement for the year ended 31 March 20X2 based on these transactions and using the indirect method, including the headings under which they should appear.

Note. The headings from FRS 1 are to be used.   **(4 marks)**

(Total: 9 marks)

65   WEASEL PLC

The balance sheets of Weasel plc at 31 August 20X8 and 20X9 are given below:

	Reference to notes	Year ended 31 August			
		20X8		20X9	
		£000	£000	£000	£000
Fixed assets	1		6,400		8,500
Current assets					
Stock		1,200		1,400	
Debtors		1,500		1,400	
Cash at bank		200		300	
		2,900		3,100	
Creditors – amounts falling due within one year					
Trade creditors		(800)		(700)	
Taxation		(400)		(500)	
Bank overdraft		(360)		(200)	
Net current assets			1,340		1,700
Total assets less current liabilities			7,740		10,200
Creditors – amounts falling due after more than one year					
10% debentures 20Y5	3		(1,000)		(1,500)
			6,740		8,700

Capital and reserves

Called up share capital	2,000	2,200
Share premium account	2,340	2,540
Revaluation reserve	–	1,000
Profit and loss account	2,400	2,960
	6,740	8,700

Notes

(1) Movements in fixed assets:

	Land	Buildings	Plant and Equipment	Total
	£000	£000	£000	£000
Cost or valuation				
At 1 September 20X8	2,000	3,000	3,400	8,400
Additions			2,500	2,500
Disposals			(1,000)	(1,000)
Revaluation	1,000			1,000
At 31 August 20X9	3,000	3,000	4,900	10,900
Accumulated depreciation				
At 1 September 20X8		400	1,600	2,000
Provision for year		60	1,140	1,200
Disposals			(800)	(800)
At 31 August 20X9		460	1,940	2,400
Net book amounts				
At 31 August 20X9	3,000	2,540	2,960	8,500
At 1 September 20X8	2,000	2,600	1,800	6,400

(2) Dividends paid during the year amounted to £500,000.

(3) Issue of debentures – A further £500,000 of 10% debentures was issued at par on 1 September 20X8. Interest on all debentures is paid on 28 February and 31 August each year.

(4) Plant sold during the year realised £250,000.

(5) The tax charge for the year in the profit and loss account was £500,000.

Required:

Prepare a cash flow statement for Weasel plc for the year ended 31 August 20X9, complying as far as possible with FRS 1 *Cash Flow Statements*, using the indirect method.

The note reconciling operating profit to operating cash flows must be shown, but *no* other notes are required. **(20 marks)**

66   FINTRY

The balance sheets of Fintry Limited at 30 September 20X1 and 30 September 20X2 are as follows:

	Reference to notes	20X1 £000	20X1 £000	20X2 £000	20X2 £000
Fixed assets					
Cost/revaluation		2,740		4,995	
Accumulated depreciation	1	700		1,000	
		——	2,040	——	3,995
Current assets					
Stock		380		490	
Debtors		410		380	
Cash		10		15	
		——		——	
		800		885	
		——		——	
Current liabilities					
Creditors		200		250	
Bank overdraft		80		70	
Proposed dividend	2	60		80	
		——		——	
		340		400	
		——		——	
Net current assets			460		485
			——		——
			2,500		4,480
12% Debentures	3		(500)		(1,000)
			——		——
			2,000		3,480
			——		——
Capital and reserves					
Ordinary shares of 50p each	5		1,000		1,500
Share premium account			600		800
Revaluation reserve			–		400
Profit and loss account			400		780
			——		——
			2,000		3,480
			——		——

Notes

(1)   Fixed assets

During the year, land carried in the accounts at cost £800,000 was revalued to £1,200,000. No depreciation had been provided on this land.

Also, fixed assets which had cost £200,000 were sold for £55,000. Their book value at the time of sale was £40,000.

(2)   Dividends

An interim dividend of 2p per share was paid on 10 May 20X2.

(3)   Debentures

£500,000 of debentures were issued on 1 October 20X1.

(4)   Bank overdraft interest

Interest on the bank overdraft for the year was £8,000.

(5)   Share issue

1,000,000 ordinary shares were issued on I July 20X2 at a price of 70p per share.

Required:

(a)   Prepare a cash flow statement for the year ended 30 September 20X2, using the indirect method and complying as far as possible with FRS 1 *Cash Flow Statements*.

Your answer should include the reconciliation of operating profit to net cash flow but the note reconciling net cash flow with movement in net debt is *not* required. Ignore taxation.   **(17 marks)**

(b)   Explain briefly how the operating cash flow would be calculated and shown in the cash flow statement if the direct method was used.   **(3 marks)**

(Total: 20 marks)

67   CRASH

The balance sheets of Crash Limited at 31 March 20X0 and 31 March 20X1 were as follows:

	Reference to notes	20X0		20X1	
		£000	£000	£000	£000
Fixed assets	1				
Cost or valuation		9,000		10,950	
Accumulated depreciation		(3,300)	5,700	(3,600)	7,350
Current assets					
Stock		1,215		1,350	
Debtors		1,350		1,290	
Cash		60		105	
Total assets		2,625		2,745	
Less:					
Current liabilities					
Trade creditors		(990)		(1,080)	
Bank overdraft		(195)		(270)	
		(1,185)		(1,350)	
			1,440		1,395
Net current assets			7,140		8,745
Less: 10% debentures			(1,500)		(750)
			5,640		7,995
Called up share capital			2,250		3,000
Share premium account			750		1,200
Revaluation reserve					750
Profit and loss account			2,640		3,045
			5,640		7,995

Notes

(1) Fixed assets

    (a) During the year fixed assets, which had cost £1,500,000 and which had a book value of £300,000 at 31 March 20X0, were sold for £375,000.

    (b) Land acquired in four years ago was revalued upwards by £750,000 in preparing the balance sheet at 31 March 20X1.

(2) Debentures

    Interest is due half-yearly on 30 September and 31 March and was paid on the due dates. The company repaid £750,000 debentures on 31 March 20X1.

(3) Profit before interest for the year ended 31 March 20X1 was £555,000. No dividends were paid during the year.

(4) Ignore taxation.

Required:

Prepare a cash flow statement for Crash for the year ended 31 March 20X1 using the indirect method, complying as far as possible with the requirements of FRS 1 *Cash Flow Statements*.

The note reconciling net cash flow with movement in net debt is NOT required. **(10 marks)**

68   JANE LTD

The balance sheets of Jane Limited at 31 December 20X7 and 20X8 were as follows:

	Reference to notes	20X7 £000	20X8 £000
Fixed assets			
Tangible assets	1	730	1,100
Investments at cost	2	100	50
		830	1,150
Current assets			
Stock		80	110
Debtors		110	180
Cash at bank		20	30
		210	320
Creditors: amounts falling due within one year		(70)	(80)
Trade creditors		(40)	(130)
Bank overdraft		(30)	(40)
Proposed dividend	3		
		(140)	(250)
Net current assets		70	70
Total assets less current liabilities		900	1,220

Creditors: amounts falling due after more than one year			
10% Debentures	4	(100)	(150)
		800	1,070
Capital and reserves			
Called-up share capital	5	300	380
Share premium		200	300
Revaluation reserve	6	100	200
Profit and loss account		200	190
		800	1,070

Notes

(1)   Tangible assets

During the year tangible assets with a net book value of £80,000 were sold for £60,000. The depreciation charge for the year on all tangible assets held at the end of the year was £100,000.

(2)   Investments

Investments which cost £50,000 were sold during the year for £40,000.

(3)   Proposed dividends

The proposed dividends are on the company's ordinary share capital. No interim dividends were paid.

(4)   10% Debentures

£50,000 of 10% debentures were issued on 1 January 20X8. All interest to 31 December 20X8 has been paid.

(5)   Called-up share capital

The company's called-up share capital at 31 December 20X7 consisted of 300,000 ordinary shares of £1 each. Another 80,000 shares were issued during the year at a price of £2.25 per share.

(6)   Revaluation reserve

The freehold land and buildings were revalued upwards by £100,000 during the year.

Required:

Prepare the company's cash flow statement for the year ended 31 December 20X8 complying with FRS 1 *Cash Flow Statements*. The reconciliation of net cash flow to movement in net debt is *not* required. Ignore taxation.   **(20 marks)**

INTERPRETATION

69 WEDEN LIMITED

The summarised financial statements of Weden Limited, a manufacturing company, are shown below:

Profit and loss account

	Year ended			
	31 March 20X1		*31 March 20X2*	
	£000	£000	£000	£000
Sales revenue		3,200		4,000
Cost of sales				
Opening stock	800		300	
Purchases	1,800		3,200	
	2,600		3,500	
less: Closing stock	300		500	
		(2,300)		(3,000)
Gross profit		900		1,000
Expenses		(400)		(450)
Interest paid		(100)		(200)
Net profit		400		350

Balance sheets

	31 March 20X1		*31 March 20X2*	
	£000	£000	£000	£000
Fixed assets		1,970		4,000
Current assets				
Stock	300		500	
Debtors – trade	600		800	
Prepayments	60		70	
Cash	50		10	
	1,010		1,380	
less: Current liabilities				
Creditors – trade	(380)		(1,400)	
Accruals	(50)		(80)	
Net current assets (liabilities)		580		(100)
		2,550		3,900
10% Debentures		(1,000)		(2,000)
		1,550		1,900
Issued share capital		600		600
Share premium account		200		200
Profit and loss account		750		1,100
		1,550		1,900

Required:

(a) Compute the following five ratios for each of the two years:

   (i) return on capital employed

   (ii) return on owners' equity

   (iii) current ratio

   (iv) stock turnover (using closing figures)

   (v) number of days' purchases in trade creditors **(5 marks)**

(b) Comment briefly on the changes in the company's results and position between the two years, as shown by the movements in these ratios, mentioning possible causes for the changes. **(5 marks)**

(Total: 10 marks)

70 HAWK

The directors of Hawk Limited wish to compare the company's most recent financial statements with those of the previous year. The company's financial statements are given below:

Hawk Limited
Profit and loss accounts

	Year ended	
	31 March 20X1	31 March 20X2
	£000	£000
Sales revenue (80% on credit and 20% cash)	1,800	2,500
Cost of sales (see note below)	(1,200)	(1,800)
Gross profit	600	700
Distribution costs	(160)	(250)
Administrative expenses	(200)	(200)
Operating profit	240	250
Interest payable	(50)	(50)
Profit before tax	190	200
Taxation	(44)	(46)
Retained profit	146	154

Note: Cost of sales figures are made up as follows:

	Year ended	
	31 March 20X1	31 March 20X2
	£000	£000
Opening stock	180	200
Purchases (all on credit)	1,220	1,960
	1,400	2,160
Less closing stock	(200)	(360)
Cost of sales	1,200	1,800

Balance sheets

	As at			
	31 March 20X1		*31 March 20X2*	
	£000	£000	£000	£000
Fixed assets – cost	3,100		3,674	
Less accumulated depreciation	1,214		1,422	
	——	1,886	——	2,252
Current assets				
Stock	200		360	
Debtors – trade	400		750	
Cash at bank	100		120	
	——		——	
	700		1,230	
	——		——	
Less current liabilities				
Creditors – trade	(210)		(380)	
– sundry	(260)		(430)	
Taxation	(48)		(50)	
	——		——	
	(518)		(860)	
	——		——	
Net current assets		182		370
		——		——
Total assets less current liabilities		2,068		2,622
10% debentures		500		500
		——		——
		1,568		2,122
		——		——
Capital and reserves				
Issued ordinary share capital*	1,000		1,200	
Share premium account*	400		600	
Profit and loss account	168		322	
	——	1,568	——	2,122
		——		——
		1,568		2,122
		——		——

*The additional share capital was issued on 1 April 20X1

Required:

(a)   Calculate, for each of the two years, eight accounting ratios which should assist the directors in their comparison, using closing figures for balance sheet items needed.

(8 marks)

(b)   Suggest possible reasons for the changes in the ratios between the two years.

(12 marks)

(Total: 20 marks)

71   CASTOR AND POLLUX

(a)   Ratio analysis of a company's performance as shown in its profit and loss account may show a decline in profit margin (gross profit as a percentage of sales revenue) compared with the previous period.

Required:

Give five possible reasons for a decline in gross profit as a percentage of sales revenue from one year to the next, briefly explaining for each why it has the effect of reducing the percentage.

Note: You are *not* required to consider factors which reduce gross profit itself, only those which reduce the gross profit *percentage* of sales. **(10 marks)**

(b) Two companies, Castor and Pollux, have the following capital structures:

	Castor	*Pollux*
	£000	£000
Ordinary share capital and reserves	200	800
10% debentures	800	200
	1,000	1,000

In the year ended 31 December 20X0, the companies both made profits of £100,000 before interest. Both companies are forecasting a profit of £200,000 before interest for the year 20X1, and £50,000 for the year 20X2. (Both companies distribute all their profit, so you may assume that shareholders' capital remains the same throughout). Ignore taxation.

Required:

Explain how gearing can have a significant effect on a company's performance, using the above details of Castor and Pollux to illustrate your answer where appropriate.

(10 marks)

(Total: 20 marks)

72 BROOD

The balance sheets of Brood Limited, at 30 April 20X1 and 30 April 20X2, are given below:

	30 April			
	20X1		*20X2*	
	£000	£000	£000	£000
Assets				
Tangible fixed assets				
Cost or valuation	51,000		63,000	
Accumulated depreciation	(12,500)	38,500	(16,300)	46,700
Current assets				
Stocks	16,400		18,400	
Trade debtors	19,100		20,600	
Sundry debtors and prepayments	3,100		4,000	
Total assets	38,600		43,000	
Less:				
Current liabilities				
Trade creditors	(11,400)		(8,400)	
Accruals	(3,400)		(4,200)	
Overdraft at bank	(13,700)		(4,800)	
	28,500		17,400	

Net current assets	10,100	25,600
	48,600	72,300
Less: 7% Debentures	(20,000)	(40,000)
(£20m issued 1 May 20X1)		
	28,600	32,300
Called up share capital	10,000	10,000
Share premium account	5,000	5,000
Revaluation reserve	5,000	5,000
Profit and loss account	8,600	12,300
	28,600	32,300

The summarised profit and loss accounts of Brood for the years ended 30 April 20X1 and 20X2, ignoring tax, are:

	Year ended 30 April	
	20X1	*20X2*
	£000	£000
Sales	58,000	66,000
Cost of sales	(43,000)	(49,000)
Gross profit	15,000	17,000
Operating expenses	(10,000)	(10,500)
Profit from operations	5,000	6,500
Interest payable	(1,400)	(2,800)
Net profit for the period	3,600	3,700

Required:

(a) Calculate the following ratios for each of the two years:

   (i) return on total capital employed

   (ii) return on owners' equity

   (iii) current ratio

   (iv) quick ratio (acid test)

   (v) gearing (leverage).

   Use year-end figures for all ratios. **(5 marks)**

(b) Comment briefly on the movements in these ratios between the two years. **(5 marks)**

(Total: 10 marks)

73 OVERTRADING

The term 'overtrading' is used to describe the condition of an enterprise which is increasing its sales revenue with insufficient working capital to support the increase.

Required:

(a) State FOUR movements in items in financial statements or in accounting ratios that could indicate overtrading.

(4 marks)

(b)   State THREE actions a company suffering from overtrading could take to rectify its position, and explain the likely effect of the actions you propose.   **(6 marks)**

(Total: 10 marks)

74   APILLON

Extracts from the financial statements of Apillon for the years ended 31 March 20X2 and 20X3 are given below:

Trading and profit and loss account			**Year ended 31 March**	
	20X2		**20X3**	
	£	£	£	£
Sales revenue (including cash sales £300,000 in 20X2 and £100,000 in 20X3)		3,100,000		3,800,000
Cost of sales:				
Opening stock	360,000		540,000	
Purchases (all on credit)	2,080,000		2,580,000	
	2,440,000		3,120,000	
less: Closing stock	540,000	(1,900,000)	720,000	(2,400,000)
Gross profit		1,200,000		1,400,000
Expenses		(900,000)		(1,100,000)
		300,000		300,000

Balance sheet			**31 March**	
	20X2		**20X3**	
	£	£	£	£
Current assets				
Stock	540,000		720,000	
Trade debtors	450,000		700,000	
		990,000		1,420,000
Current liabilities				
Trade creditors	410,000		690,000	
Bank overdraft	20,000		170,000	
		430,000		860,000

Required:

(a)   Calculate the following for each of the two years:

   (i)   Current ratio

   (ii)   Quick ratio (acid test)

   (iii)   Stock turnover period (use closing stock)

   (iv)   Debtors' collection period

   (v)   Creditors' payment period.

   Calculate items (iii), (iv) and (v) in days.   **(5 marks)**

(b)   Make *four* brief comments on the changes in the position of the company as revealed by the changes in these ratios and/or in the given figures from the financial statements.

(4 marks)

(Total: 9 marks)

Section 3

ANSWERS TO OBJECTIVE TEST QUESTIONS

GENERAL FRAMEWORK, ACCOUNTING CONCEPTS AND PRINCIPLES

1   B

The other answers are also aims of accounting, but are subsidiary to the main aim of providing financial information.

2   D

The transaction is accounted for as a drawing, with the owner taking capital out of the business. The owner and the business are treated as separate entities, for accounting purposes.

3   D

If a business is a going concern, it is reasonable to assume that fixed assets will be used over their expected useful economic life. It is therefore appropriate to value a fixed asset at cost less accumulated depreciation, which represents the consumption of value so far.

4   C

If the net realisable value (NRV) of stock is less than its cost, it is prudent to write down the stock from cost to NRV. The amount written off is recorded as a loss. The loss is taken 'now' (as soon as it is recognised), rather than at a later time, when it is sold.

5   D

If there is no new capital introduced in the period, retained profit can be measured as the rise in the value of net assets between the beginning and the end of the period. (Profit would be retained profit + drawings/dividends in the period.)

6   A

These are the five qualities of information in the ASB's Statement of Principles.

7   C

The money measurement concept is that items should only be recorded in the accounts if their value can be identified in money terms. Comparability does usually require consistency in accounting treatments from one pear to the next. Financial information should be neutral, i.e. free from bias, although this sometimes conflicts with the prudence concept. Gains are increases in ownership not resulting from contributions from owners. ('Contributions from owners' means the introduction of new capital.)

8   D

'True and fair' is partly determined by compliance with accounting standards and company law, but is more generally determined by reference to generally-accepted accounting practice (GAAP), which includes compliance with accounting standards and the law.

9   A

Comment (2) should obviously be incorrect: if it were correct, it would not be possible to have intangible assets such as goodwill in the balance sheet. Comment (3) is also incorrect: the substance over form convention means that the accounts must reflect the commercial effect of the transaction, where this differs from its legal form. An example is leasing: leased assets are legally owned by the lessor, but assets provided under a finance lease should be reported as fixed assets by the lessee.

Comment (1) is more difficult to analyse. In the Statement of principles for financial reporting, it is stated that: 'On occasion, a conflict will arise between the qualitative characteristics of relevance, reliability, comparability and understandability.' For example, a conflict can arise between relevance and reliability over the timeliness of information. A delay in providing information can make it out-of-date and so without relevance, but reporting the information sooner before all uncertainties have been resolved could affect its reliability. It is concluded, however, that: 'Although … entities should do all that they can to speed up the process necessary to make information reliable, financial information should not be provided until it is reliable.' Therefore Comment (1) is correct. Not an easy question!

10   A

The correct answer is A. FRS 18 states: Often there is uncertainty, either about the existence of assets, liabilities, gains, losses and changes to shareholders' funds, or about the amount at which they should be measured. Prudence requires that accounting policies take account of such uncertainty in recognising and measuring those assets, liabilities, gains, losses and changes to shareholders' funds.' Answer D is not correct: FRS 18 states: 'It is not necessary to exercise prudence when there is no uncertainty' so deliberately understating assets or gains or overstating liabilities or losses is not acceptable. Statement B is also incorrect: for example, contingent liabilities are not provided for and included in the balance sheet. Answer C has no relevance to the prudence concept.

11   A

You need to be familiar with the ASB's *Statement of Principles*. The characteristics that contribute to reliability are: (1) faithful representation (2) neutrality (3) being free from material error (4) completeness and (5) prudence.

12   C

The prudence concept is that gains and assets should not be overstated and losses and liabilities should not be understated. This is very different from what is stated in statement (2).

13   A

With historical cost accounting, assets are recorded at cost. When the rate of inflation is high, or when assets are held for a long time (such as land and buildings), the historical cost of assets can be significantly different from their current cost or current value.

14   C

At a time of rising prices, asset values in the balance sheet are understated: for example fixed assets have a current value higher than their original cost. Profits are overstated – for example, depreciation charges on fixed assets are based on historical cost rather than current value.

15   D

For example, when prices are rising, fixed asset replacement costs will go up. Fixed assets will therefore be valued in the balance sheet at below their current value. Depreciation charges will be based on historical cost rather than current value, so that depreciation does not properly reflect the consumption of value, and profits will therefore be overstated. (A similar argument applies in the case of stocks, with closing stocks undervalued if they are at historical cost, and the cost of sales undervalued and so profits overstated).

16   D

Profits are overstated, in the sense that the cost of sales and expenses are measured at their historical cost, not at their current value at the time of sale or consumption. Balance sheet values are understated, because they are recorded at cost rather than at their current value.

17   C

The patent certainly has commercial value to the business, and so could be called as asset of the business. However, unless an asset has been purchased, so that its value can be measured in money terms, it is not recorded in the accounts of a business or in the financial statements.

18   B

Profit is the increase in net assets between the beginning and end of the period, plus drawings taken out of the business, minus new capital introduced in the period (which is not profit).

19   B

Purchases should be recorded when the transaction takes place, which in this case is on receipt of the stock. If a business waits until receipt of the invoice to record a purchase, there could be an opportunity for 'window dressing' of the accounts at the end of the year, by asking suppliers not to send in invoices until later.

20   A

Consistency means using the same accounting policies from one year to the next. Asset valuations and profit measurements are made the same way each year, and this makes it easier to compare the financial position and performance of the business between one year and the next.

21   D

Falling prices (deflation) are not usual. If deflation does occur, historical cost accounting will overstate the current value of assets in the balance sheet. Profits will be understated. Perhaps the easiest way to think about this is that if fixed assets are valued at historical cost when their current value is much lower due to deflation, depreciation charges will be higher and profit lower.

22   £1,350

The prudence concept states that stock should be valued at the lower of cost and NRV. This should be for each item of stock individually, rather than for stocks in total. Here, stock should be valued at £750 for X and £600 for Y.

23   **A**

Stock should be valued at the lower of cost or net realisable value. The net realisable value of each stock item is calculated as follows.

	£
(1) *400 coats*	

NRV for each coat = 50% of £150, less 5% = £71.25. This is less than their £80 cost.

	£
Stock value = 400 coats × £71.25	28,500
Current stock value = 400 coats × £80	32,000
Reduction in stock value	3,500

	£
(2) *800 skirts*	
NRV = 800 × £(28 – 5), less £800	17,600
Cost = 800 × £20	16,000

Cost is lower, so no adjustment to stock value

	£
Closing stock before adjustment	284,700
Adjustment for item (1)	(3,500)
Adjusted stock value	281,200

DOUBLE-ENTRY BOOKKEEPING AND ACCOUNTING SYSTEMS

24   **£7,700**

The contra transaction should have been recorded as:

Debit:	Purchase ledger control account (creditors)	£400
Credit:	Sales ledger control account (debtors)	£400.

However, by debiting the sales ledger control account, instead of crediting it, total debtors have been over-stated by 2 × £400 (£800), and should be £7,700 rather than £8,500.

25   **A**

In the sales ledger control account (total debtors account), credit entries are for items that reduce the total of debts owed. These are mainly cash receipts from debtors, but also include sales returns, bad debts written off, settlements and discounts allowed and contra entries to supplier accounts in the purchases ledger.

26   **B**

The transaction should have been recorded as:

Debit Fixed asset account £38,000.

The fixed asset would then be depreciated and the depreciation charge for the year should be 20% of £38,000 × (3 months/12 months) = £1,900.

In error, the transaction was recorded as:

Debit Machinery repairs account £38,000.

The entire expense would be charged against profits in the year.

Cost has been overstated, and profit understated, by £38,000 - £1,900 = £36,100.

27   D

Suspense account

	£		£
Discounts received	5,100	Starting balance (836,200 – 819,700)	16,500
Debtor account (19,000 – 9,100)	9,900	Discounts allowed	3,900
Closing balance	5,400		
	20,400		20,400
		Balance b/d	5,400

Notes

A credit entry is needed in the suspense account to make total debit balances equal to total credit balances.

To decide whether to make a credit or debit entry in a suspense account, think about what the other side of the double entry transaction should be. We should credit the discounts received account, so we debit the suspense account. We should debit the discounts allowed account, so we credit the suspense account. We should credit the debtor account with an additional £9,900, so we debit the suspense account.

28   B

A suspense account is needed when, as a result of an accounting error, total credit balances and debit balances will not be equal to each other.

Error 1.   The entry should have been Credit Bank, Debt Motor Vehicles account. Instead, it was recorded as Credit Bank, Credit Motor Vehicles account. A suspense account is needed.

Error 2.   The entry should have been Debit Bank, Credit Brown, but was recorded as Debit Bank, Credit Green. Total credits and debits will not be unequal, so no suspense account needed to correct the error.

Error 3.   The entry has been recorded as: Credit Bank £9,500, Debit Rent £5,900. Credits and debits are unequal, so a suspense account is needed.

Error 4.   The transaction has been recorded as Credit Debtors, Debit Discounts Received, but should have been recorded as Credit Debtors, Debit Discounts Allowed. Total credits and debits will not be unequal, so no suspense account needed to correct the error.

Error 5.   An omission of a transaction does not need a suspense account to correct it.

29   C

	£
Overdraft in bank statement	(38,600)
Deposits not yet credited to the account	41,200
	2,600
Cheques paid but not yet presented to the bank	(3,300)
Overdraft in cash book	(700)

30   A

An entry is required in the cash book for all the correct items in the bank statement that have not yet been recorded in the cash book. These are the items that the business learns about from the bank statement, and should then record in its own accounts, in the cash book. Such items include bank charges (including overdraft interest) and details of dishonoured cheques. They are also likely to include details of credit transfers, standing orders and direct debit payments.

31   B

By crediting £40 to the Discounts Allowed account, when the discount should have been debited to the account, discounts allowed have been reduced by £40 when they should have been increased by £40. As a result of this error, profit has been overstated by 2 × £40 = £80.

32   A

	£
5 months at (£24,000/12) per month	10,000
7 months at (£30,000/12) per month	17,500
Annual rent expense	27,500

33   B

Expense		£
1 Feb – 30 Sept: (8 months)	8/12 × £90,000	60,000
1 Oct – 31 Jan: (4 months)	4/12 × £120,000	40,000
Total expense for the year		100,000

There is an accrual of one month for rent (January 20X3) for which rent has been incurred but no invoice received/payment made. Accrual = 1/12 × £120,000 = £10,000.

34   D

Rent receivable

	£		£
Opening balance	21,200	Opening balance	28,700
Profit and loss a/c (balancing figure)	475,900	Cash	481,200
Closing balance	31,200	Closing balance	18,400
	528,300		528,300

35   C

Rental income for the year to 30 November 20X2	£
December 20X1: (⅓ × £7,500)	2,500
1 January – 31 March 20X2	7,500
1 April – 30 June 20X2	9,000
1 July – 30 September 20X2	9,000
1 October – 30 November 20X2: (⅔ × £9,000)	6,000
	34,000

Rent has been received in advance for December 20X2: ⅓ × £900 = **£3,000**. It is a **credit** balance item in the balance sheet and described as income received in advance.

36   £3,770

The balance sheet figure is the original cash book balance adjusted for terms in the bank statement that need to be recorded in the cash book. See below.

37   £3,170

	£
Overdraft in cash book	(4,360)
Items in bank statement but not in cash book:	
Bank charges	(120)
Bank overdraft interest	(90)
Credit transfer into the account	2,500
Direct debit payment	(1,700)
Adjusted cash book: *balance sheet figure*	**(3,770)**
Items in cash book but not bank statement:	
Payments received	(3,600)
Payments to suppliers	4,200
Bank statement balance	**(3,170)**

38   C

Since total debits are less than total credits in the trial balance by (£1,026,480 - £992,640) £33,840, we need a debit balance of £33,840 in the suspense account to make the total debits and total credits equal.

Error 1.   does not affect the suspense account, because it is an omission and omissions do not alter debits and credits.

Error 2.   has treated a debit balance of £27,680 as a credit balance, as a result of which total credits will exceed total debits by 2 × £27,680 = £55,360.

Error 3.   does not affect the suspense account, since the error has been to debit the motor vehicle asset account instead of the bank account with £6,160.

Error 4.   has been to omit a credit balance of £21,520 for rent payable, as a result of which total debits will exceed total credits by £21,520.

To correct the errors:	£
Credit suspense account	55,360
Debit suspense account	21,520
To eliminate suspense account balance	33,840

39   C

This is a complex question. Remember that a suspense account is needed when, as a result of an accounting error, total credit balances and debit balances will not be equal to each other.

Error 1.   The original entry for the sales return would have been: Debit Sales returns, Credit Debtors. When the cash refund is paid, the entry should be Credit Cash, Debit Debtors. The error is really two errors. The wrong customer account has been used, but a debit entry has been recorded as a credit entry.

Error 5.   The entry should have been Credit Bank, Debit Plant repairs, but has been Credit Bank, Credit Plant and equipment account. A suspense account is needed to correct this error.

Errors 2, 3 and 4 do not result in total debits and total credits being unequal.

Error 2.   The wrong accounts have been used, but the debit entry and credit entry are equal. (The correct entry should be Credit Purchases, Debit Director's Current Account.)

Error 3.   The entry has been Debit Creditors, Credit discount allowed, but should have been Debit Creditors, Credit discount received. However, total debits and total *credits are equal.*

Error 4.   Presumably, these transactions have been omitted from the accounts entirely.

40   B

In an imprest system, the money in petty cash is topped up to a maximum limit from time to time. This is done by drawing cash from the bank equal to the total of petty cash expenditures since the last time petty cash was topped up. (This amount should equal the total of the payments recorded on the petty cash vouchers that are in the petty cash box.)

41   C

Items shown in the bank statement that should subsequently be recorded in the cash book are items that the business does not learn about until it receives the bank statement. These include bank charges, dishonoured cheques and standing orders and direct debit payments.

42   D

	£
Bank statement balance	(36,840)
Lodgements not yet credited	51,240
Payments outstanding	(43,620)
Correct cash book balance	(29,220)

An overdraft balance on the bank account is a credit balance item (a liability).

43   A

The cash book needs updating for dishonoured cheques and bank charges, but not for errors by the bank (irrelevant for the cash book) or transactions not yet processed by the bank (already entered in the cash book).

44   A

	£
Overdraft in bank statement	(68,100)
Deposits not yet credited to the account	141,200
	73,100
Cheques paid but not yet presented to the bank	(41,800)
Cash balance in cash book	31,300

45   B

The journal, petty cash book and sales day book are all books of prime entry. The petty cash book (like the cash book) is also an account in the double entry system (the main/general/nominal ledger). The purchase ledger is neither a day book nor a part of the double entry system.

46   B

The sales day book has been overcast by £800 (i.e. the total is £800 higher than it should be). As a result, the sales account has been credited and the sales ledger control account (total debtors) has been debited with £800 too much.

The purchase day book has been undercast by £1,100. As a result of this, the purchases account has been debited and the purchase ledger control account (total creditors) credited with £1,100 too little.

As a result of these errors, the control account balances need to be adjusted, and profit reduced by (£800 + £1,100) £1,900, by reducing sales and increasing purchases.

Neither error affects the entries in the accounts of individual debtors and creditors.

47   £603

Creditors account

	£		£
Bank	1,470	Balance b/d	540
Purchase returns	33	Purchases (on credit)	1,590
Discounts received	24		
Balance c/d	603		
	2,130		2,130
		Balance b/d	603

48   C

	Alpha's ledger account for Beta	Beta's statement
	£	£
Initial balance	4,140	8,950
Payment not yet allowed for		(4,080)
Cash discount disallowed	40	
Goods returned, not yet recorded	-	(380)
Adjusted balances	4,180	4,490

The remaining discrepancy is £4,490 - £4,180 = £310.

49   A

Credit sales are a debit entry in the sales ledger control account, because they represent an increase in debtors. Charges in the provision for doubtful debts account are not sales ledger control account items. Cash refunds are a debit item, since the bank account is credited. Sales returns by customers for which credit is given (item 6) are credited to sales ledger control account.

50   D

VAT account

	£		£
Creditors/bank	6,000	Balance b/d	3,400
Bank	2,600	Debtors/bank	10,500
Balance c/d	5,300		
	13,900		13,900
		Balance b/d	5,300

VAT on sales (outputs) = 17.5% × £60,000 = £10,500.

VAT on purchases (inputs) = (17.5/117.5) × £40,286 = £6,000

51   B

VAT is chargeable on the price after deducting the bulk purchase discount of 20%. The full purchase price is therefore 1.175 × £1,600 = £1,880. Since the trader is not registered for VAT, the purchases account should be debited with this full amount, including the tax. (A different situation arises when a trader is registered for VAT.)

52   A

Cash sales do not affect debtors.

Discounts received affect creditors, not debtors.

The provision for doubtful debts does not affect the amount of debtors, but specific bad debts written off do affect debtors.

Debtors account

	£		£
Opening balance b/d	37,500	Discounts allowed	15,750
Sales (credit sales)	357,500	Bad debts written off	10,500
		Bank (balancing figure)	**329,750**
		Closing balance c/d	39,000
	————		————
	395,000		395,000
	————		————
Balance b/d	39,000		

53   D

The purchase day book has been undercast by £500 (i.e. the total is £500 lower than it should be). As a result of this, the purchases account has been debited and the purchase ledger control account (total creditors) credited with £500 too little.

The sales day book has been overcast by £700. As a result, the sales account has been credited and the sales ledger control account (total debtors) has been debited with £700 too much.

As a result of these errors, the control account balances need to be adjusted, and profit reduced by (£500 + £700) £1,200, by reducing sales and increasing purchases.

Neither error affects the entries in the accounts of individual debtors and creditors.

54   B

The total charge for wages is the gross wages of employees, plus the employer's national insurance contributions. Here, the total is £157,326 + £33,247 = £190,573.

55   B

VAT account

	£		£
Bank	6,800	Opening balance b/f	7,200
Creditors/bank	13,800	Debtors/cash	18,261
Closing balance c/f	4,861		
	————		————
	25,461		25,461
	————		————
		Balance b/f	4,861

VAT on sales (outputs) = (17.5/117.5) × £122,610 = £18,261.

VAT on purchases = 17.5% × £78,857 = £13,800.

56   £4,009

A debit balance on the creditors ledger means that the business is owed money by its creditors, perhaps for sales returns or because of an overpayment. Here the debit balances are being transferred to the debtors ledger, and the accounting entry to record this is: Credit Creditors, Debit Debtors.

Creditors account

	£		£
Bank	271,845	Balance b/d	76,104
Discounts received	5,698	Purchases	286,932
Contra: debtors ledger	866	Debtors ledger	107
Balances written off	82		
Purchase returns (balancing figure)	4,009		
Balance c/d	80,643		
	_____		_____
	363,143		363,143
	_____		_____
		Balance b/d	80,643

57   C

Error 1.   Total sales and total debtors have been recorded £370 too much.

Error 2.   Total debtors has been recorded (£940 - £490) £450 too little.

As a result of these two errors, total debtors have been under-recorded by £450 - £370 = £80.

The errors have not affected the accounts of individual debtors.

58   A

As a result of the error, total creditors are under-stated by £259,440 - £254,940 = £4,500. To correct the error, we need to increase the balance in the creditors' ledger control account, and this is done by crediting the control account.

The error has affected the control account only, and not the entries in the individual creditor account for Figgins in the purchase ledger, so the total of creditors' balances is unaffected.

59   B

You think that you owe £150 more than the supplier has stated. With items, A, C and D the result would be that the supplier will state that you owe more, not less, than you think.

60   C

Opening stock should be a debit balance item (asset). As a result of the error with recording stock, total credit balances exceed total debit balances by 2 × £31,763 = £63,526. The question seems to be saying that a suspense account has already been opened for this error, and it needs a debit balance to make total debits equal to total credits.

Adding the total of debit balances incorrectly does not affect the suspense account balance. If it did, total credits would exceed total debits by a further £90, and the suspense account balance would need to be £90 higher. This is not a choice in the solutions.

61   A

Think of the other side of the double entry that is needed to correct the error. This will help you to decide whether the entry in the suspense account should be a debit or a credit entry.

Error 1.   To correct , we must debit gas account £180, therefore credit suspense account.

Error 2.   To correct, we need to debit discounts received £50 and debit discounts allowed £50, so we must credit the suspense account with 2 × £50.

Error 3.   To correct, we need to credit interest receivable, therefore we debit suspense account.

The account is shown below. The original balance inserted in the account is a debit balance.

Suspense account

	£		£
Balance (balancing figure)	210	Gas expense	180
Interest received	70	Discounts allowed	50
		Discounts received	50
	280		280

62   D

Discounts received should be recorded as:

Debit Creditors

Credit Discounts received.

Here, the discount has been debited instead of credited, so that the balance in the discounts received account is 2 × £200 = £400 too low. To correct, we must:

Credit Discounts received £400

Therefore Debit Suspense account £400.

63   B

The wording of this question can make it quite difficult, but the correct answer might be identified quickly.

Item B   Discounts allowed should be debited, therefore there is no error. If there is no error, we do not need a suspense account.

Item A   This is an error where a debit entry has been incorrectly recorded as a credit balance.

Item C   might cause you a problem. If the bad debt has been omitted entirely, and no accounting entry has been made, there can be no suspense account entry. Here, it would seem that the debtors balance has been reduced for the bad debt (credit Debtors) but the bad debt expense account has not recorded the bad debt. If so, credits exceed debits and a suspense account entry is needed.

Item D   The error in item D makes total debits higher by £180. These will therefore cause an entry in the suspense account.

64   C

The error you should look for is one where the correction will require:

Debit Suspense account

Credit the other account containing the error.

PAYE and National Insurance deductions are liabilities, payable to the tax authorities. If they have been recorded twice, the credit balance is too high, and the correction will need a debit entry in this account.

The contra entry has credited both the control accounts, and to correct this will require a debit entry in the account containing the error (the purchase ledger/creditors control account).

Closing stock should be a debit entry, and so a debit is needed to correct the error.

A balance for an accrual is a credit balance, but has been recorded incorrectly as a debit balance. To correct the error, the telephone expense account must be credited, and so the suspense account will be debited.

65   D

The error has been to debit the debtor account and credit the supplier (creditor) account, instead of debiting the supplier account and crediting the debtor account. As a result debtors are over-stated by $2 \times £270 = £540$, and creditors are over-stated by £540. The error should be corrected, but sales and purchases are unaffected, so profit is unaffected. Total assets (debtors) and total liabilities (creditors) are both £540 too high, so that net assets are unchanged.

66   A

To decide what entries are needed in the suspense account, you should think about the entry in the other account that is needed to correct the error. The entry in the suspense account is then the other side of the double entry. For example, stock (an asset) should be a debit balance, so to correct the error, we need to debit the stock account and credit suspense account. Similarly, VAT payable should be a credit balance, and to record the missing VAT, we need to credit the VAT account, debit suspense account.

Suspense account

	£		£
Balance (balancing figure)	2,050	Stock (1,475 + 1,745)	3,220
Telephone expense (2 × £190)	380		
VAT (£5,390 - £4,600)	790		
	3,220		3,220

The original balance in the account is a debit balance.

67   A

The VAT balance for purchases should be a debit balance, because the money is recoverable from the tax authorities. The VAT recoverable has been recorded as a credit entry (liability) instead of a debit entry, so to make the correction, we need to debit the VAT account by $2 \times £3,079 = £6,158$. The correction is Debit VAT £6,158, Credit Suspense account £6,158.

68   £14,600

	£
Profit as recorded	10,200
Reduce revenue expenditure (add to profit)	3,000
Increase revenue receipts (add to profit)	1,400
Correct net profit	14,600

69   B

If the suspense account shows a credit balance, the correcting entry to clear the account must be Debit Suspense account £130, credit the account with the error £130.

Purchase shave been over-stated by £130, and to correct this, we need to credit the Purchases account (and so debit Suspense account) with £130.

Omissions of transactions (item A and possibly item C) do not affect total debits and credits. If item C means that total debtors have been reduced by the bad debt, but the bad debts account does not yet show the bad debt, the correcting entry would be to debit the Bad debts account and credit Suspense account. The error in item D leaves total debits and credits equal.

70   B

A straightforward question compared with many others! Sales are recorded at their value excluding VAT, as credit items (income).

71   B

Debit balances represent assets or expenses (and drawings).

Credit balances represent liabilities, capital or income.

Carriage outwards is an expense and a prepayment is an asset.

72   D

Credit balances represent liabilities, capital or income, and the question is arguably incorrect to omit 'capital'. However, item D is the only possible answer.

73   B

The corrected account is shown below. You might have been puzzled by how to deal with the cash refunds to credit customers. It may help to think about the other side of the double entry: when there is a cash refund, the bank account is credited. The corresponding double entry must therefore be a debit item. The temptation may be to assume that the cash refund reduces debtors, therefore it is a credit item in the sales ledger control account. If you try doing this, however, your answer would not match any of the available answers A to D. This potentially tricky question was set in the June 2003 examination.

Sales Ledger Control Account

	£		£
Opening balance	180,000	Cash from credit customers	228,000
Sales	190,000	Sales returns	8,000
Cash refunds to credit customers	3,300	Discount allowed	4,200
		Bad debts written off	1,500
		Contras against creditors	2,400
		Closing balance	**129,200**
	373,300		373,300

74   B

An error of principle occurs when an item is incorrectly classified and posted to the wrong type of account, for example when the purchase of plant and machinery (a fixed asset) is debited to the purchases account.

75   A

Computer equipment (an asset) will be over-stated. Stationery costs (an expense) will be under-stated, which means that profit will be over-stated.

76   C

Expenses are recorded from the petty cash book by debiting the relevant expense account in the nominal ledger with the total of expense in each of the analysis columns. If the totals in the analysis columns are £20 too low, the debit entries in the expense accounts will be too low. This will make the credit balance in the trial balance higher by £20.

77   A

Item A means that although purchases have been recorded correctly (debit balance), creditors are £50 too low. Total debits exceed total credits.

Item A results in debtors (debit balance) being under-stated by £50. Item C results in the electricity expense (debit balance) being under-stated by 2 × £25 = £50. Item D results in the bank balance (debit) being under-stated. With items B, C and D, total credits would therefore exceed total debits.

78   D

A Suspense account entry is required whenever an error has resulted in a mismatch between debits and credits in the ledger accounts. If you need to work out whether an entry in the Suspense account should be a debit or a credit, think about which side of the 'other' ledger account the entry needs to be made, and the Suspense account entry is the matching debit or credit.

Item (1) is corrected by: credit Ordinary share capital £3,000, debit Suspense account £3,000.

Item (2) is corrected by: debit Plant asset account £2,800, debit Plant repairs account £2,800, credit Suspense account £5,600. You need to spot that the entry in the Plant asset account should have been a debit entry, not a credit.

Item (3) is a simple omission of a ledger balance from the trial balance, but since the opening Suspense account balance is taken from the incorrect trial balance, the correction is: debit Petty cash £500, credit Suspense account £500.

Item (4) is corrected, assuming the entry in the cash book is correct, by reducing the balance on the Motor car account. Credit Motor car account £9,000, debit Suspense account £9,000.

Item (5) is corrected by: debit purchases ledger £2,400 (2 × £1,200) and credit sales ledger £2,400 (2 × £1,200). For example, in the purchase ledger, we need to remove the credit entry of £1,200 and make a debit entry of £1,200, so the total amount to be debited is £2,400.

Items (1), (2), (3) and (4) all require a Suspense account entry to correct them.

79   A

The opening balance is a credit balance of £(864,390 − 860,930) = £3,460. It is a credit balance, to bring total credits up to being equal with total debits.

Suspense account

	£		£
(1) Ordinary shares a/c	3,000	Opening balance	3,460
(4) Motor car account	9,000	(2) Plant asset account	2,800
		(2) Plant repairs account	2,800
		(3) Petty cash	500
		Closing balance c/d	**2,440**
	12,000		12,000
Opening balance b/d	**2,440**		

Tutorial note: The closing balance is a debit balance, because total debit entries exceed total credit entries in the period. It is the opening balance brought down that determines whether the balance is a debit or a credit. Don't be confused by the fact that the closing balance c/d is entered on the credit side of the account.

80   B

Discount received should have been credited to the discount received account, not debited to the discount allowed account. The error will make total debit balances exceed total credit balances by $2 \times £400 = £800$.

With items A and D, the error makes the total credits exceed the total debits by £800. With error C, there is no debit and no credit, since the receipt has been omitted completely from the records.

81   A

This is not an easy question to solve. You should prepare a debtors account and calculate the closing balance as a debit balance. You should then look for the answer that gives the same net debit balance. Here, the closing balance is £32,125, and only answer A gives this net amount.

Debtors account

	£		£
Opening balance b/d	32,750	Opening balance b/d	1,275
Sales	125,000	Bank	122,500
		Discounts allowed	550
		Sales returns	1,300
		Closing balance (net)	32,125
	———		———
	157,750		157,750
	———		———
Opening balance (net)	32,125		

82   B

VAT on sales = $(17.5/117.5) \times £27,612.50 = £4,112.50$.

VAT on purchases = $17.5\% \times £18,000 = £3,150$.

Net amount of VAT payable (credit balance) = £4,112.50 - £3,150 = £962.50

83   C

The owner is transferring capital into the business, in the form of a car. Additions to capital are entered in the credit side of the capital account, and additions to fixed assets are entered on the debit side of the relevant fixed asset account.

84   B

The debtors account should be debited with the full amount payable, including the tax. The entry in the sales account should be for the sales value excluding VAT. VAT payable to the tax authorities should be credited to the VAT account (liability = credit balance).

85   A

The debtors account should be credited with the full amount of the sales return, including the tax. The Sales returns account should be debited with the value of the returns excluding the VAT. The VAT account should be debited with the amount of tax on the returns (since the tax is no longer payable).

86   A

The profit and loss account is a part of the double entry accounting system in the nominal ledger. When the profit for a period is being calculated, two double entry transactions to record are:

Credit Stock account (opening stock)

Debit Profit and loss account.

Debit Stock account (closing stock)

Credit Profit and loss account.

87   D

The sales day book provides totals for debtors, sales excluding VAT and VAT on the sales. These totals are transferred to the nominal ledger by debiting total debtors account with the gross amount payable, crediting the sales account with the value of sales excluding VAT and crediting VAT account with the amount of VAT payable.

88   D

Items A and B will result in an error in the control account (total debtors). Item C will result in an error in the total of individual debtor account balances. Item D will not affect either of the totals, although there are errors in the individual accounts of the two customers affected, with one account balance too high and the other too low by the same amount.

89   A

The series of transactions might be recorded as follows.

Original purchase

Debit Purchases

Credit Brad (creditor)

On payment

Debit Brad (creditor)

Credit Bank

On cancellation of the cheque

Debit Bank

Credit Purchase returns

If the second and third transactions are dealt with at the same time, they simplify to Debit Brad, credit Purchase returns.

90   A

Charge to the profit and loss account:

7 months: $7/12 \times £1,800 = £1,050$

Prepayment of rent:

5 months: $5/12 \times £1,800 = £750$.

91   £340

	£
Bank statement balance	(825)
Error in bank records	
Add direct debit incorrectly charged	160
Items in cash book but not yet in bank statement	
Unpresented cheques	(475)
Deposits not yet recorded	800
Balance in cash book (for balance sheet)	(340)

Note: Bank charges. The cash book should be brought up to date by including the bank charges of £50. These are included in the bank statement balance of £825 overdrawn.

92   A

	£
Amount to top up petty cash	500
Increase in float	(50)
	450
Cash paid in by staff (photocopying)	25
	475
Cash paid to employee in return for cheque	(90)
Petty cash expenses in the month	385

93   D

A fixed asset register is a detailed schedule of fixed assets, and is not another name for fixed asset ledger accounts in the nominal ledger.

94   £3,900

The best estimate of electricity expenses to accrue for June 20X4 is $1/3 \times £600 = £200$.

Electricity expenses account

	£		£
Bank	4,000	Opening balance b/d (accrual)	300
Closing balance c/d (accrual)	200	Profit and loss account	3,900
	4,200		4,200
		Opening balance b/d	200

The accrual carried forward is for June 20X4. The best estimate for the expense for June is $1/3 \times £600 = £200$.

95   C

P & L account charge for insurance:

(7 months): $7/12 \times £2,400 = £1,400$

Prepayment: 5 months $= 5/12 \times £2,400 = £1,000$.

96   C

The trial balance will fail to balance when a transaction is recorded but without matching debit and credit entries.

Item A   has been incorrectly recorded as Debit Machine repairs, Credit Creditors.

Item B   has been recorded incorrectly as Debit Bank, Credit Creditors.

Item C   has been recorded as Debit Sales returns, Debit Debtors, so this is the answer to the question.

Item D   is not clear, because depreciation could refer to either the depreciation charge for the period or the accumulated depreciation (provision for depreciation). Since item C is a correct answer, you needn't worry too much about the meaning of item D.

97   B

When you pay a creditor too much, the creditor will owe money to you, and so is a debtor. This would explain a debit balance on a creditor account.

98   B

It is easy to get confused about credits and debits with a bank account. In the accounts of a business, cash is shown as a debit balance and an overdraft is a credit balance. Cash paid into the account is debited and cash paid out is credited to the Bank account. To a bank, however, money in a customer's account is money that the bank owes to the customer, and to the bank, this is a credit item. This is why a bank might 'credit your account' by putting money into it. This meaning of crediting an account is used in this question.

	£
Cash book balance	(8,970)
Items on bank statement, but not in cash book	
Bank charges	(550)
Bank error	425
Items not yet on the bank statement	
Payments from the account	3,275
Receipts into the account	(5,380)
Bank statement balance	(11,200)

99   A

Error 1.   There is a missing debit balance (prepayment = asset = debit balance).

Error 2.   Wages costs have been debited to the wrong account, but this does not affect the trial balance.

Error 3.   A failure to accrue suggests that there has been no entry at all in the accounts. Omissions of this sort do not affect the trial balance.

100   A

An audit trail allows you to trace transactions through the accounting system.

101   D

Tutorial note: To work out the cost of oil used, you must first of all calculate total purchases of oil for the year.

	£
Closing creditors for oil	3,200
Payments in the period	34,600
	37,800
Less: Opening creditors for oil	(3,600)
Purchases of oil in the period	34,200

	£
Opening stock of oil	8,200
Purchases	34,200
	42,400
Less: closing stock of oil	(9,300)
Cost of oil used in the period	33,100

102   C

The accrual for May and June 20X3 is assumed to be 2/3 × £840 = £560.

Electricity expenses account

	£		£
Bank	600	Opening balance b/d	300
Bank	720		
Bank	900		
Bank	840		
Closing balance c/d	560	Profit and loss account	3,320
	3,520		3,520
		Opening balance b/d	560

103   B

The four gas bills cover the same period as the financial year of the company, and the total amount of the four invoices is £6,800. However, at the start of the year, the company had overpaid by £200. Presumably, the gas supplier reduced the next invoice to Mud by £200 as a way or dealing with the overpayment. The charge for gas in the financial year should therefore be £6,800 + £200 = £7,000.

104   A

When a debt is written off as bad, the transaction is recorded as:

        Debit Bad and doubtful debts account (expense)

        Credit Debtor account.

Any subsequent change to the provision for doubtful debts should be dealt with as a separate matter.

105 £122,000

Remember that: Opening stock plus (Purchases minus Returns) – Closing stock = Cost of sales. Here, all the figures are given except the figure for purchases.

	£
	£
Opening stock	12,000
Purchases (balancing figure)	**122,000**
Purchase returns	(5,000)
	129,000
less Closing stock	(18,000)
Cost of sales	111,000

106 £1,970

	£
Balance at start of month	2,500
Payment (£800 less 10%)	(720)
Receipt (£200 less 5%)	190
Balance at end of month	1,970

107 A

Error 1. The fixed asset has been treated as a purchase expense, and this will add to the cost of sales. As a result, both gross profit and net profit will be £50,000 lower. (This question ignores the depreciation charge that would have been made for the fixed asset.)

Error 2. The closing stock of stationery has been treated as raw materials stock, but net profit will not be affected. However, raw materials closing stock is used to measure the cost of sales, whereas stationery stock is not. The cost of sales will therefore be £10,000 lower, and gross profit will be £10,000 higher.

Taking the two errors together, gross profit will be £40,000 lower and net profit £50,000 lower, ignoring whatever the depreciation charge on the fixed asset would have been.

108 D

Stock costing £400 is sold for £1,000, giving a profit of £600. The VAT on the sale will be £175.

	Cash	Stock	Liabilities	Capital
	£	£	£	£
Start business	1,000			1,000
Buy stock		800	800	
Sell stock	1,175	(400)	175	600
	2,175 +	400 =	975 +	1,600

109   B

	£
Closing capital	4,500
Opening capital	10,000
Decrease in net assets	(5,500)
Drawings: profit taken out	8,000
Capital introduced	(4,000)
Loss for the year	(1,500)

110   B

	£
Payments for purchases	85,400
Less: Opening creditors for fuel	(1,700)
Plus: Invoices due for fuel purchased	1,300
Purchases	85,000

	£
Opening stock	12,500
Purchases	85,000
	97,500
Closing stock	(9,800)
Cost of fuel – P & L account	87,700

111   B

Items requiring an entry in the cash book are those that are correct and need to be recorded, but have not yet been recorded. These are items on the balance sheet that the company's accountant is not aware of until the bank statement is received. They are bank charges, the dishonoured cheque (assuming the company has not been notified previously) and the direct debit (assuming this too has not been previously notified). Lodgements and outstanding cheques have already been recorded correctly in the cash book. The bank's error (item 3) should not be recorded – this is something for the bank to correct in its own accounts.

112   £880

The bank statement overdraft balance of £800 omits the cheque that has not yet been presented for payment, which is correctly recorded in the cash book. The cash book balance should therefore be an overdraft of £880. The actual cash book balance at the moment is an overdraft of £750, because the business did not know about the dishonoured cheque. Having found out about the dishonoured cheque, the cash book should be updated, and the overdraft balance will become £880.

113 £389

The payment of the petrol invoice at the start of the month does not affect the expenses account.

Motor expenses account

	£		£
Opening balance (prepayment) (prepayment 4 months)	96	Profit and loss account (balancing figure)	389
Sundry creditors	245	Closing balance	72
Creditors (petrol)	120		
	461		461
Opening balance b/d (prepayment)	72		

114 A

Purchase ledger control account

	£		£
Bank	68,900	Opening balance b/d	34,500
Discounts received	1,200	Purchases (credit)	78,400
Purchase returns	4,700		
Closing balance c/d	38,100		
	112,900		112,900
		Opening balance b/d	38,100

115 B

	£
Bank statement balance	13,400
Items not recorded in the cash book	
Dishonoured cheque	300
Bank charges	50
	13,750
Unpresented cheques	(1,400)
Error: receipt recorded as a payment (2 × £195)	(390)
Cash book balance before corrections	11,960

116 D

£14.10 + £25.50 + £12.90 + (£24.00 × 1.175) = £80.70.

117 C

It might not be easy to identify the correct solution to this question. A trial balance does not confirm the accuracy of the ledger accounts, nor does it provide information for calculating adjustments. Neither does it provide all the figures necessary to prepare the final accounts, even though it provides many of them. For example, the trial balance does not include a closing stock figure. Almost by default, answer C is the correct answer.

118   A

In a computerised system, it is necessary to enter all transactions into the system, so the day book entries are almost as time-consuming as with a manual system. A computer system is most useful, however, in maintaining ledger accounts, because these are updated automatically from the day book entries.

119   £15,000

Sales ledger control account

	£		£
Opening balance b/d	14,500	Discounts allowed	350
Sales	53,500	Contra: purchase ledger	50
		Sales returns	1,400
		Bank	51,200
		Balance c/d	15,000
	68,000		68,000
Balance b/d	15,000		

120   D

The balance on the control account exceeds the total of the individual account balances by £1,802. Items A, B and C would all have the effect of making the total of the individual account balances higher by £1,802. Item D, however, by recording a credit item as a debit item in the control account, has made the control account debit balance too high by £901 × 2 = £1,802.

121   £2,185

Telephone expenses account

	£		£
Opening balance b/d (Rental prepayment 2/3 × £90)	60	Opening balance b/d (Accrued call charges)	80
Creditors	2,145	P & L account	2,185
Closing balance c/d (Accrued call charges)	120	Closing balance c/d (Rental prepayment 2/3 × £90)	60
	2,325		2,325
Balance b/d (prepayment)	60	Balance b/d (accrual)	120

Tutorial note: Prepayments are debt entries as a balance brought down and accruals are a credit entry (liability) as a balance brought down.

122   C

VAT on sales = 10% × £90,000 = £9,000.

VAT on purchases = 10% × £72,000 = £7,200.

VAT payable = £9,000 - £7,200 = £1,800.

123   D

All these codes might be used in a computerised accounting system.

124 A

The situation in the question is unusual because there is an opening accrual on the account, but a closing prepayment of $1/3 \times £1,200 = £400$ (prepayment of the rent for April 2004).

Rent account

	£		£
Bank	4,000	Balance b/d (accrual)	300
		Profit and loss account	**3,300**
		Balance c/d (prepayment)	400
	4,000		4,000
Balance b/d	400		

125 C

Rent for the year 1 July 20X2 to 30 June 20X3 was $£13,200 \times 1/1.1 = £12,000$.

Profit and loss account charge:

6 months at £12,000 plus 6 months at £13,200 = £6,000 + £6,600.

126 B

	£
Bank statement balance	(1,000)
Bank charges	100
Unpresented cheque	(750)
Deposits not recorded by bank	500
Cash book balance before adjustments	(1,150)

127 B

Presumably, there was no opening balance on this account.

Sales ledger control account

	£		£
Sales	250,000	Bank	225,000
Bank: cheque returned	3,500	Sales returns	2,500
		Bad debts	3,000
		Contra: purchase ledger	4,000
		Balance c/d	19,000
	253,500		253,500
Balance b/d	19,000		

ACCOUNTING TREATMENTS

128 £4.72 m

	£ million
Fixed assets at cost	10.40
Accumulated depreciation	0.12
Net book value	10.28
Revaluation amount	15.00
Transfer to revaluation reserve	4.72

129 **£5,000**

Depreciable amount £(60,000 – 12,000)	£48,000
Expected life	4 years
Annual depreciation charge	£12,000
Depreciation each month	£1,000
Depreciation charge in the period (5 months)	£5,000

130 **B**

With FIFO, closing stock is the most recently purchased stock, therefore when prices are rising, closing stock will have a higher value than if the average cost method of stock valuation is used. Since closing stocks will be valued higher, the cost of sales will be lower and the profit will be higher.

131 **A**

Debtors (5% of £2 million) = £100,000.

Required provision for doubtful debts (4% of £100,000) = £4,000.

Current provision for doubtful debts = £4,000 × ¾ = £3,000.

Increase in provision = £1,000.

An increase in the provision for doubtful debts reduces profits.

132 **D**

Items A and B are normal repairs and maintenance items, and so are classed as revenue expenditure. The purchase by a garage/car showroom of a car is the purchase of stock for resale. The car is a current asset, and its purchase cost is revenue expenditure. Professional fees incurred in the purchase of a fixed asset can be included in the cost of the asset.

133 **B**

The cost of the asset to the buyer is the fair value of the goods given in exchange, which is the cost of those goods, £10,000.

134 **D**

Accumulated depreciation at the time of disposal = (3 years) 3 × 20% × £12,000 = £7,200.

	£
Cost of vehicle	12,000
Accumulated depreciation	7,200
Net book value at time of sale	4,800
Sale value (trade-in value)	5,000
Profit on sale	200

135 **C**

The question presumably refers to the valuation of stock of finished goods or part-finished work in progress in a manufacturing business. Inward carriage costs (i.e. the costs of delivery of materials and components purchased from suppliers) are included in stock costs. Work in progress and finished goods should also include a share of production overhead costs.

136   A

The charge for bad and doubtful debts is the actual amount of bad debts written off plus the increase in the provision for doubtful debts, or minus the decrease in the provision.

	£
Provision at end of year (5% of £120,000)	6,000
Provision at start of year	9,000
Decrease in provision	(3,000)
Bad debts written off	5,000
Charge to P & L account	2,000

137   D

Depreciable amount £(52,000 – 4,000)	£48,000
Expected life	8 years
Annual depreciation charge	£6,000
Number of years' depreciation (20X2 – 20X6)	5
Accumulated depreciation at time of disposal	£30,000

	£
Cost	52,000
Accumulated depreciation at time of disposal	30,000
Net book value (NBV) at time of disposal	22,000
Disposal price	35,000
Profit on disposal	13,000

138   £1,725

	£
Purchase price	15,000
Transportation cost	1,500
Installation cost	750
Cost of fixed asset	17,250
Depreciation (10%)	1,725

139   D

In a period of rising prices, the replacement cost method will give the highest charge for stock issues, and so the highest cost of sales and the lowest profit.

140   C

The cost of manufactured goods should include the cost of the raw materials, including carriage inwards costs, plus conversion costs. Conversion costs are the cost of manufacturing labour and the cost of production overhead. Together, these are the costs of getting the products into their current condition. Carriage outwards and the costs of storage of finished goods should not be included, because they are costs incurred after the manufacture of the products is complete.

141   £900

Depreciable amount £(40,000 – 4,000)	£36,000
Expected life	10 years
Annual depreciation charge	£3,600
Depreciation each month	£300
Depreciation charge in the period (3 months)	£900

142 C

	Cost	Accum dep'n	NBV
	£000	£000	£000
Opening balance	860	397	
Disposal	(80)	(43)	
	780	354	
Purchase	180		
	960		
Depreciation (10%)		96	
		450	
NBV = 960 - 450			510

143 D

Depreciation: Assets held all year = £381,200 - £36,000 = £345,200.

Depreciation charge		£
Assets held all year	20% × £345,200	69,040
Assets bought on 1 Sept	$^{10}/_{12}$ × 20% × £18,000	3,000
Assets disposed of	$^{8}/_{12}$ × 20% × £36,000	4,800
		76,840

144 A

Statement 1   Incorrect, because applied research costs may not be capitalised.

Statement 3   Incorrect. There is no specific time restriction on the amortisation period.

Statement 4   Incorrect, because if capitalisation of development costs is no longer justified, it should be written off in full immediately.

145 £54,183

	£
Item (3)	
Net realisable value of component P (200 × £208)	41,600
Less selling costs	(500)
	41,100
Units of component P: original cost (200 × £250)	50,000
Amount to write down	8,900

	£
Original valuation	72,857
(1) Overvaluation of nails: 8,000 × £0.99	(7,920)
(2) Copying error has overvalued stock by (8,726 – 6,872)	(1,854)
(3) Write-down of component P	(8,900)
Correct year-end stock value	54,183

146 A

The net realisable value of stock items is the selling price less the 4% commission payable.

	NRV	Lower of cost or NRV	
	£	£	
Henry VII	2,784	2,280	(cost)
Dissuasion	3,840	3,840	(NRV)
John Bunion	1,248	1,248	(NRV)
		7,368	

147 A

	NRV (discounted price)	Lower of cost or NRV
	£	£
Liszt	56.0	50.0
Delius	49.5	49.5
Offenbach	202.5	150.0
Bax	17.5	17.5
		267.0

148 C

With LIFO, closing stock will be valued at the cost of the earliest stock items acquired.

149 C

Costs incurred after production has been completed cannot be included in the cost of finished goods. These costs include finished goods storage costs and outward delivery (carriage outwards) costs.

Carriage inwards is a part of the materials purchase costs, and depreciation of plant and factory supervisors' wages are production overhead costs. A share of production overhead costs is included in the value of stock.

150 C

Answer C is the most appropriate of the three definitions given, although it is not a strictly accurate definition.

151 A

Depreciation charge:	£
For plant disposed of in the year (20% of £30,000 × 9/12)	4,500
For other plant held at the start of the year (20% of £(380,000 − 30,000))	70,000
For plant acquired during the year (20% of £51,000 × 9/12)	7,650
Total charge for depreciation of plant	82,150

152   A

The nominal ledger account for fixed assets shows a net book value that is £10,000 higher than the figure in the fixed assets register. This could be due to having omitted to deduct an asset with a NBV of £10,000 from the ledger. A fixed asset will have a NBV on disposal when it is sold for £15,000 and the profit on disposal is £5,000.

153   B

The accumulated depreciation at the start of the year is the difference between the cost of the assets and their net book value: £380,000 - £278,000= £102,000. The accumulated depreciation at the time of the revaluation is the depreciation at the start of the year (£102,000) plus the depreciation charge for the year up to the date of the revaluation. This is 2% × £380,000 = £7,600.

	£000
Freehold property at cost	380.0
Accumulated depreciation at time of revaluation (102 + 7.6)	109.6
Net book value at time of revaluation	270.4
Revaluation amount	411.0
Transfer to revaluation reserve	140.6

Answer B is the only one with this correct amount for the transfer to the revaluation reserve. The other book-keeping entries in answer B are also appropriate for recording the revaluation.

154   £62,210

	£
Sale value of asset	4,000
Loss on disposal	1,250
Net book value at time of disposal	5,250
Balance on fixed asset register before disposal	67,460
Balance on fixed asset register after disposal	62,210

155   C

1 Jan – 30 June: 3% of £380,000 × 6/12 = £5,700.

1 July – 31 December: 3% of £450,000 × 6/12 = £6,750.

Charge for the year: £5,700 + £6,750 = £12,450.

156   B

	£
Cost of asset	126,000
Depreciation to 31 October 20X3 (4/12 × 15%)	6,300
	119,700
Depreciation to 31 October 20X4 (15%)	17,955
	101,745
Depreciation to 31 October 20X5 (15%)	15,262
	86,483
Depreciation to 31 October 20X6 (15%)	12,972
	73,511
Depreciation to 30 September 20X7 (11/12 × 15%)	10,108
Net book value at time of disposal	63,403
Disposal price	54,800
Loss on disposal	8,603

157 D

> *Tutorial note*: Remember that when you calculate a provision for doubtful debts as a percentage of total debtors, you calculate the percentage on the value of debtors after removing the bad debts written off. It is incorrect to calculate a doubtful debt provision on bad debt items! You need to remember too that a reduction in the provision for doubtful debts is a negative expense, and adds to profit.

	£
Provision for doubtful debts at end of year	36,200
(10% of (400,000 – 38,000))	
Provision for doubtful debts at start of year	50,000
Reduction in the provision	13,800
Bad debts written off	(38,000)
Charge for bad and doubtful debts	(24,200)

158 C

	£120,000
Debtors (4% of £3 million)	
	£
Required provision for doubtful debts (3%)	3,600
Provision last year (£3,600 × 100/125)	2,880
Increase in provision	720
Bad debts written off	3,200
Bad debts recovered	(150)
Charge to P & L account	3,770

159 C

The calculations are a bit complex here. The general provision is 2% of the total debtors after deducting the specific provision. £13,720 therefore represents 98% of the total debtors after deducting the specific provision. This means that total debtors before deducting the specific provision are £13,720/0.98 = £14,000.

	£
Provision for doubtful debts at start of year:	
Specific	350
General (2% of £14,000)	280
	630
Required provision at end of year (3% of £17,500)	525
Reduction in provision (credit P & L account)	105

160 B

The receipt has been accounted for by:

> Debit Bank, Credit Sales ledger control account.

It should have been accounted for as:

> Debit Bank, Credit Bad debts.

> (The debtor was removed from the accounts when the bad debt was written off. The receipt is the recovery of a bad debt, which is credited to the bad debts account.)

To correct the error:

> Debit Sales ledger control account, Credit Bad debts.

161 £4,200

The charge to the profit and loss account is the bad debt written off (£4,000) plus the increase in the provision for doubtful debts (£200).

162 £950

Net realisable value = Sales price £1,200 less modification costs (£150) and selling costs (£100). NRV is therefore £950. Stock is valued at the lower of cost or NRV. Cost is £1,000, so the stock item should be valued at £950.

163 B

	£
Opening valuation	10,250
Purchases	3,450
	13,700
Value of disposals	(2,175)
	11,525
End of year valuation	8,000
Depreciation charge for the year	3,525

Tutorial note: You might have been able to reach this answer logically. This method of depreciation is not in common use.

164 B

Cost = Purchase price + Installation costs = £85,000. Training of staff and costs of testing are revenue expenditures.

165 B

	Net realisable value	Lower of cost or NRV	Units	Value
	£	£		£
Basic	8	6	200	1,200
Super	8	8	250	2,000
Luxury	10	10	150	1,500
Total value				4,700

166 D

Do not include the road tax in the cost of the car. Road tax is a revenue expense item.

	£
Cost of asset	10,000
Depreciation 20X1 (25%)	2,500
	7,500
Depreciation 20X2 (25%)	1,875
	5,625
Depreciation 20X3 (25%)	1,406
	4,219
Depreciation 20X4 (25%)	1,055
Net book value at time of disposal	3,164
Disposal value	5,000
Profit on disposal	1,836

167   £2,950

	In	*Out*
Opening stock	50 at £40	
7 February	100 at £45	
14 February		50 at £40
		30 at £45
21 February	50 at £50	
28 February		60 at £45

Closing stock = 10 units at £45 (£450) plus 50 units at £50 (£2,500) = £2,950.

168   A

		£
Opening stock	700 units × £190	133,000
1 July purchases	500 units × £220	110,000
		243,000
1 November sales	400 units × £190	(76,000)
		167,000
1 February purchases	300 units × £230	69,000
		236,000
15 April sales	250 units × £190	(47,500)
Closing stock, 30 April		188,500

169   D

Statement 1 is incorrect: Stocks are normally valued at the *lower* of cost and net realisable value. Statement 2 is incorrect: the cost of manufactured stock will include some production overhead cost. Statements 3 and 4 are correct. Valuing stock at sales price less estimated profit margin might be appropriate for closing stock valuation in a retail business.

170   A

The asset disposed of had a net book value at the time of disposal = sales proceeds + loss on sale = £25,000 + £5,000 = £30,000.

	£
Net book value at 1 August 20X2	200,000
Net book value of asset disposed of	30,000
	170,000
Depreciation charge	20,000
Net book value at 31 July 20X3	150,000

171   B

Only purchased goodwill is recorded in the accounts of a business, not internally-generated ('inherent') goodwill. Purchased goodwill is classified as an intangible fixed asset.

172   C

	£
Profit	8,000
Add depreciation (not a cash expense)	12,000
	20,000
Purchase of new fixed assets	(25,000)
Fall in cash balance	(5,000)

173 A

You need to know the sales proceeds to calculate the length of ownership, or you need to know the length of ownership to calculate the sales proceeds. For example, this asset might have been sold after one year (NBV = £1,000) for £5,500, or it might have been sold after two years (NBV £8,000) for £3,500, and so on.

174 C

'Material' means of significance (typically 'of a significant monetary amount'). When assets have along useful life but are of an insignificant value, it is simpler (and permissible) to write off the full purchase cost in the year of purchase. This avoids the need to calculate a depreciation charge each year, and maintain a fixed asset register records for the items, and so on.

175 B

	£
Cost of asset	2,400.0
Depreciation Year 1 (20%)	480.0
	1,920.0
Depreciation Year 2 (20%)	384.0
	1,536.0
Depreciation Year 3 (20%)	307.2
Net book value at time of disposal	1,228.8
Disposal value	1,200.0
Loss on disposal	28.8

176 B

	£
Purchase of raw materials	112,000
Decrease in raw material stocks	8,000
	120,000
Carriage inwards	3,000
Direct wages	42,000
Production overhead	27,000
Cost of production	192,000
Increase in work in progress	(10,000)
Cost of finished production	182,000

177 C

	Units	Average cost £	Total cost £
Opening balance	30	2.00	60
5 August	50	2.40	120
	80	2.25	180
10 August	(40)	2.25	(90)
	40	2.25	90
18 August	60	2.50	150
	100	2.40	240
23 August	(25)	2.40	(60)
Closing balance	75	2.40	180

178   B

Development costs could be capitalised (subject to certain conditions), but research costs should not be capitalised. Research costs should always be treated as a revenue expense.

179   B

There is no requirement about having to amortise development costs within 5 years. Capitalised development costs should be amortised over the period expected to benefit from the development expenditure.

180   C

Statements (1) and (3) are incorrect. Statement (1): If certain conditions are met, development expenditure may be capitalised, but does not have to be capitalised. Statement (3): capitalised development expenditure should be amortised over the period of years expected to benefit from the expenditure. Statements (2) and (4) are correct.

181   £93,000

Net cash outflow is assumed to mean the cash paid for new additions minus the cash received from disposals.

	£
Net book value of assets disposed of (79,000 – 64,000)	15,000
Loss on disposals	6,000
Cash received from disposals	9,000
Cash paid for new additions	(102,000)
Net cash outflow	(93,000)

182   A

	£
Cost of asset	9,000
Depreciation Year 1 (30%)	2,700
	6,300
Depreciation Year 2 (30%)	1,890
	4,410
Depreciation Year 3 (30%)	1,323
Net book value at time of disposal	3,087
Disposal value	3,000
Loss on disposal	87

183   D

A provision for doubtful debts is a type of current liability. In the balance sheet, it is subtracted from debtors. An increase in a provision for doubtful debts will therefore reduce net current assets, i.e. it will reduce working capital.

184   B

Goods sold on a sale or return basis cannot be treated as a genuine sale until they have been sold on by the customer. It is necessary to eliminate the 'profit' on the sale. Stock should include the goods on sale or return, valued at cost. Debtors should exclude 'debts' for the sale-or-return goods.

	Stock £	Debtors £
As originally stated	87,000	124,000
Adjust for sale or return goods	4,500	(6,000)
Balance sheet values	91,500	118,000

185 A

	£
Cost of asset	5,000
Depreciation Year 1 (20%)	1,000
	4,000
Depreciation Year 2 (20%)	800
	3,200
Depreciation Year 3 (20%)	640
Net book value at time of disposal	2,560
Disposal value	2,200
Loss on disposal	360

186 D

The reducing balance method charges more depreciation in earlier years than in later years. It is therefore appropriate to use for fixed assets such as motor vehicles that lose a large part of their value in the earlier years of their life.

187 A

	£
Bad debts written off (800 + 550)	1,350
Bad debt recovered	(350)
Reduction in provision for doubtful debts	(200)
Charge for bad and doubtful debts to P & L	800

FINANCIAL STATEMENTS

188 B

Net cash outflow is assumed to mean the cash paid for new additions minus the cash received from disposals.

	£
Net book value of assets disposed of	2,000
Profit on disposal	2,000
Cash received from disposals	4,000
Cash paid for new additions	(15,000)
Net cash outflow	(11,000)

189 D

The reconciliation of operating profit to net cash flow from operations is not a part of the cash flow statement itself. It is a note to the cash flow statement. 'Profit on disposal' appears in this reconciliation, but is not part of the cash flow statement.

New purchase (additions) are given in the question as £2,000. The assets disposed of had a cost of £3,000 and accumulated depreciation at the time of disposal of £1,500. Their net book value at disposal was therefore £1,500. The profit on disposal was £500, so the cash received from the disposal was £2,000.

190   A

	£000
Operating profit	180
Depreciation	30
Profit on sale of fixed asset	(75)
	135
Increase in working capital (50 – 40)	(10)
Net cash flow from operating activities	125

191   D

	£
Depreciation	980,000
Profit on sale of fixed assets	(40,000)
Increase in stocks	(130,000)
Decrease in debtors	100,000
Increase in creditors	80,000
Net effect on cash flow	+ 990,000

192   C

Surplus on the revaluation of a fixed asset, proposal dividends and bad debts written off are not cash flow items.

193   D

A loss on the sale of a fixed asset should be added back, because it is not a cash loss. The cash proceeds from the sale are shown in the cash flow statement itself.

194   D

Statement 1 is incorrect: net cash flow from operating activities is the same, whichever method of presentation is used.

Statement 2 is incorrect. Companies with high profits can be cash-negative, due to high spending on new fixed assets and/or a large build-up of working capital.

Statement 3 is incorrect. Profits and losses on fixed asset disposals are shown in the note to the cash flow statement that reconciles the operating profit to the net cash flow from operating activities.

195   D

Items added in this note include the depreciation charge for the period, any losses on disposals of fixed assets, reductions in stocks and debtors (including prepayments) and any increase in trade creditors (including accruals).

196

Disposals were £350,000.

Additions were £5,100,000. See workings below.

	£000
Net book value of assets disposed of	500
Loss on disposal	150
Fixed asset disposals – sales value	350

	£000
Net book value of assets at end of year	6,000
Net book value of assets at start of year	2,400
Increase in NBV	3,600
NBV of assets disposed of	500
	4,100
Depreciation charge for the year	1,000
Fixed asset additions	5,100

197 C

	£000
Change in working capital	
Decrease in stock	30
Increase in debtors	(10)
Decrease in creditors (30 + 20) – (35 + 5)	(10)
Net cash inflow	10

198 D

	£000
Profit for the year	18,750
Depreciation	1,250
Fixed asset purchases	(8,000)
Decrease in stocks	1,800
Increase in debtors	(1,000)
Increase in creditors	350
Net cash inflow	13,150

199 C

	£000
Profit for the year	63,400
Depreciation	2,700
Fixed asset purchases	(17,300)
Loss on disposal	3,000
Increase in stocks	(2,500)
Decrease in debtors	600
Increase in creditors	900
Net cash inflow	50,800

200 B

Discounts allowed are the balancing figure in the debtors account, after all the other figures have been entered in the account. Provisions for doubtful debts are credited to a separate provision account, not to the debtors account.

Debtors

	£		£
Balance b/d	800	Bank	6,730
Sales	6,800	Bad debts	40
		Discounts allowed	**280**
		Balance c/d	550
	7,600		7,600
Balance b/d	550		

201 B

Current assets	£	£
Employee loan, repayable in four months	12,000	
Unpaid accrued interest owed by employee (12,000 × 2%)	240	
		12,240
Prepayment of insurance (8 months Jan – Aug): 8/12 × £9,000		6,000
Debtor for rent, unpaid as at 31 December 20X2		4,000
Current assets		22,240

202 D

Creditors

	£		£
Bank	542,300	Balance b/d	142,600
Discounts received	13,200	Purchases (balance)	**578,200**
Purchase returns	27,500		
Balance c/d	137,800		
	720,800		720,800
		Balance b/d	137,800

203 B

	£
Opening stock	386,200
Purchases	989,000
	1,375,200
Closing stock	(422,700)
Cost of sales	952,500
Gross profit (× 40/(100 – 40))	635,000
Sales revenue	1,587,500

Alternatively, having calculated the cost of sales:

Sales revenue = £952,500 × 100/60 = £1,587,500

204 D

	£	£
Sales		612,000
Gross profit (25%)		153,000
Cost of sales		459,000
Opening stock	318,000	
Purchases	412,000	
	730,000	
less: Stock held	214,000	
Cost of sales and stock shortfall		516,000
Stock shortfall		57,000

205 C

Cost of goods sold = £5,000 (half of £10,000).

Profit mark-up = 120% = £6,000.

Sale price = £5,000 + £6,000 = £11,000.

Discounts allowed = 5% of £11,000 = £550.

	£
Gross profit	6,000
Discounts allowed	550
Net profit	5,450

206   A

The figure for sales can be calculated by setting up a workings account for debtors, and calculating credit sales as the balancing figure. Having calculated credit sales, total sales equals credit sales plus cash sales.

It is assumed here that refunds to credit customers are refunds for overpayments.

Debtors (Workings account)

	£		£
Balance b/d	29,100	Cash from debtors	381,600
Refunds to customers	2,100	Expenses paid with cash from debtors	6,800
Sales (credit sales)	**412,400**	Bad debts	7,200
		Discounts allowed	9,400
		Balance c/d	38,600
	443,600		443,600

Total sales = Credit sales + Cash sales = £412,400 + £112,900 = £525,300.

207   D

Gross profit = 40% of sales.

Cost of sales = 60% of sales.

	£
Opening stock	17,000
Purchases	91,000
	108,000
Closing stock	(24,000)
Cost of sales	84,000

Gross profit = 40% sales, so cost of sales = 60% of sales.

Sales = £84,000/0.60   £140,000

208   A

	D £000	E £000	F £000	Total £000
First half year				
Salaries		12.0	12.0	24
Share balance of profit (5: 3: 2)	108	64.8	43.2	216
				240
Second half year				
Salaries		18.0	12.0	30
Share balance of profit (3: 1: 1)	126	42.0	42.0	210
				240
Total share	234	136.8	109.2	480

209 £216,000

	X £000	Y £000	Z £000	Total £000
First half year				
Share of profit	100	100		200
Second half year				
Bad debt	(20)	(20)		(40)
Share of profit (40:40:20)	136	136	68	340
				300
	216	216	68	500

210 A

It is assumed that Q had no salary before 1 January 20X2.

	P £	Q £	R £	Total £
1 July – 31 Dec				
Share of profit (3:2)	144,000	96,000		240,000
1 Jan – 30 June				
Salaries		10,000	6,000	16,000
Share of remaining profit (50:25:25)	112,000	56,000	56,000	224,000
				240,000
	256,000	162,000	62,000	480,000

211 A

	S £000	T £000	U £000	Total £000
First half year				
Salary	15			15
Share balance of profit	96	64		160
				175
Second half year				
Salary	25			25
Share balance of profit	60	60	30	150
				175
	196	124	30	350

212 B

	£
Bad debts written off	18,000
Reduction in provision for doubtful debts	(17,000)
Net charge for bad and doubtful debts	1,000

A charge item is an expense, which is a debit balance item.

213 £32,640

Gross profit = 30% of sales.

Cost of sales = 70% of sales = 70% of £64,800 = £45,360.

	£	
Opening stock	28,400	
Purchases	49,600	
	78,000	
Cost of sales	45,360	
Closing stock	32,640	= stock destroyed by fire

214   A

	£000
Profit for the year	63,200
Depreciation	15,900
Profit on disposal of fixed asset	(7,000)
Fixed asset purchases	(18,000)
	54,100
Increase in stocks	(3,500)
Increase in debtors	(4,000)
Decrease in creditors	(1,600)
Net cash inflow	45,000

215   B

	£
Money banked	50,000
Money from sale of car	(5,000)
Money banked from sales	45,000
Wages paid in cash	12,000
Drawings in cash	2,000
Increase in cash in till in the month	100
Sales (all cash)	59,100

216   £18,950

	£
Sales	230,000
Money banked (160,000 + 50,000)	210,000
	20,000
Increase in debtors (3,000 – 2,000)	(1,000)
Increase in cash in till (100 – 50)	(50)
Money unaccounted for = stolen	18,950

217   B

	£000
Sales	148
Gross profit	40
Cost of sales	108
	£000
Opening stock	34
Purchases	100
	134
Cost of sales	108
Closing stock	26

218   C

	£
Purchases	20,000
Purchase returns	(4,000)
Change in stock	0
Cost of sales	16,000
	£
Sales	40,000
Sales returns	2,000
Net sales	38,000

Gross profit = £38,000 - £16,000 = £22,000.

219 A

This question calls for a good knowledge of the items in a cash flow statement, including the reconciliation of operating profit to net cash flow from operations. Here, you start with a cash flow figure and have to work back to calculate the operating profit. It is quite a complicated calculation, because you need to work out what to add and what to subtract.

	£000
Cash from share issue	1,000
Cash paid to redeem debenture	(750)
Cash paid to purchase fixed assets	(200)
Cash increase not attributable to profit	50
Actual cash increase	750
Cash increase attributable to profit	700
Increase in working capital	575
Depreciation	(100)
Profit for the year	1,175

220 B

	Share capital £	Share premium £
At start of year	50,000	180,000
Bonus issue (1 for 2)	25,000	(25,000)
	75,000	155,000
Shares issued for cash (premium 30p/share)	30,000	18,000
At end of year	105,000	173,000

221 D

	£
Ordinary dividend: (10 million ordinary shares × 5p)	500,000
Preference dividend: (8% × £500,000)	40,000
	540,000

222 B

The issue price is 80p (50p + 30p) for each share, so the cash raised from 1 million shares is £800,000. The receipt of cash is debited to the bank account. The credit entries are £500,000 in the share capital account (1 million × 50p) and £300,000 in the share premium account (1 million × 30p).

223 C

The addition to share premium with the rights issue is 200,000 shares at (£1.30 - £0.50) each, i.e. £160,000.

	Share capital £000	Share premium £000
At start of period	500	300
Rights issue	100	160
	600	460
Bonus issue	150	(150)
At end of period	750	310

224   D

The addition to share premium with the rights issue is 60,000 shares at (£1.20 - £0.25) each, i.e. £57,000.

	Share capital £000	Share premium £000
At start of period	75	200
Rights issue	15	57
	90	257
Bonus issue	30	(30)
At end of period	120	227

225

Share capital **£240,000**

Share premium **£522,000**.

The addition to share premium with the rights issue is 120,000 shares at (£1.10 - £0.25) each, i.e. £102,000.

	Share capital £000	Share premium £000
At start of period	150	480
Rights issue	30	102
	180	582
Bonus issue	60	(60)
At end of period	240	522

226   D

Recovered bad debts add to profit, so answer D is correct. The issue of shares (answer A) has no bearing on profit, and the revaluation of fixed assets is not recorded in the profit and loss account. The disposal of the fork-lift truck is at a loss, and so would reduce profit.

227   A

This is a difficult question, because you need to know the detail of section 130 of the Companies Act 1985. This states that the share premium account may be applied:

1   to pay up shares allotted as fully paid bonus shares

2   to write off the company's preliminary expenses

3   to write off the expenses of or discount allowed on the issue of any shares or debentures

4   to provide for the premium payable on the redemption of debentures.

Answer A is the required answer because it refers to the issue of partly-paid bonus shares.

228   B

	£
Ordinary dividend (4,000,000 shares × £0.02)	80,000
Preference dividend (6% × £250,000)	15,000
Total dividend	95,000

229   A

This is a straightforward definition of revenue reserves.

230   D

Purchased goodwill is the difference between the price paid for a business and the fair value of its separable identifiable assets at the time of the purchase. For example, if a business buys another business for £2 million, and the fair value of its separately identifiable assets is just £1.5 million, there is purchased goodwill of £0.5 million. Purchased goodwill is an intangible fixed asset.

231   C

	£
Ordinary dividend (1,000,000 shares × £0.05)	50,000
Preference dividend (5% × £50,000)	2,500
Total dividend	52,500

232   B

Issued share capital and reserves are credit balances in the nominal ledger accounts (since capital balances are credit balances). The money raised is 200,000 × £1.30 = £260,000, of which £200,000 is share capital (nominal value) and £60,000 is share premium.

233   B

The loan was included as a current liability, but should be treated as a long-term liability. Correcting the error will reduce total current liabilities, and this will increase net current assets (= current assets minus current liabilities).

234   A

FRS3 requires the separate disclosure of the aggregate profit or loss on discontinued operations, and also any extraordinary items. It also calls for disclosure of the costs of any fundamental reorganisation, profit or loss on sale of part of the business and profits or losses on fixed asset disposals. There is no specific mention of the loss from writing off a bad debt.

235   A

Extraordinary items are now very rare. FRS 3 requires separate disclosure in the profit and loss account of:

(1)   extraordinary income or charges

(2)   tax on this extraordinary profit or loss

236   B

Item 3: The gain on a revaluation of a fixed asset is taken straight to reserves (revaluation reserve) and is not taken through the P & L account.

237   B

Salaries of company directors, loan interest and donations to charities are all expenses for a limited company, and come out of profit before taxation. Dividends, in contrast, are an appropriation of after-tax profit.

238   £85,000

	£
Ordinary dividend:	
Interim: 400,000 shares × £0.05	20,000
Final: 400,000 shares × £0.15	60,000
Preference dividend (5% × £100,000)	5,000
Total dividend	85,000

239 C

Giving customers more time to pay will result in an increase in debtors. An increase in debtors has a negative effect on cash flow, because it takes longer for the money to come in. A business can therefore make a profit but still suffer a fall in its bank balance due to an increase in debtors.

240 A

Preference shares are not regarded as equity capital (except perhaps that preference shares might be treated as equity for the purpose of some loan or bond documentation). Equity capital is therefore ordinary share capital plus reserves.

241 £43,080

	Change in assets	Change in liabilities	Change in capital	Change in working capital
	£	£	£	£
Pay creditors	(3,000)	(3,000)		0
Write off bad debt	(250)		(250)	(250)
Sell stock at a profit	(100)			
	230		130	130
				(120)
Opening working capital				43,200
Closing working capital				43,080

242 C

Ordinary share capital = 800,000 shares of £1.

Dividend = £120,000 = (£120,000/800,000) £0.15 per share.

243 B

The accruals concept applies to dividends as well as to income and expenses. The P & L account shows the dividends payable out of profits of the current year, regardless of whether or not the dividend has been paid yet. Typically, the dividends in the profit and loss account consist of an interim dividend already paid and a final dividend that has not yet been paid. This final dividend is shown in the balance sheet as a current liability.

244 D

	£
Dividends paid (cash)	27,000
Dividends payable from previous year	(25,000)
	2,000
Dividends payable at end of year	30,000
Dividends in profit and loss account	32,000

245 C

	£
Net assets acquired, 1 January 20X0: 80% of (100,000 + 90,000)	152,000
Cost of investment	180,000
Cost of goodwill	28,000
Annual amortisation (£28,000/4 years)	£7,000

	£
Goodwill at cost	28,000
Accumulated amortisation (3 years × £7,000)	21,000
Value of goodwill at 31 December 20X2	7,000

246 A

$20\% \times £260,000 = £52,000$.

247 D

Post acquisition retained profits of Beta = £160,000 – 90,000) = £70,000.

	£
Profit and loss account of Alpha	210,000
Group share of retained post-acquisition profits of Beta (80% of £70,000)	56,000
Amortisation of goodwill	(21,000)
Consolidated profit and loss account balance	245,000

248 B

The share capital and reserves (net assets) of S at the date of acquisition were £100,000 + £40,000 = £140,000.

	£
Net assets acquired (80% of £140,000)	112,000
Purchase cost	160,000
Purchased goodwill	48,000
Amortisation each year (over 5 years)	9,600

	£
Purchased goodwill	48,000
Accumulated amortisation over three years to 31 December 20X7	28,800
Amount for goodwill in group balance sheet	19,200

249 D

	£
S share capital	100,000
S reserves	200,000
Total share capital and reserves	300,000
Minority interest (25%)	75,000

250 C

	£
S share capital	100,000
S reserves	180,000
Total share capital and reserves	280,000
Minority interest (40%)	152,000

251 C

The share capital and reserves (net assets) of S at the date of acquisition were £(200,000 + 120,000) £320,000.

The post-acquisition reserves of S are £(180,000 – 120,000) £60,000. The group's share is 75% of £60,000 = £45,000.

	£
Net assets of S acquired by H (75% of £320,000)	240,000
Purchase price of shares in S	280,000
Purchased goodwill	40,000

	£
Consolidated reserves	
Reserves of H Limited	480,000
Group share of post-acquisition reserves of S	45,000
Purchased goodwill amortised	(40,000)
Consolidated profit and loss account reserve	485,000

252 D

Minority interests are shown separately in the consolidated balance sheet, not as a current liability.

INTERPRETATION

253 D

Stock turnover is the number of times stock is used up in the year. It is measured as the cost of stock consumed in the year (cost of goods sold) divided by the average stock level in the year, valued at cost.

254 A

Accepted 'norms' are 2.0 for the 'ideal' current ratio and 1.0 for the 'ideal' acid test ratio or quick ratio. However, these 'ideal' ratios are only a rough guide, since 'norms' vary greatly between companies in different industries. In this question, the current ratio is (1,390/420) 3.3 times and the acid test ratio is [(380 + 40)/420] 1.0 times. The current ratio is therefore high and the acid test ratio is 'ideal'.

255 A

Gearing is usually measured as the ratio of long-term debt to equity.

At 31.10.X8, gearing was 20/(15 + 3 + 22) × 100% = 50%.

At 31.10.X9, gearing was 40/(30 + 18 + 12) × 100% = 66.7%.

Gearing has therefore risen. Higher gearing increases the financial risk for ordinary shareholders.

256 D

The average debt collection period, measured as (debtors/sales) × 365 days, will increase when debtors rise but annual sales remain the same (or when debtors remain the same but annual sales fall). An increase in debtors without any increase in sales can happen as a result of poor credit control and debt collection procedures, or when debtors are abnormally high, perhaps due to a large credit sale or to seasonal sales being high.

A downturn in trade should result in a fall in both total debtors and annual sales, and there is no reason why the debtor collection period should change.

257 D

The ratio of stock to annual sales will increase when stock levels rise but there is no increase in annual sales. This could happen when stock control is poor and stocks are allowed to increase, or when there has just been a large purchase (temporarily increasing the stock level) or when stock levels are high due to high seasonal sales.

An increase in sales should result in some increase in stock levels, and there is no reason why the rate of stock turnover should change.

258 B

The answer calls for a simple definition of working capital.

259 C

Shareholders' return is usually measured as profit after tax, but in this question the figure for profit before tax must be used, since the profit after tax is not given.

Profit before tax = £200,000

Shareholders' equity = (in £000) 500 + 200 + 800 = £1,500,000.

Return on shareholders' equity = (200/1,500) × 100% = 13.3%.

260 A

To compare like with like, we must measure ROCE as the profit before interest and taxation as a percentage of total share capital and long-term debt.

Return = £300,000.

Capital employed = £2,500,000.

Return on capital employed = (300/2,500) × 100% = 12%.

261 D

Stock turnover should normally be measured by comparing the cost of average stock with the annual cost of sales. However, in this question you are asked how many days of stock are in hand at the end of the year, so you should use the figure for closing stock.

	£
Opening stock	1,750
Purchases	10,200
	11,950
less: Closing stock	1,950
Cost of sales	10,000

Days of sales in stock at the year-end =
(1,950/10,000) × 365 = 71 days.

262 A

The current ratio is the ratio of current assets to current liabilities. When a business has net current liabilities, the current ratio is less than 1.0.

A short-term loan will add to both current liabilities and to current assets (cash) by the same amount. When the current ratio is less than 1.0, an equal increase in current assets and current liabilities will alter the current ratio so that it is closer to 1.0 (although still less than 1.0). In other words, the current ratio will increase. Since the 'ideal' current ratio is 2.0, such an increase would improve the ratio.

263 B

An increase in debtors (answer C) and prepayments (answer D) would result in a reduction in cash flow, not an increase. Drawings also reduce cash flow (answer A).

The sale of fixed assets, either at a loss or a profit, will bring cash into the business, and could explain an increase in cash despite making a loss.

264 C

Stock turnover is the number of times that stock is used up during a year, and is measured as the ratio of the cost of sales to average stock (at cost) during the year. The turnover ratio is 6 times when the cost of goods sold is £180,000 and average stock is £30,000.

265 D

The normal formula to calculate stock turnover is the total cost of sales in a year divided by average stock (at cost) during the year.

266 D

$12\% \times 2 = 24\%$

$$\text{ROCE} = \frac{\text{Profit before interest and tax}}{\text{Sales}} \times \frac{\text{Sales}}{\text{Capital employed}}$$

267 C

$$\text{ROCE} = \frac{\text{Profit before interest and tax}}{\text{Sales}} \times \frac{\text{Sales}}{\text{Capital employed}}$$

268 A

Return on capital employed (ROCE) compares the profit before interest and tax with the total long-term capital of the company, both share capital (and reserves) and long-term debt. This contrasts with return on shareholder capital (ROSC), which compares profit after interest (and usually after tax as well) with share capital and reserves.

269 C

This is possibly a confusing question, because debtor days can be calculated in different ways. Strictly, debtor days should be calculated as (debtors including VAT/credit sales including VAT) × 365. This would give (23,500/50% of 235,000) × 365 = 73 days.

In practice, debtor days might be calculated as (debtors including VAT/total sales including VAT) × 365. This is because information is not always available about the division of total sales between cash sales and credit sales. In this question, debtor days would then be (23,500/235,000) × 365 = 37 days.

Even more often in practice, it is usual to measure debtor days approximately as (total debtors including VAT/total sales excluding VAT) × 365 days. This measurement is often used by stock market analysts, who can extract these figures easily from the published financial statements of a company. In this question, the debtor days would then be (23,500/200,000) × 365 days = 43 days.

This means that answers A, B and C could all be correct. However, given the information in the question, you are probably expected to compare like with like, i.e. debtors including VAT should be compared with credit sales including VAT.

270   C

When you are asked to calculate a gearing ratio, you ought to be given information about the basis on which the ratio is calculated, because there are different ways of measuring gearing. In particular, gearing might be measured as the percentage ratio of long-term debt to total shareholders' capital and reserves. Alternatively, gearing could be measured as the percentage ratio of (long-term debt plus some short term loans) to shareholders' capital and reserves.

In this question, the problem is deciding what to do about the overdraft of £50,000, which the company has apparently had for the second half of the year.

1   If gearing is measured as long term debt to share capital and reserves, the ratio would be (75/500) × 100% = 15%. This is not an option in the question.

2   If gearing is measured as (long term debt plus overdraft) to share capital and reserves, the ratio would be (125/500) × 100% = 25%. This is not an option in the question.

3   It might be assumed that since the overdraft has only been in place for one half of the year, just one half of it (£25,000) should be included in debt, together with the long-term debt of £75,000. This would give a gearing percentage of (100/500) × 100%. = 20%. This is an option in the question.

Although it is possibly not the best way of measuring gearing, it is the most plausible of the four available answers.

271   A

	£
Increase in stock	250
Decrease in bank balance	(400)
Increase in creditors	(1,200)
Change in working capital	(1,350)

272   C

When fixed assets are purchased on credit, creditors (= current liabilities) increase without any increase in current assets. Working capital is therefore reduced, in this case by £500.

When goods costing £3,000 are sold for £3,500, there is an increase in current assets and so an increase in working capital. (Stocks are reduced by £3,000 but debtors or cash increase by £3,500, and there is a profit of £500.) The sale of a fixed asset at a loss increases working capital, because cash is received from the sale and there is no other change in current assets or current liabilities.

273   D

This is another question that could be confusing because there are different ways of calculating the creditors' payment period. You should try to compare like with like in this type of question. Here, since creditors arise from purchases on credit, we should try to compare average creditors with purchases during the year. (A figure for purchases should be used rather than the figure for cost of sales.)

	£
Cost of sales	32,500
Add: Closing stock	3,800
	36,300
Less: Opening stock	(6,000)
Purchases	30,300

Creditors' payment period = (£4,750/£30,300) × 365 = 57 days.

274 A

Gross profit = £60,000.

Mark-up = 50%.

Cost of sales = (£60,000/0.50) = £120,000.

Average stock = £(12,000 + 18,000)/2 = £15,000.

Stock turnover = £120,000/£15,000 = 8 times.

275 B

Gross profit margin = £800 = 33.33% of sales.

Sales = £800/0.3333 = £2,400.

Net profit = gross profit – expenses = £800 - £680 = £120.

Net profit percentage = net profit/sales = (£120/£2,400) × 100% = 0.05 or 5%.

276 D

Event A is unlikely to be the cause. There is no necessary reason why an increase in sales volume will result in a higher gross profit margin percentage, i.e. there is no reason why the sales prices should go up or unit cost of sales come down.

Event B is also unlikely to be the cause. The cost of sales is opening stock + purchases – closing stock. The effect of the mistake in B is to reduce opening stock but increase purchases by the same amount, so that there is no effect on cost of sales or gross profit.

Cost of sales will be affected, however, if opening stock is understated or closing stock is overstated. Stock at 31 December 20X1 is the opening stock for 20X2, so gross profit could have been increased if this stock had been *understated* in value, so answer D is correct.

277 A

Profit after tax = £22 million

Equity shareholders' funds = £500 million

Return on equity shareholders' capital employed = 22/500 = 0.044 or 4.4%.

278 A

Average stock = £(4,000 + 6,000)/2 = £5,000.

Stock turnover = Cost of sales/average stock = £24,500/£5,000 = 4.9 times.

279 D

A payment of dividends reduces equity (shareholders' funds) without affecting the amount of long-term loans. Gearing will therefore rise.

Answers A and B are not correct. A decrease in long-term loans and a decrease in shareholders' funds will affect the gearing ratio. However, whether the gearing ratio rises or falls will depend on both the size of the decreases and on the level of gearing before the reductions occur.

280 A

Working capital is increased because by issuing shares for cash, current assets increase (cash) but current liabilities are unaffected. Gearing is reduced because equity (ordinary share capital plus reserves) is increased. The value of the share premium account will increase, since the new shares will be issued at a price above their nominal value. The value of investments will be unaffected.

281 A

A rights issue adds to share capital and reserves without affecting debt capital. The gearing ratio will therefore fall.

Item B would increase gearing by adding to debt capital. Item D would add to gearing by reducing share capital and reserves. Item C would not affect gearing at all, because total share capital plus reserves would remain the same.

282 C

Gross profit is profit before deducting selling and distribution costs. Reducing the value of closing stock to less than cost will increase the cost of sales and so reduce the gross profit percentage. Changes in stock levels should not affect gross profit. Lower sales volume will reduce total gross profit, but it need not reduce the gross profit percentage.

283 C

This is another difficult question to answer, because all the possible answers seem sensible. Liquidity ratios can vary enormously between well-managed companies, particularly companies in different industries.

Many businesses operate efficiently with a bank overdraft. Similarly many businesses operate without difficulty with an acid test ratio of less than one. (Supermarkets, for example, have high stock levels but even higher amounts of creditors, and they operate comfortably with an acid test ratio well below 1.0.)

The correct answer, however, is C. The current ratio of the company is (2,900:1,100) 2.6 times, which is much higher than the industry norm of 1.8 times. This suggests that stock levels or debtor levels are unusually high for the industry, or creditor levels are unusually low. This is a possible sign of poor control over working capital, operating cash flows and liquidity.

284 C

You should calculate the gross profit mark-up for each answer until you get to one with a mark-up of 40%.

Answer C. Mark-up = £100,800 - £72,000 = £28,800.

Mark-up percentage = (£28,800/£72,000) × 100% = 40%.

285 B

Accepted 'norms' are 2.0 for the 'ideal' current ratio and 1.0 for the 'ideal' acid test ratio or quick ratio. Remember that these 'ideal' ratios are only a rough guide, since 'norms' vary greatly between companies in different industries. In this question, the current ratio is (2,698/1,349) 2.0 times and the acid test ratio is [(863 + 95)/1,349) 0.7 times. The current ratio is therefore 'ideal' and the acid test ratio is on the low side of ideal.

286 C

Capital employed at the start of the year (in £000) = 11,200

Capital employed at the end of the year (in £000) = 11,200 + retained profit 600 = 11,800.

Average capital employed (in £000) = (11,200 + 11,800)/2 = 11,500.

Return = profit before interest and taxation = (in £000) 1,200.

Return on average capital employed = (1,200/11,500) × 100% = 10.43%

287   C

Longer payment periods for debtors will increase total debtors (current assets) and longer payment periods from suppliers will increase total creditors (current liabilities). Although changes in total debtors and total liabilities will also have an effect on cash, it would appear that answer C is the correct answer here.

The change in working capital will depend on the extent of the change in the debtors' payment period and creditors' payment period, which means that neither answer A nor answer B is necessarily correct.

288   A

There are different ways of measuring gearing. In particular, gearing might be measured as the percentage ratio of long-term debt to total shareholders' capital and reserves (including preference share capital). Alternatively, gearing could be measured as the percentage ratio of (long-term debt plus preference share capital) to ordinary share capital and reserves.

Answer A is a correct definition. Answer C is incorrect, because preference share capital cannot be included both above the line with long-term debt and below the line as part of shareholders' capital.

289   C

If the cost per unit goes down, but the sales price and sales quantity remain the same, the gross profit margin must go up.

The gross profit margin might go up if both cost per unit and sales price go up, but it might also fall, depending on the size of the rise in each. (Answer A is therefore incorrect.) When sales volume goes up, there need not be any change in the gross profit margin as a percentage, so answer B is inappropriate.

290   A

Gearing at 31.10.X3 = $[15/(20 + 10 + 43)] \times 100\% = 21\%$.

Gearing at 31.10.X4 = $[50/(30 + 20 + 36)] \times 100\% = 58\%$.

There has been an increase in gearing and as a result the financial risk for shareholders is higher.

291   B

20X8

> Average stock = $(75 + 85)/2 = 80$.
>
> Cost of sales = 1,250
>
> Stock turnover = $1,250/80 = 15.6$ times.

20X9

> Average stock = $(85 + 115)/2 = 100$.
>
> Cost of sales = 1,300
>
> Stock turnover = $1,300/100 = 13$ times.

Stock turnover has fallen. A reduction in the rate of stock turnover results in an increase in stock levels (unless there is also a fall in the cost of sales). This has a negative effect on cash flow and so has a possible detrimental effect on liquidity.

292 C

Sales next period = £130,000 × 1.40 = £182,000.

Stock turnover this year = £60,000/£7,500 = 8 times.

Stock turnover in the next period (8 × 2) 16 times.

Average stock in the next period (given) £7,500.

Cost of sales in the next period = £7,500 × 16 = £120,000.

Gross profit next period = £182,000 - £120,000 = £62,000.

Gross profit mark-up = £62,000/£120,000 = 0.517 or 51.7%.

293 C

In 20X4 the company had a higher current ratio than in 20X3 but a lower acid test ratio. The current ratio is the ratio of current assets to current liabilities. The acid test ratio is the ratio of current assets excluding stocks to current liabilities.

If the current ratio has increased but the acid test ratio has fallen, the change is most likely to be due to an increase in stocks. An increase in stocks will increase the current ratio but not the acid test ratio. If the increase in stocks ties up some cash and so reduces the bank balance, the acid test ratio could fall.

Section 4

ANSWERS TO PRACTICE QUESTIONS

GENERAL FRAMEWORK; ACCOUNTING CONCEPTS AND PRINCIPLES

1   STANDARD-SETTING PROCEDURE

Key answer tips

A good answer to this question relies upon knowledge of the basics of the regulatory structures in the UK.

(a)   (i)   **Financial Reporting Council (FRC)**

The FRC is a body with responsibilities for financial reporting in the UK. It is responsible for ensuring that the arrangements of its 'subsidiary' operating bodies, the ASB and the FRRP, are economical, efficient and effective, and for the proper funding of these bodies. It is financed in roughly equal proportions by the accountancy profession, City Institutions and the Government. Although the FRC is the parent organisation of the ASB and the FRRP, these two operational bodies operate independently of the FRC and of each other. The FRC provides general policy guidance to the ASB. It also publishes an annual report on the state of financial reporting.

(ii)   **Accounting Standards Board (ASB)**

The aims of the ASB are to establish and improve standards of financial accounting and reporting for the benefit of users, preparers and auditors of financial information. The main role of the ASB is to issue accounting standards (Financial Reporting Standards). Another objective of the ASB is to principles that will be applied in setting accounting rules in standards. These are contained in the ASB's Statement of Principles for Financial Reporting. The ASB can issue new accounting standards without the need for approval from any other body. However, it discusses widely when it is developing new standards, and issues at least two consultation documents, a Discussion Paper and an exposure draft.

(iii)   **Financial Reporting Review Panel (FRRP)**

Like the ASB, the FRRP is an operational body. The FRRP's main task is to look into companies whose financial statements show material departures from accounting standards or the provisions of the Companies Act 1985. The FRRP deals with public companies and large private companies. The Department of Trade and Industry deals with other cases. If the FRRP considers that any departures are not justified in the cause of providing a true and fair view, it will seek to persuade the company to take corrective action. Failing that it will seek remedy through the courts.

    (iv)   **Urgent Issues Task Force (UITF)**

          The UITF is a committee of the ASB. Its main role is to deal with problems arising with existing accounting standards. It does not develop new material but issues a consensus statement to resolve unsatisfactory or conflicting interpretations of accounting standards. These consensus statements are issued in the form of UITF Abstracts. Companies are required to comply with relevant UITF Abstracts if their accounts are to give a 'true and fair view'.

(b)   The stages that the ASB goes through in the development of an FRS are as follows.

    (i)   There is a debate of the issue by the Board.

    (ii)   The Board prepares and publishes a Discussion Paper to stimulate debate and the submission of comments to the ASB. At this stage the ASB might not have reached any firm decisions, and the discussion Paper might therefore include a list of questions, for which the Board invites opinions and responses.

    (iv)   Having studied the responses to the discussion Paper, the Board reaches a view, and develops and publishes a Financial Reporting Exposure Draft (FRED), which sets out the proposed standard. A further opportunity is given for comment, in response to the FRED. The strength and nature of the responses enable the ASB to gauge the level of acceptance of its proposals.

    (v)   Sometimes an amended FRED is issued when substantial revisions to the original one prove necessary.

    (vi)   The ASB does not just wait to receive comments. It also discusses proposals for a new standard with a wide variety of interested parties.

    (vii) The FRS is then issued in its final form, with a date specified for implementation.

(c)   In general, the requirements of statute take precedence over accounting standards. However, the Companies Act 1985 allows a departure from any of the requirements of the Act relating to the form and content of the financial statements if there are special circumstances, such that compliance with the Act is inconsistent with the requirement to show a true and fair view. This is known as the 'true and fair override'. It could be used by the ASB to publish an FRS requiring or allowance non-compliance with an aspect of the Companies Act, on the grounds that it is necessary to show a true and fair view.

2   SOLE TRADER V LIMITED LIABILITY COMPANY

Key answer tips

This question asks for eight differences between operating as a sole trader and operating as a company. Marks would be awarded for any valid points, not just for those in the answer below.

	Sole trader	*Limited company*
Legal background	There is comparatively little statutory control over a sole trader's business. There is no legal requirement for the public disclosure of accounting information.	Companies are governed by the Companies Acts. The CA1985 requires disclosure of accounting information and details of directors and shareholders. This must be filed with the Registrar of Companies.

Legal status	The business is not a separate legal entity from the proprietor as an individual. All the assets and rights belonging to the business and all the liabilities of the business are those of the proprietor personally.	A company constitutes a separate legal entity from its owners, the shareholders. A company can own assets, owe money, enter contracts, and sue or be sued in a court of law as a legal person, separate from its owners.
Owner's liability	The proprietor has unlimited personal liability to the creditors of the business, to the full extent of his or her private as well as business assets. If the business owes money that it cannot pay, the proprietor is liable for the debt and must pay if necessary out of his private assets.	The liability of the owners (the shareholders) is limited to the company's own assets plus any uncalled share capital. If the shares are fully paid and the company becomes insolvent, the shareholders have no further liability for the unpaid debts of the company.
Constitution	No formal constitution is required for the business of a sole trader. The owner is not bound by any rules of conduct.	A company must have a written constitution, set out in its memorandum and articles of association. The memorandum includes matters such as the objects of the company and its authorised share capital. The articles set out various rights, duties and procedural requirements, for example relating to shareholders' rights, directors' powers and company general meetings.
Audit	No annual audit is required.	An annual audit is required unless the company is exempt as a 'small company'.
Capital structure	The owner's capital is contributed by just one person	With the exception of very small private companies, capital is contributed by several persons who own shares in the capital (shareholders).
Management	The owner normally manages the business, although this is not always the case.	Often, shareholders do not run the company themselves but appoint directors to do so. (Shareholders may, of course, also be directors, and many smaller companies are run by shareholder-directors).
Share in profit	The sole proprietor is entitled to the whole of the profit, and decides how much of the profits to draw for personal benefit.	The shareholders may receive dividends out of their share of the profits. however, dividend decisions are made by the directors. The shareholders can vote to approve a dividend recommended by the directors (or even reduce it) but cannot vote to increase it.

Other points would be considered on their merits.

3   DEFINITIONS

(a)   Accruals

The accruals concept is that revenue and expenses are recognised in the profit and loss account as they are earned or incurred, not as the money from the revenue income is received or as the payments for the expenses are paid. It also includes the matching concept that accrued costs should be set against related accrued revenues in arriving at the profit or loss for a period.

Example: Rent due but not yet paid is recognised as an expense of the period to which it relates and is therefore set against revenue for the same period, as an accrued expense. Similarly, rent paid in advance for a period falling in a future accounting period is treated as a prepayment (a short-term asset in the balance sheet) and will not be set as an expense against profit until the future period to which the expense relates.

(b)   Money measurement

The money measurement concept is that financial accounts can only recognise items that are capable of being expressed in monetary terms.

Example: Financial accounting can recognise a piece of plant or equipment, because its value can be recognised in money terms, based on its original purchase cost, or conceivably its replacement cost. In contrast, the expertise of the workforce of a business, which could be a hugely valuable asset for a business, cannot be properly measured in money terms, and so is excluded from financial statements.

(c)   Substance over form

When there is a difference between the real effect of a transaction (substance) and its legal form (form), the concept of substance over form is that the real effect should be recognised in the financial statements rather than the legal form, provided this is legally permissible.

Example: When an asset is acquired by a business on hire purchase terms over a number of years, it will be recognised as a fixed asset in the balance sheet, with an associated liability to a hire purchase creditor. This is because in substance, the business has become the long-term owner of the asset, despite the fact that the legal ownership of the asset does not pass to the business until the last instalment due under the agreement has been paid.

(d)   Consistency

Accounting treatment of like items within each accounting period and from one period to the next should be the same, unless either a change is required by legislation or a new accounting standard, or unless circumstances change.

Example: Depreciation rates should remain the same from period to period unless there is clear evidence that changed circumstances require them to change.

(e)   Duality

The recording of every transaction must reflect the fact that two accounts are affected by that transaction. This is represented to some extent by the concept of the accounting equation, that total assets must always equal the sum of total liabilities plus total capital. An transaction affecting the value of an asset must be offset by a matching transaction such that the accounting equation still holds true.

Example: The receipt of cash from a credit customer requires the recording of an increase in cash and an equal decrease in the customer's sales ledger balance. In other words, the increase in the cash balance is offset by a matching decrease in the debtors balance (leaving the total value of assets unchanged in this particular example).

(f) **Prudence**

In preparing financial statements, prudence requires that provision should be made for all known liabilities, including those based on estimates because exact information is not available. Prudence also requires that revenue and profits should not be included in the profit and loss account until their realisation is reasonably certain.

Example: A provision for doubtful debts should be created out of profits whenever the realisation of all trade debts in full is uncertain, and any increase is this provision will be set against profits of the current period in which the increase is made. The effect of applying the prudence concept is to recognise losses in the financial statements now, even though it has not yet happened and might never happen.

4   ASB STATEMENT OF PRINCIPLES

Key answer tips

In a question split, like this one, into several parts, it is very important to attempt ALL parts. Also, allow the full measure of time to written questions, rather than over-running on computational questions and leaving yourself insufficient time to earn enough marks from what you are able to write in a rush.

(a)   An item of information is material to the financial statements if its misstatement or omission might reasonably be expected to influence the economic decisions of users of those financial statements, including their assessments of management's stewardship. Material items should therefore be included in the financial statements. In contrast, immaterial items need not be included and should be excluded if the effect of their inclusion is to reduce the understandability of the statements.

Factors enabling materiality to be judged include:

(i)   The size of the item;

(ii)   The nature of the item.

(b)   Information is relevant if it has the ability to influence the economic decisions of users and is provided in time to influence those decisions. Information is relevant if it has either predictive value or confirmatory value. Information has predictive value if it helps users to evaluate past, present or future events, as a means of predicting the future. Information has confirmatory value if it helps users to confirm or correct their past evaluations. Maximising the relevance of information involves maximising predictive plus confirmatory value.

(c)   Information is reliable if it provides a faithful representation, is neutral, is complete (within the bounds of materiality) and is free from material error, and if prudence has been applied to exercising judgement and making estimates.

(i)   Neutrality means that the information is financial statements should be free from deliberate or systematic bias. Financial information is not neutral if it is selected or presented in such a way as to influence decisions or judgements, or to achieve a predetermined result.

Prudence means that a degree of caution is needed in judgements when making estimates about uncertain items, so that gains are not over-stated and liabilities and losses are not under-stated.

(ii)   The potential conflict between the two is that whereas neutrality requires freedom from bias, the exercise of prudence is a potentially biased concept since an exercise of judgement is required. In resolving the conflict, a balance should be found that neither overstates nor understates assets, gains, liabilities and losses.

(d) Three safeguards to ensure that a company's financial statements are free from material error are as follows.

    (i) The fact that they have been audited by an independent professional, who give an opinion that the financial statements give a true and fair view.

    (ii) The existence of sound internal controls within the company, to prevent errors and or detect errors that occur.

    (iii) The existence of an internal audit function within the company, to provide checks on the efficiency and effectiveness of the internal controls system.

5 ACCOUNTING CONCEPTS

(a) **Going concern**

The going concern assumption means that financial statements are prepared on the basis that the business will continue for the foreseeable future.

The application of the concept is relevant to many items in the financial statements.

    (i) Stock is valued on the basis that it will be disposed of in sales in the normal course of business rather than in a forced bulk sale.

    (ii) Fixed assets are valued at cost less depreciation rather than their immediate sale value.

    (iii) Long-term liabilities are distinguished from current liabilities in assessing a company's liquidity position.

(b) **Accruals**

The accruals concept is that income and expenses are recognised in the period to which they relate and not in the period in which they are paid.

The relevance of the concept is that profit or loss figures would be meaningless if the inclusion of items of income or expense depended on whether they had been received or paid.

(c) **Substance over form**

Substance over form means that if the real nature and effect of a transaction differ from its legal form, the real nature and effect should be recognised instead of the legal form, unless legislation prohibits this.

The relevance of the concept is that its application improves the usefulness of the financial statements by preventing certain creative accounting practices.

(d) **Historical cost**

The historical cost convention is that assets are recorded at their initial cost and are not subsequently revalued upwards, and liabilities valued at the amount initially received in exchange for the obligation.

The relevance of the convention is that figures remain objectively based on verifiable figures, but in times of high inflation historical cost can become a dubious convention to follow.

6   CHARACTERISTICS AND CONCEPTS

Key answer tips

The answer to the first part of this question is largely taken from the ASB's Statement of Principles for Financial Reporting. Answers in your own words should contain the essential points indicated in the suggested answer here.

(a)   **Comparability** is defined in the ASB's Statement of Principles as follows: 'Users must be able to compare the financial statements of an enterprise over time to identify trends in its financial position and performance. Users must also be able to compare the financial statements of different enterprises to evaluate their relative financial position, performance and financial adaptability. Hence the measurement and display of the financial effect of like transactions and other events must be carried out in a consistent way throughout an enterprise and over time for that enterprise and in a consistent way for different enterprises.'

Example: if certain types of tools purchased are treated as fixed assets in one period, similar tools purchased in subsequent periods should also be treated as fixed assets.

(b)   **Objectivity** is often referred to as comprising verifiability or faithful representation and neutrality. Financial statements must represent faithfully the effect of transactions and other events it either purports to represent or could reasonably be expected to represent and where possible be based on verifiable evidence. According to the ASB SOP, financial statements are not neutral if by the selection or presentation of information they influence the making of a decision or judgement in order to achieve a predetermined result or outcome.

Example: internally generated goodwill should not be included in the balance sheet as a fixed asset because its value cannot be determined objectively.

(c)   The **consistency** concept requires that the financial effect of like transactions and other events should be given similar treatment within a single set of accounts and from one period to the next.

Consistency of treatment improves the comparability of information in financial statements.

Example: The accounting policy that a business uses for fixed asset depreciation should be consistent, such that the depreciation method selected for each class of fixed assets should be applied consistently from period to the next.

7   HISTORICAL COST ACCOUNTING

Key answer tips

Note that the four points are made in respect of each part of the answer – exactly as required by the question.

(a)   **Limitations of historical cost accounting**

(i)   Profit on a sale is taken as the difference between the proceeds of sale and the historical cost of the item sold. This ignores the fact that if prices have risen due to inflation during the time the goods were held it will cost more to replace them. The result is that profit is overstated during a time of rising prices, and if the business just breaks even in profit terms, or if its owners take out all the reported profit, the physical capital of the business will be eroded.

(ii) If the depreciation charge in the profit and loss account is based on the historical cost of the fixed assets, and the current value of the fixed asset is higher due to inflation than its historical cost, the charge understates the true value of the benefit enjoyed from the use of the assets. Once again, historical cost profit tends to be overstated.

(iii) The balance sheet does not show the value of the business. In times of inflation, valuing fixed assets at their historical cost minus accumulated depreciation is likely to lead to a serious understatement of their actual value.

(iv) Users of financial statements often assess the performance of a business by means of ratio analysis. A widely-used performance ratio is return on capital employed. In a period of inflation, the ROCE of a business can be very misleading, since for reasons already explained, profit tends to be overstated while capital employed (which depends on asset values) is understated. Return on capital employed using financial statements based on the historical cost convention is therefore reported at a much higher level than the real situation would justify.

(b) **Reasons for continuing with historical cost accounting**

(i) It is a simple accounting convention and cheap to operate. Alternative methods of accounting tend to be complicated and expensive, especially for smaller businesses, and there is no general agreement on an acceptable alternative.

(ii) In practice, fixed asset revaluation is permitted or encouraged, so that many businesses (companies in particular) do not apply the historical cost convention in this respect to all its fixed assets. As a result, much of the adverse effect of HCA on fixed asset values and depreciation charges is avoided.

(iii) The profit concept of historical cost accounting is well understood and expert users of financial statements are able to make allowances for its limitations. Alternatives to HCA such as current cost accounting or current purchasing power accounting involve some quite complex concepts of profit, capital maintenance and asset valuation.

(iv) Compared with other methods which rely more on valuation, figures in historical cost accounts are objective and verifiable, because they are tied to an actual transaction (the original purchase cost of an asset for example) and not dependent upon a subsequent subjective valuation.

8   EXPLAIN

(a) (i) **Materiality**

Information is material to the financial statements if its misstatement or omission might reasonably be expected to influence the economic decisions of users of those statements.

Example: The amount of stock write-down through obsolescence will only be disclosed in financial statements if material.

(ii) **Prudence**

Prudence in accounting means that a degree of caution is necessary when making estimates that are required under conditions of uncertainty, so that gains or assets are not overstated and losses or liabilities are not understated.

Example: In deciding whether to make a provision for a doubtful debt, a provision should be made whenever there is doubt as to the eventual receipt of the cash.

(b) **Comparability is promoted by two main means:**

(i) The requirement to treat similar items in the same way within each accounting period and from one period to the next, subject to the need to change treatments if, for example, a new accounting standard requires a change. There is also a requirement, when there is a change, to disclose full details of its effect.

(ii) The requirement to disclose accounting policies and changes in them. This makes comparisons with other entities easier.

ACCA marking scheme			
			Marks
(a)	(i)	Explanation	2
		Example	1
	(ii)	Explanation	2
		Example	1
(b)		Consistency of treatment of items	2
		Disclosure of policies	2
Total			10

DOUBLE-ENTRY BOOKKEEPING AND ACCOUNTING SYSTEMS

9 SUSPENSE ACCOUNT

Key answer tips

Suspense accounts can be confusing. It might help to assume that the suspense account is part of the double entry system, because you can then think about the double entry in the accounts that is needed to make the correction. Here, some of the errors seem to have occurred in writing up the trial balance manually, but you can ignore this.

Suspense account			
	£		£
Discounts received		Trial balance – difference	14,000
(7,000 × 2)	14,000	Discounts allowed	
Current account of senior		(3,000 × 2)	6,000
partner's wife	9,600	Creditors control account	
		(237,386 – 233,786)	3,600
	23,600		23,600

Notes

(1) The discount received of £7,000 should be credited to the discount received account (a form of income, like sales), but has been debited instead. To make the correction, to get from debit £7,000 to credit £7,000, we must add £14,000 to the credit side. The correction is therefore: Credit discount received £14,000, and debit the suspense account £14,000. A similar adjustment, but on the other side, needs to be made for the error with the discount allowed.

(2) The creditors control account balance (a credit balance) is overstated by £3,600. This is corrected by reducing it. The double entry required is: Debit Creditors control account £3,600, credit Suspense account £3,600.

(3) The omission from the sales day book means that the transaction does not appear in the accounts at all, and is missing from both the sales account balance and the debtors control account balance. It therefore has no effect on the difference between the total debits and credits in the trial balance.

(4) The omission of the current account for a partner is an omission of a credit balance. This is corrected by: Credit Partner current account, Debit Suspense account. Here it is the balancing figure of £9,600.

10 REASONS FOR CONTROL ACCOUNTS

Key answer tips

This question demonstrates that it is not enough to be able to operate control accounts. It is also necessary to fully understand the rationale behind them.

(a) A purchase ledger is required to give to the business information on the transactions with and the amounts owing to **each** individual supplier. It therefore contains a separate account for individual supplier. For a small business, the purchase ledger might be part of the double entry system. However, it is more usual to have a separate purchase ledger outside the main double entry accounting system of the nominal ledger. The nominal ledger then contains a debtors control account, which records the total value of transactions with and the total amounts owed by debtors.

A purchase ledger control account can then act as a check on the accuracy of the entries made in the purchase ledger. At any time the sum of the balances on the individual accounts in the purchase ledger should equal the balance on the debtors control account in the nominal ledger.

The effectiveness of the check is considerably improved if the preparation of the control account and the purchase ledger is performed by different people.

(b) (i) Total creditors are understated by £198. To correct, increase the purchase ledger control balance by £198.

(ii) Total creditors are overstated by £100. To correct, reduce the purchase ledger control balance by £100.

(iii) The error affects an individual account in the purchase ledger and has no effect on the purchase ledger control account in the nominal ledger.

(iv) The contra entry should reduce the net amount owed to £200, and both the sales ledger control account and the purchase ledger control account should be reduced by £400. The purchase ledger control account has not been altered yet. To correct, reduce the purchase ledger control balance by £400.

(v) The error has added £60 to total creditors instead of reducing creditors by £60. The creditors total is therefore overstated by £120. To correct, reduce the purchase ledger control balance by £120.

(c) In a computerised accounting system there is effectively only one preparer of accounting information – the accounting program. Assuming that information is keyed in correctly, the program will generate totals from the individual transactions keyed in and post the transactions and totals to the purchase ledger and control account respectively. There is thus no independent check and the control account serves little useful purpose.

Some form of control will still be required but this must take place outside the computer and in different ways from the preparation of a control account.

11 RHEA LIMITED

(a) **Journal entries**

	Debit	Credit
	£	£
Trial balance (no ledger entry)	48,900	
Suspense account		48,900
Correction for carriage outwards balance omitted from trial balance		
Discount received	38,880	
Discount allowed	38,880	
Suspense account		77,760
Suspense account	136,400	
Discount received		68,200
Discount allowed		68,200
Correction of discount totals		
Wrong discount amount posted to the wrong side		
Ordinary share capital account	300,000	
Share premium account		300,000
Correction of error in recording issue of shares – £300,000 wrongly credited to ordinary share capital account.		

Tutorial note. Item (3)

The correct entry should have been:

	Debit	Credit
Fixed asset account	400,000	
Ordinary share capital account		100,000
Share premium account		300,000

Instead, the entry was:

	Debit	Credit
Fixed asset account	400,000	
Ordinary share capital account		400,000

The journal entry corrects this error.

(b)

Suspense account

	£		£
Opening balance (difference)	386,400	Trial balance (carriage inwards)	48,900
Discount accounts	136,400	Discount accounts	77,760
		Balance	396,140
	522,800		522,800

12   OTTER LIMITED

Sales ledger control account

	£		£
Opening debit balance	386,430	Opening credit balance	190
Sales (163,194 + 1,386)	164,580	Cash received	158,288
Cash refund (note 1)	350	Discounts allowed	2,160
		Returns inwards	590
		Contra: purchase ledger control a/c	870
		Bad debts written off	1,360
Closing balance	370	Closing balance	388,272
	551,730		551,730

Purchase ledger control account

	£		£
Opening balance	520	Opening balance	184,740
Cash paid (103,040 − 350) (note 1)	102,690	Purchases (98,192 + 36) (note 3)	98,228
Discounts received	990	Bad debt written off (note 4)	420
Returns outwards (1,370 + 2,000) (note 2)	3,370		
Contra: sales ledger control account	870		
Closing balance	175,048	Closing balance	100
	283,488		283,488

Notes

(1)   The error in recording the cash refund could be corrected by means of: Credit Purchase ledger control account, Debit Sales ledger control account with £350. Here, instead of crediting the purchase ledger control account, payments to suppliers have been reduced by £350.

(2)   When a credit note is issued by a supplier, this may be recorded as 'purchases returns' or 'returns outwards'. Total returns are £1,370 plus item (5).

(3)   The error in keying in the invoice meant that the total value of invoices was understated by £1,395 - £1,359 = £36. Both total purchases and total creditors are understated, and the error is corrected by: Debit Purchases £36, Credit Purchase ledger control account £36. In the solution, £36 has been added to the double entry for Purchases.

(4)   The debit balance in the purchase ledger represents money owed by a supplier to Otter Limited. As this is being written off as irrecoverable, the double entry required is Debit Bad debts, Credit Purchase ledger control account.

(5)   The error between B Jones and R Jones does not affect the control account, only the purchase ledger accounts for the individual suppliers

13   ANDROMEDA LIMITED

Key answer tips

The question specifically requires narratives to support the journal entries. If narrative is not supplied, marks will be lost.

			Suspense account		
20X0		£	20X0		£
31 Dec	Jason loan account	40,000	31 Dec	Original difference (bal. figure)	42,130
31 Dec	Discounts	2,130			
		42,130			42,130

		Dr	Cr
1	Suspense account	40,000	
	Jason loan account		40,000
	Correction of error – entry on wrong side of loan account		
2	Motor expenses	28,600	
	Motor vehicles asset account	28,600	
	Supplier account		57,200
	Correction of error in recording purchase of motor vehicle on credit		
3	Bad debts recovered	800	
	A Smith Sales ledger account		800
	Correction of misposting of cheque from A Smith, wrongly credited to bad debts recovered.		
4	Bank charges	380	
	Cash book		380
	Recording of bank charges not entered in cash book.		
5	Discount allowed	1,840	
	Suspense account	2,130	
	Discount received		3,970
	Correction for December 20X0 discount totals not posted.		
6	Plant	16,000	
	Plant repairs		16,000
	*Depreciation expense	3,200	
	Provision for depreciation		3,200
	Correction of error in posting cash paid for purchase of plant and insertion of necessary depreciation.		
	***Note.** Acceptable alternative	3,200	
	Profit and loss account		3,200
	Provision for depreciation		

Notes

(1)   Error 1. Jason loan account has been debited with £20,000 instead of credited with £20,000. The correction is made by crediting £40,000 to the loan account, to get from

debit £20,000 to credit £20,000. No other account is involved, so the error should be part of the reason for the Suspense Account balance.

(2) Error 2. The correct entry should be Debit Motor Vehicles £28,600, Credit Supplier Account £28,600. Instead, the entry was recorded as Debit Supplier Account, Credit Motor Expenses Account. The journal entries are needed to correct the error and record the transaction correctly.

(3) Error 3. The transaction has been entered as Credit Bad Debts Recovered £800 instead of Credit A Smith Account £800. The journal correction required is therefore to Debit Bad Debts Recovered and credit A Smith Account. (In this question, the purchase ledger is obviously a part of the nominal ledger, and there is no sales ledger control account or purchase ledger control account.)

(4) Error 5. The cash book balance is correct. The error only affects the discounts accounts, and it will be part of the reason for the Suspense Account balance. The entries needed in the discounts accounts are Debit Discounts Allowed £1,840 and Credit Discounts Received £3,970. The corresponding double entries are Credit Suspense Account £1,840 and Debit Suspense Account £3,970. Only the net debit of £2,130 is shown in the solution.

(5) Error 6. Here, the incorrect debit to Plant Repairs is corrected by means of Credit Plant Repairs £16,000, Debit Plant Account £16,000. The question gives a strong hint, though, that you must also record an entry for depreciation, with Debit Depreciation (expense) Account and Credit Provision for Depreciation Account.

ACCA marking scheme					
	Entry	*Narrative*		*Marks available*	*Max*
(1)........................	1	1	2		
(2)........................	1	1	2		
(3)........................	1	1	2		
(4)........................	1	1	2		
(5)........................	2	1	3		
(6)........................	2	1	3	14	
Suspense Account entries					
1 mark per entry				2	
Original Difference				1	
Total				17	16

14 WHOLESALERS

Sales ledger control account

	£		£
Opening balance b/f	50,000	Sales returns	5,000
Sales	107,000	Cash book receipts	111,000
		Discounts allowed	3,000
		Bad debts	2,000
		Contra	6,000
		Closing balance c/f	30,000
	157,000		157,000
Balance b/f	30,000		

Provision for doubtful debts

	£		£
Bad and doubtful debts expense a/c	800	Opening balance b/f	2,000
Closing balance c/f	1,200		
	2,000		2,000
		Balance b/f	1,200

Note: closing provision is 4% of the closing debtors balance of £30,000.

Summary memorandum ledger accounts

All figures in £000; credits in brackets

	A	B	C	D	E	F	G	Totals
Opening balance	10	20	8	9	6	(2)	(1)	50
Sales	30	35		18	9	8	7	107
Sales returns	(2)					(3)		(5)
Cash receipts	(35)	(30)	(5)	(20)	(12)	(5)	(4)	(111)
Discounts allowed	(2)					(1)		(3)
Bad debts			(2)					(2)
Contra					(2)		(4)	(6)
	1	25	1	7	1	(3)	(2)	30

15 DEBTORS CONTROL

Key answer tips

The memorandum accounts for individual debtors do <u>not</u> form part of the double entry bookkeeping system. The solution shows corrections that are required to the memorandum individual debtors ledger accounts (outside the general ledger double entry system) as well as the correction of general ledger errors.

		Dr	Cr
		£000	£000
(a)	Sales	180	
	Debtors control		180

	Memorandum individual debtor		180
(b)	Memorandum individual debtor	800	
(c)	Discounts allowed	70	
	Debtors control		70
	Memorandum individual debtor		70
(d)	Sales	198	
	Debtors control		198
	Memorandum individual debtor		198
(e)	Purchases (creditors) control	600	
	Debtors control		600
	Memorandum individual creditor	600	
	Memorandum individual debtor		600
(f)	Memorandum individual debtors		160

Tutorial notes

1   Item (a). The credit note was recorded as Debit Debtors control a/c £90, credit Sales £90 and the debit and credit are the wrong way round. To correct, we need to reduce sales by (2 x £90) £180 and reduce the balance on the debtors control account by the same amount.

2   Item (b). This error affects the memorandum debtors ledger, but not the general ledger double entry system.

3   Item (c). This is an omission that has to be entered in the records in full.

4   Item (d). This error affects both the general ledger total and the memorandum debtors ledger, because the error relates to an individual transaction entered in the day book. Sales and debtors have been over-stated by (£321 – 123) £198.

5   Item (e). The solution shows all the adjustments needed. The question does not mention the memorandum individual creditors (purchases ledger) but the required adjustments to memorandum creditors are shown for the sake of completeness.

6   Item (f). Only the individual debtors accounts in the memorandum debtors ledger need to be adjusted, because the question states that the transaction has otherwise been recorded properly.

16   UPRIGHT

Key answer tips

Not all errors have an impact on the suspense account balance. The errors that affect the suspense account are those that will result in the total of debit balances and the total of credit balances being different. Errors or omissions that maintain equal debits and credits do not affect the suspense account balance.

Upright, year ended 31 October 20X5

(a)   **Adjustments to profit**

			+	–
			£	£
	Profit per draft accounts		48,200	
(i)	Insurance: opening balance omitted			1,305
(ii)	Profit on sale of vehicle		1,600	
	Reduction in sales figure			6,000

(iii)	Depreciation:		
	Reduction 20% × £22,000	4,400	
(iv)	Insurance paid in advance omitted	1,500	
(v)	Rent receivable understated	400	
		56,100	7,305
			7,305
	Revised profit	£48,795	

(b)

Suspense account

	£			£
Opening balance	1,175	(i)	Insurance account (opening balance omitted)	1,305
(v) Rent receivable	400	(vi)	Purchase ledger account	270
	1,575			1,575

Tutorial notes

1   Item (i). The opening balance of the prepayment has been omitted. As a result, it has not been charged against the profit for the period. The adjustment to correct the error will therefore reduce profit. Since a debit balance has been omitted, the suspense account is affected. The correction is to enter the opening prepayment balance in the suspense account, debit Insurance, credit Suspense account.

2   Item (ii). The profit on the disposal of the fixed asset is the sale proceeds (£6,000) minus the net book value of the asset at the time of disposal (£22,000 - £17,600) £4,400. The profit on disposal is therefore £1,600. The profit has been omitted from the profit and loss account. However, the sale proceeds of £6,000 have been treated as sales revenue, which is incorrect. The £6,000 is not sales revenue, but instead goes into the calculation of the profit on disposal of the asset. Although the disposal has not been entered in the accounts, the omission has not put total debits and total credits out of balance, so the suspense account is not affected.

3   Item (iii). The accounts have not recorded the disposal of the asset, which means that depreciation has been charged on the asset (20% × £22,000 = £4,400). The question states that we have to make a correction for this, which involves removing the depreciation charge and adjusting profit accordingly.

4   Item (iv). A prepayment to carry forward has been omitted. This will reduce the total insurance expense for the year, and so profit must be adjusted upwards. The omission does not affect the suspense account.

5   Item (v). Rent receivable has been understated and so should be increased. As it is income, the adjustment will add to profit. The total credits have been undercast, so total debits and credits differ and the suspense account is affected. To decide which side of the suspense account needs to show the £400, think in terms of the double entry nature of the correction. The correction should be credit rent receivable balance, and so debit suspense account.

6   Item (vi). The error does not affect profit, because it relates to amounts owed, not sales revenue or expenses. However, the purchase has been recorded as £630 in the creditor's account. Since the company does not maintain a creditors' ledger control account, the individual creditor accounts are part of the double entry system, and the total credits have been over-stated by £630 - £360 = £270. Since this puts total debits and total credits out of balance, the suspense account is affected. The required correction is to reduce the creditor balance, i.e. debit Creditor's account, credit Suspense account.

17   TURNER

Key answer tips

Journal narratives are not required in this question, so don't waste time in providing them. Read the question carefully so that the requirements are fully understood. Note that the balance on the suspense account is a debit balance, to make total debits = total credits.

(a)

Suspense account

	£		£
Opening balance (1,852,817 – 1,796,100)	56,717	Sales returns	8,980
Discounts received	919	Purchase returns	8,980
		Discount allowed	836
		Insurance	580
		Telephone (trial balance)	38,260
	57,636		57,636

Journal entries		£	£
(i)	Sales returns account	8,980	
	Suspense account		8,980
	Purchases returns account	8,980	
	Suspense account		8,980
(ii)	Plant	9,600	
	Plant repairs		9,600
	Plant depreciation (expense a/c)	960	
	Provision for depreciation of plant		960
	Profit and loss account	960	
	Plant depreciation		960
(iii)	Discount allowed	836	
	Suspense account		836
	Suspense account	919	
	Discount received		919
(iv)	Insurance account	580	
	Suspense account		580
(v)	Trial balance (no ledger entry)	38,260	
	Suspense account		38,260

(vi)	Sales account	4,800	
	Motor vehicle disposal account		4,800
	Motor vehicles disposal account	12,000	
	Motor vehicles asset account		12,000
	Motor vehicles depreciation account	8,000	
	Motor vehicles disposal account		8,000
	Motor vehicle disposal account	800	
	Profit and loss account		800

(b) **Adjustment to profit**

		−	+
		£	£
Profit as in draft profit and loss account			141,280
(i)	Sales returns adjustment (2 × 8,980)	17,960	
(ii)	Plant:		
	reduction in plant repairs		9,600
	depreciation 6/12 × 20% × £9,600	960	
(iii)	Discount allowed	836	
	Discount received		919
(iv)	Insurance – opening balance omitted	580	
(v)	Telephone expense omitted	38,260	
(vi)	Profit on sale of car		800
	Proceeds taken out of sales	4,800	
		_____	_____
		63,396	152,599
			63,396
			_____
	Revised net profit		89,203
			_____

Tutorial notes

1   Item (i). The error was to enter what should have been a debit entry (sales returns) as a credit entry (purchases returns). this puts total debits and total credits out f balance, so the suspense account is affected. The correction is made by reducing purchases returns (debit Purchases returns, credit Suspense account) and increasing sales returns (debit Sales returns, credit Suspense account).

2   Item (ii). The Plant account (asset account) should have been debited, not the Plant repairs account (an expense account). In addition, no entries have yet been made for depreciation of this item of plant.

3   Item (iii). The cash discount totals have not been posted, which means that total debits (discounts allowed) and total credits (discounts received) are both too low. Each error affects the suspense account. The corrections are therefore debit Discounts allowed, credit Suspense account and credit Discounts received, debit Suspense account.

4   The missing opening debit balance (a prepayment = asset) makes total debits lower than total credits, and this affects the suspense account. To enter the missing balance, debit Insurance account, credit Suspense account.

5   Item (v). The omission of the telephone expenses balance (debit) has made the total credits higher than the total debits. There is no adjustment to make in the general ledger, since there is no error in the accounts. However, the omission has created a suspense account effect. To decide which side of the suspense account to make the entry, think of the hypothetical 'correction' that would be needed if the balance had been missing from the accounts: debit Telephone expenses, so credit Suspense account.

6   Item (vi). The sales income from disposal of the motor vehicle should be taken to a disposal account, not sales. A correction is needed to reduce total sales: debit Sales , credit Motor vehicles disposal account. The remaining journal entries are those required to record the other entries for the motor vehicle disposal account

18   USE OF COMPUTERS

Key answer tips

12 marks are available for part (c); it is therefore important to list as many separate points as possible – one or two will not suffice.

(a)   (i)   **Error of posting**

In a manual system errors can occur in transferring items from one record to another, for example from a sales day book to the nominal ledger or to individual debtor accounts in the sales ledger. In a computer system, postings are made automatically, so errors will not occur.

(ii)   **Errors in additions**

In a manual system, an error might be made in totalling entries in a record. For example, the total of credit sales might be added up incorrectly in the sales day book. Addition errors will not occur in a computer system.

(iii)   **Errors in extracting balances**

In a manual system, a balance may be omitted or miscalculated when listing sales ledger balances. Errors of this sort will not happen in a computer system.

(Only two of these examples are required for a solution.)

(b)   (i)   **Omission of a transaction**

The complete omission of a transaction can occur in either system.

(ii)   **Item entered to the incorrect account**

For example, in either a manual system or a computer system, a telephone expense might be incorrectly recorded and coded as an electricity expense. Some errors of this kind might be prevented in a computer system by the use of check digits in accounts codes, but check digits cannot avoid all errors.

(iii)   **Transaction incorrectly keyed or written in**

In a manual system a transaction may be incorrectly entered, and the same type of error can occur in a computer system. For example, an expense of £9,814 might be written in or keyed in as £9,184.

(Only two examples required for a solution.)

(c)   (i)   **Advantages of computers over manual system:**

–   *Speed of operation*

The speed of operation is incomparably greater, allowing huge volumes of data to be processed very quickly.

– *Accuracy*

Although there can be errors in programs, computers are very accurate. Errors are in any case very unusual in off-the-shelf accountancy software packages.

– *Lower cost of operation*

Running costs should be much lower with a computer system than with a manual system, due to the faster speed of processing, lower error rate and greater productivity.

– *Improved filing*

The use of electronic media for storage means that relatively little space is required to hold the main accounts data. Stored data may be rapidly accessed and updated. (However, even with a computer system, paper records of accounting transactions are retained and filed.)

(ii) **Disadvantages of computers compared with manual systems:**

– *High initial costs*

Some initial capital expenditure on hardware and software is needed, so the set-up costs for a new computer system might be high.

– *Inflexibility*

It is much more difficult to change a computer system, because re-programming can be time-consuming, error-prone and costly.

– *Vulnerability*

The huge volume of work handled by a computer plus a small team of operators can come to a sudden halt if the machine breaks down or is damaged. This dependence on a single source can cause a crisis for the organisation, unless back-up arrangements are in place in the event of a system breakdown.

Overall, the advantages far outweigh the disadvantages, and accounting systems could not operate as they do today without computers.

19 GEORGE

Key answer tips

Work through each of the ten points in the question. For each, work out if there is a cash back effect and/or a profit effect and enter the figures in either the cash account or profit statement as appropriate.

(a)

George – cash book

	£		£
Balance b/f	4,890	Bank charges (3)	320
Correction of error		Plant (4)	10,000
– interest (8)	320		
Balance c/f	11,890	Cheque dishonoured (5)	980
		Correction of error in	
		entering cheque	4,800
		Error in addition	1,000
	_____		_____
	17,100		17,100
	_____		_____

Tutorial notes

1   Item 6. The cheque payment that was incorrectly entered as a money receipt (debit entry in the cash book) is corrected by a credit entry of 2 x £2,400 = £4,800 in the cash book.

2   Item 8. The receipt of bank interest that was incorrectly entered as a payment (credit entry in the cash book) is corrected by a debit entry of 2 x £160 = £320 in the cash book.

3   The carried forward balance is a credit balance, which means a bank overdraft.

(b)   **Bank reconciliation at 31 March**

	£
Balance per cash book - overdraft	(11,890)
Lodgements not credited in the bank statement (2)	(2,890)
	(14,780)
Dishonoured cheque (5)	(980)
Outstanding cheque payment (1)	1,000
	(14,760)
Balance per bank statement – overdrawn	

Tutorial notes

Item 5   The cheque is not dishonoured until after 31 March, so at 31 March, it has been recorded as a receipt in the cash book, but will not have been credited in the bank statement.

Item 1   The cheque payment has been recorded as a payment in the cash book, but will not appear in the bank statement.

(c)   **Statement of effect on profit**

	+	−
	£	£
Profit per draft accounts	81,208	
Bank charges so far omitted (3)		320
Depreciation under-charged (10% of £10,000) (4)		1,000
Bad debt to be written off (5)		980
Motor expenses not yet charged (6)		2,400
Additional depreciation on motor vehicles (6)		600
Purchases understated (7)		1,000
Interest adjustment: income recorded as expense (8)	320	
Repairs to premises = drawings, not expense (9)	870	
	82,398	6,300
	6,300	
Adjusted profit	£76,098	

Tutorial note: The additional depreciation expense for the motor vehicle is needed because one of the errors was to credit £2,400 to the motor vehicles account. This reduces the balance on the account and understates the cost of motor vehicles. Depreciation (at 25%) has therefore not been charged on the £2,400 of motor vehicle cost.

(d) **Journal**

		£	£
George –	Drawings	870	
	Repairs to premises		870

Repairs to George's house mistakenly charged
as a business expense

		£	£
*Paul – purchases ledger account		540	
George – Drawings			540

Business account paid by personal cheque

Note: A debit to purchases ledger control account is also an acceptable answer for
this entry.

ACCOUNTING TREATMENTS

20 DEPRECIATION / AMORTISATION

(a) The values of the land and the buildings need to be separated, because the land would
not normally require depreciation.

The revalued amount of the buildings should be depreciated over the estimated
remaining useful economic life at the time of the revaluation. The straight-line method
is usually adopted, but other methods such as the reducing balance method may be
used.

(b) The expenditure should be held without amortisation until commercial production
begins, and should then be amortised on a systematic basis in each accounting period
in which the product is used or sold.

If the circumstances justifying the deferral of the expenditure cease to apply at any
time, the expenditure should be written off to the extent that it is no longer
recoverable.

(c) Investments of this kind do not depreciate, though they may fluctuate in value.
Accordingly no depreciation is provided for them.

21 DIAMOND

Key answer tips

Start by opening T accounts for the accounts you should see are needed – freehold land, freehold
buildings and office equipment, and provision for depreciation accounts for freehold buildings and
office equipment. Add extra accounts when you see they will be needed – here a disposal of office
equipment account and a revaluation reserve will be needed.

(a)

Freehold land – cost or valuation

20X5		£'000	20X5			£'000
1 Jan	Balance b/f	1,000	31 Dec	Balance c/f		1,000
20X6			20X6			
1 Jan	Balance b/f	1,000	31 Dec	Balance c/f		1,200
31 Dec	Reval reserve	200				
		1,200				1,200
20X7						
1 Jan	Balance b/f	1,200				

Freehold buildings – cost

20X5		£'000	20X5		£'000
1 Jan	Balance b/f	500	31 Dec	Balance c/f	550
31 Dec	Cash (extension)	50			
		550			550
20X6					
1 Jan	Balance b/f	550			

Freehold buildings – provision for depreciation

20X5		£000	20X5		£000
31 Dec	Balance c/f	221	1 Jan	Balance b/f	210
			31 Dec	Freehold building depreciation	11
		221			221
20X6			20X6		
31 Dec	Balance c/f	232	1 Jan	Balance b/f	221
			31 Dec	Freehold building depreciation	11
		232			232
			20X6		
			1 Jan	Balance b/f	232

Tutorial note: The annual depreciation charge is 2% of £550,000 in each year.

Office equipment – cost

20X5		£000	20X5		£000
1 Jan	Balance b/f	40	10 Jun	Office equipment disposal a/c	8
10 Jun	Cash	12	31 Dec	Balance c/f	48
	Office equipment disposal a/c (trade-in value)	4			
		56			56

20X6			*20X6*		
1 Jan	Balance b/f	48	1 Mar	Office equipment disposal a/c	8
			31 Dec	Balance c/f	40
		48			48
20X7					
1 Jan	Balance b/f	40			

Office equipment – provision for depreciation

20X5		£000	*20X5*		£000
10 Jun	Office equipment disposal (8–1)	7	1 Jan	Balance b/f	24
31 Dec	Balance c/f	23	31 Dec	Office equipment depreciation	6
		30			30
20X6			*20X6*		
1 Mar	Office equipment disposal (8–2)	6	1 Jan	Balance b/f	23
31 Dec	Balance c/f	22	31 Dec	Office equipment depreciation	5
		28			28
			20X7		
			1 Jan	Balance b/f	22

Office equipment – disposal

20X5		£000	*20X5*		£000
10 Jun	Office equipment cost	8	10 Jun	Office equipment prov for depreciation	7
31 Dec	Profit and loss – profit	3		Office equipment cost (trade-in)	4
		11			11
20X6			*20X6*		
1 Mar	Office equipment cost	8	1 Mar	Office equipment prov for depreciation	6
31 Dec	Profit and loss – profit	1		Cash – proceeds of sale	3
		9			9

Tutorial note: Office equipment depreciation is 12.5% of £48,000 in 20X5 and 12.5% of £40,000 in 20X6.

Revaluation reserve

			20X6		£000
			31 Dec	Freehold land	200

(b) In order for the financial statements to reflect properly all the costs of the enterprise, it is necessary for there to be a charge against income in respect of the use of all fixed assets which have finite useful economic lives. The purpose of depreciation is thus mainly to ensure that the cost or valuation of a fixed asset is spread fairly over the years benefiting from its use.

The factors to be taken into account in assessing depreciation are:

(i) the carrying amount of the asset (cost or valuation)

(ii) the expected useful economic life to the business, having due regard to the incidence of obsolescence

(iii) the estimated residual value of the asset at the end of its useful economic life in the business.

22 AGATHA LTD

Key answer tips

Part (a) of this question is a test of basic bookkeeping skills. Be careful with the calculation of the depreciation for plant and machinery and accounting for the part exchange of the motor vehicle.

Part (b) calls for the preparation of the schedule of movements in fixed assets required by the Companies Acts. Do not merely present a statement of cost less depreciation as might be found in a detailed balance sheet.

(a)

Plant and machinery – cost

20X8		£000	20X9		£000
1 Jan	Balance b/d	819,000	31 Mar	Balance c/d	864,900
10 Jan	Cash (see note)	45,900			
		864,900			864,900

Note: (41,200 + 300 + 800 + 3,600) = £45,900.

Plant and machinery – accumulated depreciation

20X9		£000	20X8		£000
31 Mar	Balance c/d	522,169	1 Jan	Balance b/d	360,000
			20X9		
			31 Mar	Plant and m/c depreciation (W1)	162,169
		522,169			522,169

Motor vehicles – cost

20X8		£000	20X8		£000
1 Jan	Balance b/d	148,000	18 Apr	MV disposal a/c	12,000
18 Apr	MV disposal a/c (trade-in)	5,000	20X9		
	Cash	13,000	31 Mar	Balance c/d	154,000
		166,000			166,000

Motor vehicles – accumulated depreciation

20X8		£000	20X8		£000
18 Apr	MV disposal a/c (Working)	6,750	1 Jan	Balance b/d	60,000
20X9			20X9		
31 Mar	Balance c/d	101,000	31 Mar	MV depreciation a/c (W2)	47,750
		107,750			107,750

Motor vehicles – disposal

20X8		£000	20X8		£000
18 Apr	Motor vehicles – cost	12,000	18 Apr	MV accumulated depreciation (W3)	6,750
				MV cost – trade-in value	5,000
				Profit and loss a/c loss on sale	250
		12,000			12,000

(b)

Movements on fixed assets

	Plant and machinery £000	Motor vehicles £000	Total £000
Cost: at Jan 20X8	819	148	967.0
Additions	45.9	18	63.9
Disposals		(12)	(12.0)
	864.9	154	1,018.9
Accumulated depreciation			
At 1 January 20X8	360	60	420.0
Disposals		(6.8)	(6.8)
Charge for year (Workings)	162.2	47.8	210.0
	522.2	101	623.2
Net book value	342.7	53	395.7

Workings:

(W1) **Depreciation charges** £

Plant and machinery

	£
£819,000 × 15% × 15 months	153,563
£45,900 × 15% × 15 months	8,606
	162,169

(W2) **Motor vehicles**

	£
£136,000 × 25% × 15 months	42,500
£18,000 × 25% × 12 months	4,500
£12,000 × 25% × 3 months	750
	47,750

(W3) **Accumulated depreciation** on motor vehicle disposed of

	£
Accumulated depreciation at 1 January	6,000
Depreciation for 3 months in year of disposal (3/12 × 25% × £12,000)	750
Accumulated depreciation to date of disposal	6,750

23 ROOK

			Dr £	Cr £
(a)		Salaries account	2,000	
		Suspense account		2,000
		Correction of error-undercasting of debit side of salaries account		
(b)		Motor vehicles	6,000	
		Bad debts	1,500	
		Wren Limited sales ledger account		7,500
		Acceptance of car in settlement for trade debt, and writing off of balance.		
(c)		Factory buildings	46,100	
		Purchases		27,600
		Wages		18,500
		Materials and labour used in constructing extension to factory.		
(d)		Motor vehicles	18,000	
		Plant and machinery	33,000	
		Purchases	20,000	
		Crow Limited loan account		71,000
		Purchase of sundry assets from Crow Limited with delayed settlement.		
(e)	(i)	Motor vehicles - cost	20,000	
		Car dealer		8,000
		Disposal of motor vehicles account		12,000
		Purchase of car on credit and in part-exchange for a car traded in		
	(ii)	Disposal of motor vehicles account	18,000	
		Motor vehicles - cost		18,000
		Transfer of cost of car given in part exchange		
	(iii)	Motor vehicles - accumulated depreciation a/c	6,000	
		Disposal of motor vehicles account		6,000
		Transfer of accumulated depreciation on car given in part exchange		

Tutorial notes

1   Item (a). A debit entry is needed in the salaries account, so the correcting entry is debit Salaries account, credit Suspense account.

2   Item (b). The payment is not in cash but in the form of a fixed asset. There is also a bad debt of £1,500 to write off. Bad debts are an expense, so the bad debts account is debited.

3   Item (c). The internal costs of building the extension are included in the cost of the extension (factory buildings – fixed asset), so debit the fixed asset account and credit the expense accounts for the materials (purchases) and labour costs (wages account).

4   The entries for item (e) could validly be combined into a single compound journal entry.

24   PENTLAND

Key answer tips

Start by opening all the accounts you can see that you need, and enter the opening balances. Then add other accounts as you find that you need them. A complexity in this question is that you are fairly clearly expected to calculate depreciation on the various fixed asset items up to the date of their revaluation or disposal, and then to calculate the depreciation from the date of revaluation or after the disposal.

Buildings – cost or valuation

20X0		£000	20X1		£000
1 Jul	Balance b/d	2,200	30 Jun	Balance c/d	3,400
20X1					
	Revaluation reserve	1,200			
1 Jan		3,400			3,400
20X1					
1 July	Balance b/d	3,400			

Revaluation reserve

20X1		£000	20X1		£000
30 Jun	Balance c/d	2,022	1 Jan	Buildings – cost/valuation	1,200
			1 Jan	Buildings – accum depreciation (see W1)	822
		2,022			2,022
			20X1		
			1 Jul	Balance b/d	2,022

Buildings – accumulated depreciation

20X1		£000	20X0		£000
1 Jan	Revaluation reserve	822	1 Jul	Balance b/d	800
			31 Dec	Profit and loss account – Depreciation to 31 Dec 20X0 2% × £2,200,000 × 6/12	22
		822			822
			20X1		
30 Jun	Balance c/d	34	30 Jun	Profit and loss account – Depreciation to 30 June 20X1 (W2)	34
		34			34
			1 Jul	Balance b/d	34

Land

20X0		£000	20X1		£000
1 Jul	Balance b/d	4,000	30 Jun	Balance c/d	4,000
		4,000			4,000
20X1					
1 Jul	Balance b/d	4,000			

Plant and machinery – cost

20X0		£000	20X1		£000
1 July	Balance b/d	1,600	1 Jan	Plant and machinery disposal	300
20X1					
1 Jan	Bank	400	30 Jun	Balance c/d	1,700
		2,000			2,000

Plant and machinery – accumulated depreciation

20X1		£000	20X0		£000
1 Jan	Plant and machinery disposal (230 + 22.5)	252.5	1 July	Balance b/d	600
			20X1		
30 Jun	Balance c/d	595	30 Jun	Profit and loss account (W3)	247.5
		847.5			847.5
			20X1		
			1 July	Balance b/d	595

Plant and machinery – disposal

20X1		£000	20X1		£000
1 Jan	Plant and machinery – cost	300	1 Jun	Plant and m/c – accumulated depreciation	252.5
30 Jun	Profit and loss account: profit on disposal	2.5		Bank	50
		302.5			302.5

Motor vehicles – cost

20X0		£000	20X1		£000
1 Jul	Balance b/d	600	1 Apr	Motor vehicles – disposal	20
20X1					
1 Apr	Bank	18	30 Jun	Balance c/d	610
	Motor vehicles – disposal (trade in value)	12			
		630			630

Motor vehicles – accumulated depreciation

20X1		£000	20X0		£000
1 Apr	Motor vehicles – disposal (W4)	13	1 Jul	Balance b/d	200
30 Jun	Balance c/d	307.5	20X1		
			30 Jun	Depreciation of motor vehicles (W5)	120.5
		320.5			320.5

Motor vehicles – disposal

20X1		£000	20X1		£000
1 Apr	Motor vehicles – cost	20	1 Apr	Motor vehicles – cost (trade-in value)	12
30 Jun	Profit and loss account: profit on sale	5		Motor vehicles – accumulated depreciation	13
		25			25

Workings

(W1) The depreciation charge on the buildings from 1 July 20X0 to the date of revaluation is £2,200,000 × 6/12 × 2% = £22,000. Total accumulated depreciation at the date of revaluation is therefore £800,000 + £22,000 = £822,000.

(W2) The depreciation charge on the buildings in the period after the revaluation to the end of the financial year is £3.4 million × 2% × 6/12 = £34,000. This is accounted for by: debit Depreciation of buildings account, credit Buildings – accumulated depreciation account.

(W3) **Plant and machinery – depreciation**

		£000
Depreciation		
Plant sold	15% × £300,000 × 6/12	22.5
Remaining plant	15% × £1,300,000	195.0
New plant	15% × £400,000 × 6/12	30.0
		247.5

(W4) Accumulated depreciation on motor vehicle disposed of = £20,000 - £10,000 = £10,000 at the start of the year, plus £20,000 × 9/12 × 20% to the date of disposal in the current year. This is £10,000 + £3,000 = £13,000.

(W5) **Motor vehicles – depreciation**

		£000
Vehicle given in part exchange	20% × £20,000 × 9/12	3.0
Remaining vehicles	20% × £580,000	116.0
New vehicles	20% × £30,000 × 3/12	1.5
		120.5

25 RUBENS

Key answer tips

This question tests knowledge and understanding of SSAP 13 very thoroughly. You can use it for both learning and revision of accounting for research and development expenditure. Part (c) of the answer is needed to prepare an answer to part (b).

(a) For development expenditure to be capitalised, the following criteria must apply.

(i) There is a clearly defined project.

(ii) There is identifiable expenditure.

(iii) The project is assessed as technically feasible.

(iv) The ultimate commercial viability of the project is reasonably assured.

(v) Related revenues will cover the remaining development costs plus production, selling and administrative costs.

(vi) Adequate resources exist, or are reasonably expected to be available, to enable the project to be completed, including the provision of any necessary increased working capital.

(b)   £000

Profit and loss account (Note 1)

Research and development   3,940 (included in cost of sales)

Balance sheet (Note 3)

Deferred development expenditure (W2)   7,560 (separate heading under Intangible Fixed Assets)

(c) **Accounting policy**

The company's accounting policy for research and development is as follows:

(i) Research expenditure: All research expenditure, other than capital expenditure on research facilities, is written off as incurred

(ii) Development expenditure: Development expenditure meeting the criteria in SSAP 13 Research and Development is capitalised and amortised on the straight line basis over five years, beginning in the year in which sales revenue is first earned.

Note 1   Profit and loss account

Research and development expenditure was made up as follows:

	£000	£000
Current year's expenditure (W1)		2,100
Past years' expenditure written off	1,200	
Amortisation of deferred expenditure from previous years (W2)	640	1,840
		3,940

Note 2   Profit and loss account

Exceptional item

During the year development of a project was abandoned. The total expenditure written off was £1,500,000, of which £1,200,000 was spent in earlier years and £300,000 in the current year.

Note 3   Balance sheet

	£000	£000
Deferred development expenditure		
Balance at 30 September 20X7 (W2)		7,800
Written off during year	1,200	
Amortisation (W2)	640	1,840
		5,960
Expenditure in year recognised as an asset (W2)		1,600
Balance at 30 September 20X8		7,560

Workings

Only project D does not meet the criteria for capitalisation of development expenditure.

(W1)	£000
Current year's expenditure	
Research (per question)	1,800
Development costs written off (Project D)	300
	2,100

(W2) Deferred development expenditure

Project	Balance 30.9.X7 £000	Expenditure in 20X7/X8 £000	Written off £000	Amortisation £000	Capitalised £000	Balance 30.9.X8 £000
A	600			200		400
B	2,400			440		1,960
C	3,600				400	4,000
D	1,200	300	1,500			nil
E					800	800
F					400	400
	7,800	**300**	**1,500**	**640**	**1,600**	**7,560**

Further workings

1 Project A amortisation each year = £1 million/5 years = £200,000.

2 Project B amortisation each year = £2,400,000/5 = £480,000 = £40,000 each month. Amortisation in the period 1 November 20X7 to 30 September 20X8 = 11 months × £40,000 = £440,000.

26 LOMOND

Key answer tips

To answer this question on research and development expenditure you have to state the conditions for the capitalisation of development expenditure and then deal with simple calculations and disclosure requirements.

(a) (i) There is a clearly defined project.

(ii) The related expenditure is clearly identifiable.

(iii) The outcome of the project has been assessed with reasonable certainty as to:

– technical feasibility

– commercial viability.

(iv) Future sales revenues will exceed development costs to date plus future development costs plus production, selling and administration costs.

(v) Adequate resources exist to enable the project to be completed.

(b)

	Profit and loss account £	Balance sheet £
Project A		
Amortisation of deferred development expenditure (£200,000/5)	40,000	
Balance sheet (£120,000 - £40,000)		80,000
Project B		
Expenditure written off (£175,000 + £55,000)	230,000	Nil
Project C		
Development expenditure to date		255,000
Project D		
Research expenditure (cannot be capitalised)	80,000	Nil
	350,000	335,000

(c)   **Disclosure requirements**

(i)   Total research and development expenditure charged in the profit and loss account was £350,000 analysed as follows:

	£
Expenditure during the year	135,000
Amortised or written off from deferred expenditure	215,000
	350,000

Tutorial note: Total expenditure in the year = £55,000 on project B and £80,000 on project D. Amortised or written off = £40,000 on project A and £175,000 on project B.

(ii)   **Movements on deferred development expenditure**

	£
Balance at 1 July 20X3	380,000
Expenditure in current year	225,000
	605,000
Amortised during year	(40,000)
Expenditure on abandoned project written off	(230,000)
Balance at 30 June 20X4	335,000

Tutorial note: Total expenditure in the current year = £55,000 on project B and £170,000 on project C.

27   SAMPI

Key answer tips

Ten marks are available for part (a) – ensure that the full time allocation is used on this part of the question to provide good quality, thorough written answers.

(a)   (i)   **LIFO**

LIFO means that goods sold or consumed are assumed to be those most recently purchased ('last in'). The stock is therefore taken to be made up of the earliest purchases and priced accordingly.

(ii)   **Three acceptable methods of stock costing**

(1)   *Unit cost*

Stock is priced at the actual amount paid for each individual item of stock held.

(2)   *First in, first out (FIFO)*

Stock is assumed to be composed of the items most recently purchased, regardless of whether this is actually the case. Stock is therefore valued according to the price paid for the most recent purchase. If this purchase is insufficient to cover the quantity in stock, the price of the next most recent purchase is taken as necessary.

(3)   *Average cost (AVCO)*

Stock is priced at the weighted average price at which each stock line was purchased during the accounting period, or brought forward from the previous period.

All three of these methods are acceptable under SSAP 9 because they are either the actual cost of the stock (method 1) or a reasonably close approximation to that actual cost (methods 2 and 3). SSAP 9 does not accept LIFO for general use because it does not normally give an acceptably close approximation to the actual cost of the items in stock at the balance sheet date.

(iii) The cost of a stock of finished goods would normally be arrived at by taking the labour and materials consumed in manufacturing the items plus an allocation of overheads. The overhead allocation should be based on the normal level of production and should exclude selling expenses and general management expenses.

(b) (i) **Value of stock using LIFO**

	Opening stock	Deliveries from factory	
		8 March	22 March
	units	units	units
	4,000	3,800	6,000
Sales			
12 March sales	(1,200)	(3,800)	
	2,800	–	
18 March sales	(2,000)		
	800		
24 March			(3,000)
			3,000
28 March			(2,000)
			1,000

The closing stock is therefore:

	£
800 at £12	9,600
1,000 at £18	18,000
	27,600

(ii) **Value of stock using weighted average cost basis**

	Number of units	Weighted average cost £	Total value of closing stock £
Opening stock	4,000	13.00	52,000
8 March	3,800	15.00	57,000
Balance	7,800	13.974	109,000
12 March	(5,000)	13.974	(69,870)
	(2,800)	13.974	39,130
18 March	(2,000)	13.974	(27,948)
	800	13.974	11,182
22 March	6,000	18.00	108,000
	6,800	17.527	119,182
24 March	(3,000)	17.527	(52,581)
	3,800	17.527	66,601

28 March	(2,000)	17.527	(35,054)
	1,800	17.527	31,547

Note: There are some rounding errors in these calculations, because average costs are taken to just 3 decimal places.

Summary:

		£
Stock value:	FIFO	32,400
	LIFO	27,600
	Weighted average cost	31,547

28   LAMORGAN

Tutorial note: The amount of credit sales can be calculated by opening up a T account for total sales and entering the transaction details. Credit sales is the balancing figure. Purchases can be calculated in part (b) in the same way. Do not forget cash sales for your answer to part (a).

(a)   **Sales**

Sales total account

	£		£
Opening debtors	41,600	Cash received from customers	218,500
Refunds to customers	800	Discounts allowed	2,600
		Bad debts written off	1,500
Credit sales (balancing figure)	225,100	Contra, purchases	700
		Closing debtors	44,200
	267,500		267,500

Credit sales as above	225,100
Cash sales £114,700 + £9,600	124,300
Total sales	349,400

(b)   **Purchases**

Purchases total account

	£		£
Payment to suppliers	114,400	Opening creditors	22,900
Contra sales	700	Drawings – goods taken	400
Closing creditors	24,800	Purchases (balancing figure)	116,600
	139,900		139,900

(c)   **Stock**

	£
Cost from stock taking	77,700
Damaged item valued at net realisable value: £1,700 – £300 – £100	1,300
Goods on approval with customer (not yet sold)	3,000
	82,000

ACCA marking scheme			Marks	Max.
(a)	½ mark per item	9 × ½ + ½ layout	5	
(b)	½ mark per item	5 × ½ + ½ layout	3	
(c)	(i)		2	
	(ii)		½	
Total			10½	10

29   PERSEUS LIMITED

Key answer tips

This question tests a range of issues, including knowledge of the application of FRS 3 in respect of prior period adjustments. Where several adjustments are involved (in this case to current assets) it is very important to approach the question in a methodical way.

(a)   (i)   The opening balance of reserves should be restated. Comparative information should be restated.

(ii)   FRS 3 *Reporting Financial Performance* requires:

–   The effect of the adjustments to be noted at the foot of the statement of recognised gains and losses.

–   The effect on the results from the previous period to be disclosed if practicable.

(b)

	£
Stock (W1)	4,249,800
Trade debtors (W2)	2,674,300
Prepayments (W3)	773,400
Cash at bank	940,000

Workings

(W1)   *Stock*

		£	£
As originally taken			4,190,000
(1) Defective stock: reduce to net realisable value			
Original cost		16,000	
Net realisable value (10,400 – 600)		9,800	
Reduction in stock value			(6,200)
(2) Goods on sale or return at cost			66,000
Re-stated stock value			4,249,800

(W2)   *Debtors*

	£
As originally stated	2,980,000
Less: Goods on sale or return	88,000
	2,892,000
Less Debts written off	92,000
	2,800,000
Less: Provision for doubtful debts (5% of £2,800,000)	140,000
	2,660,000
Add: Purchases ledger debit balances	14,300
	2,674,300

Full credit is also given if the deduction of the provision for doubtful debts is shown on the face of the balance sheet.

(W1)	*Prepayments*	£	£
	As originally stated		770,000
	Payments on account	25,000	
	Less: Commission due	21,600	
	Prepayment of commission (2/102 × £1,101,600)		3,400
	Prepayments as adjusted		773,400

Tutorial note: When a business has money in an account with one bank and a bank overdraft with another bank, the plus and minus cash amounts should not be netted off against each other. The bank overdraft should be shown separately as a current liability.

ACCA marking scheme		
		Marks
(a)	Adjusted on opening balance of reserves.	2
	Comparative information restated	2
	Disclosures	
	1 mark per valid item 2 × 1	
(b)	Stock	
	Reduction to net realisable value	1
	Including selling costs	1
	Goods on sale or return added	
	Trade debtors	
	Gross debts taken	1
	Goods on sale or return excluded	2
	Debts written off	1
	Provision based on final figure	1
	Purchase ledger debit balances	
	Prepayments	
	Calculation of commission	2
	addition to arrive at final figure	
	(Credit also given if included with trade	
	debtors under heading 'debtors').	
	Cash at bank	1
	No offsetting overdraft	
Total		20

30 THETA

Key answer tips

Over a third of the marks in this question are for part (c). Do not neglect to answer it fully. We are told that there are no ledger control accounts; therefore the individual supplier and customer accounts must be treated as a part of the double entry system.

(a) **Journal entries**

		£	£
(i)	Zeta Limited purchases ledger account	1,080	
	Zeta Limited sales ledger account		1,080
	Account settled by contra		
(ii)	Bad and doubtful debts expense account	3,590	
	P		840
	Q		120
	R		360
	S		2,090
	T		180
	Bad debts written off after review of accounts		

(iii) Bad and doubtful debts expense account   2,140

       Provision for doubtful debts   2,140

       Increase in provision for doubtful debts

       after review of accounts

(iv) Vau Limited – sales ledger   200

       Tau Limited – sales ledger   200

       Transfer to correct error in posting cash received

(b)

(i) Debtors – sales ledger £

	£
	384,600)
less: contra settlement	(1,080)
	383,520
less: bad debts written off	(3,590)
	379,930
less: provision for doubtful debts	(5,200)
	374,730
add: Purchases ledger debit balances	1,860
	376,590

(ii) Creditors: amounts falling due within one year

Creditors: purchase ledger	222,230
less: contra settlement	(1,080)
	221,150
less: long-term (liabilities over 12 months = 2 × £14,000)	(28,000)
	193,150
add: Sales ledger credit balances	2,900
	196,050

(iii) Creditors: amounts falling due after more than one year (see above)   28,000

(c) A provision is an amount set aside to provide for any liability or loss, or diminution in value of assets, which is either likely or certain to occur, but where the amount is uncertain. An example is a provision for depreciation.

A reserve is part of the ownership interest in a company. Any undistributed gains or surpluses above the nominal value of the share capital represent types of reserve. The accumulated profits form part of the reserves of a company, and a reserve may also come into existence as a result of the issue of shares at a premium (share premium account) or the revaluation of fixed assets (revaluation reserve). An example is a revaluation reserve arising on the revaluation of fixed assets.

The essential difference between the two is that a provision is a credit balance created to cover a liability or loss, whereas a reserve is a credit balance representing owners' equity.

31   DOUBTFUL DEBTS

Key answer tips

Allow enough time to provide a full answer to part (b).

Debtors

		£		£
1.1.20X1	Balance b/d	10,000	Sales returns	1,000
	Sales	100,000	Bank	90,000
			Bad and doubtful debts	500
			Discounts allowed	400
			31.12.20X1 Balance c/d	18,100
		110,000		110,000
1.1.20X2	Balance b/d	18,100	Sales returns	1,800
	Sales	90,000	Bank	95,000
			Creditors	3,000
			Bad and doubtful debts	500
			Discounts allowed	500
			31.12.20X2 Balance c/d	6,300
		108,100		108,100
1.1.20X3	Balance b/d	6,300		

Provision for doubtful debts

		£			£
31.12.20X1	Balance c/d		1.1.20X1	Balance b/d	400
	Specific	200		Bad and doubtful debts	695
	General 5% × (18,100 − 200)	895			
		1,095			1,095
	Bad and doubtful debts	780	1.1.20X2	Balance b/d	1,095
31.12.20X2	Balance c/d (5% × 6,300)	315			
		1,095			1,095

32   PROVISION FOR DOUBTFUL DEBTS

Key answer tips

In the provision for doubtful debts account, it should be noted that the required provision gives the closing balance, NOT the charge to the profit and loss account.

There are two different methods of recording bad debts written off. A debit may be made in the bad debts expense account. Alternatively, and more unusually, a bad debts expense might be debited to the provision for doubtful debts account. The net amount shown as bad debt expenses will be the same using the two methods and also the balance sheet will look exactly the same whichever method is used.

The question requires bad debts to be charged to the provision and so this method must be followed.

Provision for doubtful debts account

		£			£
Year 1	Debtors	2,345	Year 1	Balance b/d (50,000 × 2%)	1,000
	Balance c/d (60,000 × 2%)	1,200		Bad and doubtful debts (bal fig)	2,545
		3,545			3,545
Year 2	Debtors	37	Year 2	Balance b/d	1,200
	Bad and doubtful debts (bal fig)	463			
	Balance c/d	700			
		1,200			1,200
			Year 3	Balance b/d	700

Tutorial note: In Year 1 the charge to the bad and doubtful debts expense account (or direct to P & L account) is the bad debt written off plus the increase of £200 in the provision for doubtful debts. In year 2 there is a negative charge to the bad and doubtful debts account (or direct to the profit and loss account) equal to the reduction of £500 in the provision for doubtful debts minus the bad debt of £37 written off.

33 JURIEN

To:	The Directors of Jurien Limited
From:	Financial Adviser
Date:	

Accounting treatment of items in current financial statements

You asked for advice on three matters, and I set out my response below.

(a) FRS 12 *Provisions, Contingent Liabilities and Contingent Assets* will require a provision to be recognised for the best estimate of the amount needed to settle the obligation, because there is a probable present obligation arising from a past event.

(b) In accordance with SSAP 17 *Accounting for Post Balance Sheet Events*, the criterion is whether the discovery of the financial difficulties provides evidence that the debtor had difficulties at the balance sheet date. Unless there is clear evidence that there were no difficulties at the balance sheet date, a provision should be made.

(c) SSAP 9 *Stocks and Long-Term Contracts* contains reasonably clear rules on the allocation of overheads to stocks of finished goods:

    (i) Only overheads relating to production may be included.

    (ii) The allocation of fixed production overheads must be based on the normal level of activity in the period.

Two examples of overheads to be excluded are:

    (i) selling costs

    (ii) administrative overheads not contributing to bringing stocks to their present condition and location.

ACCA marking scheme			Marks	Max.
(a)	Reference to FRS 12		1	
	Provision required		1	
	Reason		_1_	_3_
(b)	Reference to SSAP 17		1	
	Evidence of position at balance sheet date		1	
	Provision required		_1_	_3_
(c)	Reference to SSAP 9		1	
	Relating to production		1	
	Normal level of production		1	
	Examples 2 × 1		_2_	_4_
	Memorandum format		_2_	
	Total		_13_	_10_

34   ACCOUNTING TREATMENTS

Key answer tips

This question requires a good knowledge of three accounting standards.

(a)   **Research and development**

The company's policy as regards research and development is contrary to the requirements of SSAP 13. All research expenditure should be written off to the annual profit and loss account as it is incurred. The only exception is capital expenditure on research facilities.

All development expenditure should also be written off immediately unless it satisfies the criteria in SSAP 13:

–   defined project

–   identifiable expenditure

–   technically feasible

–   commercially viable

–   profits will cover past and future development costs

–   resources adequate to complete the project.

If all of these conditions are met the company may if it wishes capitalise the development costs to be written off systematically in the periods during which the product is to be sold.

(b)   **Post balance sheet events**

SSAP 17 defines post balance sheet events as those events both favourable and unfavourable which occur between the balance sheet date and the date on which the financial statements are approved by the board of directors.

The liquidation of a major debtor during this period is what SSAP 17 calls an adjusting event. This is defined as an event which provides additional evidence of conditions existing at the balance sheet date. SSAP 17 requires that a provision should be made in the financial statements for this bad debt.

(c)   **Contingency**

FRS 12 explains the appropriate accounting treatment for contingent assets and liabilities which do not meet the recognition criteria for actual assets and liabilities due to their inherent uncertainty.

A loss should be accrued in financial statements as a liability where it is probable that a future event will confirm a loss which can be estimated with reasonable accuracy on the date at which the financial statements are approved by the board of directors. However a contingent liability need only be disclosed in a note to the financial statements, unless it is remote in which case it can be ignored. As the claim is unlikely to succeed, FRS 12 requires the estimated amount of the damages to be disclosed by note. However, as the legal costs are to be incurred in any case, provision should be made for them in the company's financial statements.

35   OCHIL

Key answer tips

The question presents details of six events. You are asked first to explain the accounting treatment of post balance sheet events and contingent liabilities according to SSAP 17 and FRS 12, then apply the treatments to the given events.

(a)   The relevant requirements of SSAP 17 *Post Balance Sheet Events* and FRS 12 *Provisions, Contingent Liabilities and Contingent Assets* are:

(i)   **Post balance sheet events**

These are divided into two types – adjusting events and non-adjusting events. The financial statements must be adjusted for material adjusting events. Material non-adjusting events are usually disclosed by way of a note only.

(ii)   **Contingent liabilities**

The accounting treatment of contingent liabilities depends on their degree of probability.

If it is probable that the liability will actually arise, and its amount can be measured reliably, the item should be accrued for.

If it is not probable, disclosure by way of a note is required.

If there is only a remote possibility of the liability arising, no disclosure is required.

(b)   The correct accounting treatments of the six items according to SSAP 17 and FRS 12 are:

(i)   This is an adjusting post balance sheet event under SSAP 17. The stock should be reduced by £40,000 in the trading account and balance sheet (SSAP 17).

(ii)   This is another adjusting post balance sheet event under SSAP 17, The provision for doubtful debts should be reduced by £65,000 and profit and loss account credited (SSAP 17).

(iii)   The £50,000 claim is a contingency which requires disclosure by note only as it is not probable that a liability will arise. Provision should be made in the March 20X1 accounts for the £10,000 legal fees (FRS 12).

(iv)   Provision should be made for the £100,000 probable liability under the guarantee (FRS 12).

(v)   The proposed merger is a non-adjusting post balance sheet event and should be disclosed by note in the financial statements for the year ended 31 March 20X1 (SSAP 17).

(vi)   This is an adjusting balance sheet event under SSAP 17 and the stock figure should be increased by £30,000.

(c)   **Effect on profit**

			£	£
Profit as shown in draft accounts				350,000
Add:	(ii)	Reduction in doubtful debt provision	65,000	
	(vi)	Stock omitted	30,000	
				95,000
				445,000
Less:	(i)	Reduction in value of stock	40,000	
	(iii)	Provision for legal expenses	10,000	
	(iv)	Provision for guarantee	100,000	
				150,000
Revised profit				295,000

36   GERMAINE LTD

Key answer tips

Part (a) requires factual knowledge of SSAP 17 and FRS 12 but the actual wording of SSAPs and FRSs is not necessary provided that your answer embodies the necessary points.

Part (b) requires application of the facts to two specific situations.

Make sure you provided the advice required as well as the journal entries.

(a)   (i)   For an adjustment to be required to the financial statements the event must be material, and either provide additional evidence of conditions existing at the balance sheet date or cast doubt on the application of the going concern concept to the whole or a material part of the enterprise.

(ii)   (1)   A possible obligation that arises from past events and whose existence will be confirmed only by the occurrence of one or more uncertain future events not wholly within the entity's control; or

(2)   A contingent liability is a present obligation that arises from past events but is not recognised because:

- it is not probable that a transfer of economic benefits will be required to settle the obligation; or

- the amount of the obligation cannot be measured with sufficient reliability.

Note: This definition is given in FRS 12. Your own answer, of course, can give a definition in your own words, but check that you have covered all the necessary points..

(iii)   The following table summarises the accounting treatment required by FRS 12 for material contingencies:

Degree of probability	Contingent loss	Contingent gain
Virtually certain	Recognise in financial statements	Recognise in financial statements
Probable	Recognise in financial statements	Disclose by note in financial statements
Possible	Disclose by note in financial statements	No disclosure
Remote	No disclosure	No disclosure

(iv) The date the financial statements are approved by the board of directors.

(b) (i) A provision of £30,000 is required for the legal costs which will be incurred in any case, because this is an action relating to a condition which existed at the balance sheet date. SSAP 17 requires this.

As the outcome of the case is 70%, this will be categorised as 'possible' rather than 'probable', the damages and costs to be incurred if the case is lost would be required by FRS 12 to be disclosed by note.

Journal entry:

	£	£
Profit and loss account	30,000	
Provision for legal costs		30,000

Provision for legal costs in relation to action brought by customer.

Disclosure note

A customer has brought an action against the company claiming damages for alleged supply of faulty components. Your company will vigorously defend the action and expects to succeed. If the customer's action is successful, damages and costs could amount to £180,000. A provision of £30,000 has been made to cover costs which will be incurred whether the action is successful or not.

(ii) This is an event requiring adjustment and the provision for doubtful debts should be reduced by £84,000 in the financial statements.

	£	£
Provision for doubtful debts	84,000	
Profit and loss account		84,000

Reduction in provision for doubtful debts following payment after the balance sheet date.

FINANCIAL STATEMENTS

OBJECTIVES OF FINANCIAL STATEMENTS AND USERS OF FINANCIAL STATEMENTS

37 FRS 3 AND USERS

Key answer tips

Choose five user groups and explain why they need information about the company. Each group is only worth two marks, so do not spend too long on any one user group.

In part (b), remember to explain how the provisions of FRS (regarding layout) benefit the users.

(a) **Five from:**

(i) Investors, as the providers of risk capital to the enterprise (and their advisers), are interested in information that helps them to assess the performance of management. They are also concerned with the risk inherent in, and return provided by, their investments, and need information that helps them to assess the ability of the enterprise to pay dividends, and to determine whether they should buy, hold or sell their investments.

(ii) Employees: Employees and their representative groups are interested in information about the stability and profitability of their employers. They are also interested in information that enables them to assess the ability of the enterprise to provide remuneration, employment opportunities and retirement benefits.

(iii) Lenders: Lenders are interested in information that enables them to determine whether their loans will be repaid and the interest attaching to them paid, when due.

(iv) Suppliers and other creditors: Suppliers and other creditors are interested in information that enables them to decide whether to sell to the enterprise and to assess the likelihood that amounts owing to them will be paid when due. Trade creditors are likely to be interested in an enterprise over a shorter period than lenders unless they are dependent upon the continuation of the enterprise as a major customer.

(v) Customers: Customers have an interest in information about the continuance of an enterprise, especially when they have a long term involvement with or are dependent on the enterprise.

(vi) Government and their agencies: Governments and their agencies are interested in the allocation of resources and therefore the activities of enterprises. They also require information in order to regulate the activities of enterprises, assess taxation and provide a basis for national statistics.

(vii) The public: Enterprises affect members of the public in a variety of ways. For example, enterprises may make a substantial contribution to a local economy by providing employment and using local suppliers. Financial statements may assist the public by providing information about the trends and recent developments in the prosperity of the enterprise and the range of its activities.

Other answers would be considered on their merits.

Key answer tips

You were asked why each user group needed information, not what information they required.

Make sure that you explain how the requirements of FRS 3 benefit users as well as what those requirements are.

(b) **FRS 3 Reporting Financial Performance**

(i) **Profit and loss account**

In the profit and loss account, FRS 3 requires an analysis of figures, down to profit before interest and tax, into continuing operations, new acquisitions and discontinued operations. This assists users to compare current performance with the previous year and to forecast future performance more accurately.

Exceptional and extraordinary items are clearly defined, with three 'super exceptional' items to be disclosed on the face of the profit and loss account. This makes it more difficult for directors to manipulate the reported profit figures.

The method of calculating the gain arising on the disposal of a revalued fixed asset is defined.

(ii) **Statement of recognised gains and losses**

FRS 3 includes a requirement for a statement of recognised gains and losses. This shows all gains and losses during the year, including the profit as shown by the profit and loss account and gains and losses arising on revaluation. This is convenient for users as it brings together all information relating to gains and losses.

(iii) **Reconciliation of movements in shareholders' funds**

This statement gives details of movements in share capital and reserves during the year. Although this information can be picked up from the balance sheet it is useful to have it summarised.

(iv) **Note of historical cost profits and losses**

The disclosure of what the profit or loss would have been if strict historical cost accounting had been applied may be helpful to some users who consider such results assist comparison between companies.

SOLE TRADERS AND INCOMPLETE RECORDS

38 ALTESE

(a)

	£
Opening capital	128,000
New capital introduced	50,000
	178,000
less: Drawings	48,000
	130,000
Closing capital	184,000
Profit is therefore	54,000

(b)

Creditors

	£		£
Payments to suppliers	888,400	Balance brought forward	130,400
Discounts received	11,200	Drawings: goods taken by Senji	1,000
Balance carried forward	171,250	Refunds from suppliers	2,400
		Purchases (balancing figure)	**937,050**
	1,070,850		1,070,850

(c)

	£	£
Cost of sales:		
Opening stock		243,000
Purchases	595,400	
less: Returns	41,200	554,200
		797,200
less: Closing stock		261,700
Cost of sales		535,500
Gross profit: 33.33% of sales = 50% of cost		267,750
Sales		803,250

39   GOSHAWK

Key answer tips

Part (a) is a fairly straightforward incomplete records question. Ensure that you adjust the sales receipts figure for opening and closing balances and other items to arrive at sales. Tick off the items in the question as you deal with them in the trading, profit and loss account.

Part (b) requires you to demonstrate familiarity with gross profit mark-ups in a somewhat unfamiliar context.

(a)   **Goshawk**

Trading and profit and loss account for the year ended 31 March 20X2

	£	£
Sales revenue (W1)		300,000
Opening stock	28,500	
Purchases (W2)	220,830	
	249,330	
Less: Closing stock	37,100	
Cost of sales		212,230
Gross profit		87,770
Less: Expenses		
Staff wages	25,870	
Insurance (800 + 2,000 − 1,000)	1,800	
Miscellaneous expenses (W3)	3,780	
Amortisation of lease (£200,000/40 years)	5,000	
Depreciation of shop fittings (W4)	5,460	
Loan interest (10% of £100,000)	10,000	
		51,910
Net profit		35,860

Goshawk

Balance sheet as at 31 March 20X2

	Cost £	Accumulated depreciation £	Net book value £
Fixed assets			
Leasehold shop	200,000	10,000	190,000
Shop fittings	36,400	9,660	26,740
	236,400	19,660	216,740
Current assets			
Stock		37,100	
Trade debtors		1,460	
Prepayment		1,000	
Cash at bank (W5)		16,940	
		56,500	

Less: Current liabilities			
Trade creditors	48,000		
Accruals (2,100 + 5,000 loan interest)	7,100		
		55,100	
			1,400
			218,140
Less: Loan			100,000
			118,140
Capital			
As at 1 April 20X1			112,280
Add: profit for year to date			35,860
			148,140
Less: drawings			30,000
			118,140

Workings

(W1)
Sales total account

	£		£
Opening debtors	1,380	Cash received	300,880
		(299,580 + 1,300)	
Refunds to customers	960	Closing debtors	1,460
Sales (balancing figure)	300,000		
	———		———
	302,340		302,340

(W2)
Purchases total account

	£		£
Cash paid	211,830	Opening creditors	39,000
Closing creditors	48,000	Purchases	220,830
		(balancing figure)	
	———		———
	259,830		259,830

(W3)

Miscellaneous shop expenses	£
Payments in year	2,180
Cash paid out of sales revenue	1,300
Accrued expenses at year end	2,100
	5,580
Less: accrued expenses at start of year	1,800
Shop expenses for the year	3,780

(W4) **Depreciation of shop fittings**

Depreciation rate for shop fittings = £4,200/£28,000 × 100% = 15% per year.

Depreciation charge for the year = 15% × (£28,000 + £8,400) = £5,460.

(W5) Closing bank balance

	£
Balance at 31 March 20X1	3,600
Receipts during year	299,580
	303,180
Less: Payments by cheque (total)	286,240
Closing balance	£16,940

(b) Possible loss through theft of stock

Sales	Mark-up on cost		Gross profit
£			£
14,000	40%	(× 40/140)	4,000
34,000	25%	(× 25/125)	6,800
252,000	50%	(× 50/150)	84,000
300,000		Theoretical gross profit	94,800
		Actual gross profit	87,770
		Possible cost of stock stolen	7,030

40 CYGNUS

Key answer tips

To avoid running out of time on part a) of the question keep workings brief, but set them out neatly so that key information does not get lost. Remember to use total accounts to derive missing figures. Finally, do NOT neglect part b) of the question – four fairly straightforward marks are available.

(a) **Capital as at 1 February 20X0**

	£	£
Assets		
Shop equipment		7,900
Stock		146,400
Trade debtors		14,400
Rent in advance		1,000
Cash in hand		800
		170,500
Less: Liabilities		
Loan – Draco	24,000	
Trade creditors	12,100	
Accrued expenses	2,300	
Bank overdraft	2,600	41,000
Opening capital		129,500

(b) **Trading and profit and loss account for the year ended 31 January 20X1**

	Reference to workings	£	£
Sales revenue	2		202,400
Less: Cost of sales			
Opening stock		146,400	
Purchases	1	83,500	
		229,900	

Less: Closing stock		128,700	
			101,200
Gross profit			101,200
Less: Expenses	3		
Rent (8,250 + 1,000 – 1,500)		7,750	
Sundry expenses (18,600 – 2,100 + 3,300)	4	19,800	
Depreciation		1,490	
Profit on sale of equipment (300 – 200)	5	(100)	
Interest on loan (2,400 – 200 + 100)		2,300	
Net profit			31,240
			69,960

Balance sheet as at 31 January 20X1

	£	£
Fixed assets		
Cost (W4)	15,800	
Accumulated depreciation (6,900 – 600 + 1,490) (W4)	7,790	
		8,010
Current assets		
Stock	128,700	
Trade debtors	15,700	
Prepayment: rent in advance (W3)	1,500	
Cash at bank	4,850	
Cash in hand	900	
		151,650
		159,660
Capital		
As at 1 February 20X0 (see (a))	129,500	
Profit for year to date (see (b))	69,960	
	199,460	
Less: Drawings (W6)	69,400	
As at 31 January 20X1		130,060
Non-current liabilities		
Loan – Draco		12,000
Current liabilities		
Trade creditors	14,200	
Accrued expenses (3,300 + 100)	3,400	
		17,600
		159,660

Workings

(W1) *Calculation of purchases*

Purchases total account

	£		£
Cash paid for purchases	81,400	Opening balance	12,100
Closing balance	14,200	Purchases (balancing figure)	83,500
	95,600		95,600

(W2) *Calculation of sales revenue*

Sales prices are fixed by doubling cost – sales revenue is therefore double the cost of sales = £101,200 × 2 = £202,400.

(W3) *Calculation of rent expense*

Rent went up in July 20X0 from £500 each month to £750 each month. The prepayment at the year end is for two months of rent (February and March). At 31 January 20X1 the prepayment is therefore 2 × £750 = £1,500. The rent expense for the year is £8,250 rent paid + £1,000 opening prepayment - £1,500 closing prepayment = £7,750.

(W4) *Fixed assets and depreciation*

	Cost	Accumulated depreciation
	£	£
As at 1 February 20X0	14,800	6,900
Less: Items sold	(800)	(600)
	14,000	6,300
Additions	1,800	
	15,800	
Depreciation for year		
£14,000 at 10%		1,400
£1,800 at 10% for six months		90
As at 31 January 20X1	15,800	7,790

(W5) *Interest*

Accrued interest at the year end = 1 month of interest = 1/12 × 10% × £12,000 = £100. Interest expense for the year = Interest paid £2,400 – opening accrual £200 + closing accrual £100 = £2,300.

(W6) *Calculation of drawings*

A figure for cash from customers is needed to establish how much cash has been taken in drawings.

Sales total account

	£		£
Opening balance	14,400	Cash for sales (balancing figure)	201,100
Sales (W2)	202,400	Closing balance	15,700
	216,800		216,800

Cash summary

	£		£
Opening balance	800	Banked	131,600
Cash from customers (see above)	201,100	Drawings (balancing figure)	69,400
		Closing balance	900
	201,900		201,900

(b) (i) Use of gross profit percentage on sales to compute a missing figure in the trading account.

This technique will almost certainly create inaccuracies because of the near impossibility in most cases of obtaining an accurate gross profit percentage. As a result the missing figure (purchases for example) will be imprecise and the profit understated or overstated.

(ii) Estimating proprietor's drawings as a balancing figure in the summary of cash received and paid.

More cash than the balancing amount could have been taken as drawings, thus causing the sales and profit figures to be too low.

41   HALBERD

Key answer tips

Allow plenty of space for setting out the key statements so that figures can be slotted in as they become available. The calculations of cash sales and credit sales in workings 1 and 2 are important. you also need to take care with the calculation of some expense items, where there a e prepayments or accruals at the beginning and end of the year.

Halberd
Trading and profit and loss account for the year ended 30 June 20X7

	£	£
Sales (W1)		154,610
Less: Cost of sales		
Opening stock	680	
Purchases (W3)	81,070	
	81,750	
Closing stock	810	
		80,940
Gross profit		**73,670**
Expenses		
Staff wages	21,400	
Rent and rates (8,600 + 850 − 1,000)	8,450	
Insurance (1,400 + 300 − 350)	1,350	
Van expenses (3,270 − 320)	2,950	
Miscellaneous expenses (3,600 + 200 − 120)	3,680	
Depreciation:		
Refrigeration equipment (10% of 8,400)	840	
Shop fittings (15% of (1,630 + 1,570))	480	
Van (25% of 9,200)	2,300	
Increase in provision for doubtful debts (1,860 − 0)	1,860	
Interest on loan (10% × 10,000 × 6/12)	500	
		43,810
Net profit for year to date		29,860

Halberd
Balance sheet as at 30 June 20X7

	Cost £	Aggregate depreciation £	Net book value £
Fixed assets			
Refrigeration equipment	8,400	3,360	5,040
Shop fittings	5,290	2,570	2,720
Van	9,200	6,900	2,300
	22,890	12,830	10,060
Current assets			
Stock		810	
Trade debtors	6,190		
Less: Provision for doubtful debts	1,860		
		4,330	
Prepayments (350 + 1,000)		1,350	
Cash at bank		8,370	
Cash in hand		150	
		15,010	
Less: Current liabilities			
Accrued sundry expenses	200		
Loan interest	500		
		700	
Net current assets			14,310
			24,370
Loan			10,000
			14,370
Capital account:			
As at 1.7.X6			21,110
Profit for year to date			29,860
			50,970
Less: Drawings (20,600 + 15,600 + 400)			36,600
			14,370

Workings

	£
(W1) *Sales*	
Cash sales banked	108,600
Taken for drawings	15,600
Credit sales (see Working 2)	30,360
Increase in cash balance (150 – 100)	50
Total sales	154,610

(W2) *Credit sales*

Sales ledger total account

	£		£
Opening debtors	4,270	Cash from customers	28,440
Credit sales (balancing figure)	30,360	Closing debtors	6,190
	34,630		34,630

(W3)

	£
Purchases – per bank summary	81,470
Less: Personal consumption	400
	81,070

42 ERNIE

Key answer tips

Here, there are important workings needed for total sales, total purchases and opening capital. Again, you also need to be careful computing various expenses, where there are prepayments or accruals at the start and end of the year.

Ernie
Trading and profit and loss account for the year ended 30 June 20X8

		£	£
Sales (W1)			204,490
less: Cost of sales			
Opening stock (W2)		14,160	
Purchases		84,620	
		98,780	
less: Closing stock		12,170	
			(86,610)
Gross profit			117,880
Profit on disposal of van	(3,000 – net book value 2,500)		500
			118,380
Wages		68,200	
Salaries (wife)		5,000	
Rent	$(3,600 + 750 - 900)$	3,450	
Telephone	$(860 + 240 - 210)$	890	
Electricity	$(890 + 220 - 180)$	930	
Insurance	$(700 + 800)$	1,500	
Miscellaneous expenses	(1,280 + 490 accrual)	1,770	
Bad debts		1,280	
Depreciation: plant	$(25\% \times (6,800 + 8,400))$	3,800	
Depreciation: motor van	$(6/12 \times 25\% \times 12,800)$	1,600	
Loan interest	$(10\% \text{ of } 10,000 \times 3/12)$	250	
			(88,670)
Net profit for year to date			29,710

Ernie
Balance sheet as at 30 June 20X8

	Cost	Aggregate depreciation	Net book value
	£	£	£
Fixed assets			
Plant and equipment	21,000	9,600	11,400
Motor vans	12,800	1,600	11,200
	33,800	11,200	22,600
Current assets			
Stock		12,170	
Debtors		9,580	
Prepayments (900 + 800)		1,700	
Cash in hand		890	
		24,340	
Less:			
Current liabilities			
Creditors: Trade	4,090		
Creditors: Sundry	6,200		
(5,000 + 240 + 220 + 490 + 250 loan)			
Overdraft	2,100	12,390	
			11,950
			34,550
Loan			10,000
			24,550
Capital at 30 June 20X7 (W3)			32,640
add: Net profit for year to date			29,710
			62,350
less: Drawings (8,000 + 29,800)			37,800
Capital at 30 June 20X8			24,550

Workings

(W1) *Sales*

Sales total account

	£		£
Opening debtors	9,490	Received from customers:	
		Cash	52,640
		Bank	150,880
Refund to customer	400	Bad debts	1,280
Sales (balancing figure)	204,490	Closing debtors	9,580
		(10,860 – 1,280)	
	214,380		214,380

> *Tutorial note:* The bad debt written off is an expense, not a reduction in sales. It must therefore be included in the calculation of total sales.

(W2) *Purchases*

Purchases total account

	£		£
Paid to suppliers	83,990	Opening creditors	3,460
Closing creditors	4,090	Purchases (balancing figure)	84,620
	88,080		88,080

(W3) **Capital at 30 June 20X7**

	£	£
Assets		
Plant and equipment (12,600 – 5,800)		6,800
Motor van (9,000 – 6,500)		2,500
Stock of materials		14,160
Debtors		9,490
Rent in advance		750
Insurance in advance		700
Cash at bank		1,860
Cash in hand		230
		36,490
Less: Liabilities		
Creditors for supplies	3,460	
Telephone	210	
Electricity	180	3,850
		32,640

PARTNERSHIP ACCOUNTS

43   ALAMUTE AND BRADOR

(a)

Alamute and Brador
Trading and Profit and Loss Account for the year ended 31 March 20X3

	£	£
Sales revenue		448,700
Cost of sales:		
Opening stock	15,600	
Purchases	184,600	
	200,200	
less: Closing stock	21,400	
Cost of sales		(178,800)
Gross profit		269,900
Less: Expenses:		
Salaries	88,000	
Rent (30,000 + 110% of 10,000)	41,000	
Insurance (4,000 – 1,500 prepayment)	2,500	
Sundry expenses	39,400	
Depreciation (note 1)	7,100	
Bad and doubtful debts (note 2)	1,900	
		(179,900)
Net profit		90,000

Appropriation account	*Alamute* £	*Brador* £	*Total* £
Net profit			90,000
Interest on capital (5%)	2,500	2,500	(5,000)
			85,000
Share of residual profit (60:40)	51,000	34,000	(85,000)
Total profit share	53,500	36,500	-

Notes:

1   Net book value of office equipment = £(48,300 – 12,800) = £35,500

     Depreciation = 20% of £35,500 = £7,100.

2

	£
Year-end provision for doubtful debts	3,300
(5% of £(68,400 – 2,400))	
Provision at start of year	3,800
Reduction in provision	(500)
Bad debts written off	2,400
Charge for bad and doubtful debts	1,900

(b)

Alamute Current Account

	£		£
Drawings	48,400	Opening balance c/d	3,800
Closing balance c/d	8,900	Share of profit	53,500
	57,300		57,300

Brador Current Account

	£		£
Opening balance b/d	2,600	Share of profit	36,500
Drawings	36,900	Closing balance c/d	3,000
	39,500		39,500

44   WEASEL AND STOAT

Key answer tips

Note that the appropriation of profit is dealt with through the partners' current accounts.

Profit and loss appropriation account
year ended 31 December 20X0

	Weasel £	*Stoat* £	*Total* £
Net profit for year			316,500
Salaries	20,000	15,000	(35,000)
Interest on capital	18,000	13,500	(31,500)
Share of balance of profit 60:40	150,000	100,000	(250,000)
	188,000	128,500	–

Note: Interest on capital for Stoat = 10% of 12,000 + (10% of 60,000 × 3/12) = £13,500.

Capital accounts

	Weasel	Stoat		Weasel	Stoat
	£	£		£	£
20X0			20X0		
31 Dec Balance c/f	180,000	180,000	1 Jan Balance b/f	180,000	120,000
			30 Sep Cash		60,000
	180,000	180,000		180,000	180,000

Current accounts

	Weasel	Stoat			Weasel	Stoat
	£	£			£	£
20X0			20X0			
1 Jan Balance b/f		2,700	1 Jan	Balance b/f	3,000	
Drawings	186,000	129,000	31 Dec	Profit shares	188,000	128,500
31 Dec Balance c/f	5,000			Balance c/f		3,200
	191,000	131,700			191,000	131,700
20X1			20X1			
I Jan Balance b/f		3,200	1 Jan	Balance b/f	5,000	

LIMITED COMPANY ACCOUNTS

45 CRONOS LIMITED

Cronos Limited

Profit and Loss account for the year ended 30 September 20X2

	£	£
Sales		3,210,000
Cost of sales (W1)		(1,823,100)
Gross profit		1,386,900
Distribution costs (W2)	(188,500)	
Administrative expenses (W3)	(944,680)	(1,133,180)
Operating profit		253,720
Interest payable (30,000 + 30,000)		(60,000)
Profit for the financial year		193,720

Working 1

	£	£
Opening stock		186,400
Purchases		1,748,200
Carriage inwards		38,100
Wages and salaries	694,200	
	5,800	
10% charged to cost of sales	700,000	70,000
		2,042,700
Closing stock		(219,600)
Cost of sales		1,823,100

Working 2

		£
Carriage outwards (47,250 + 1,250)		48,500
Wages and salaries	694,200	
	5,800	
20% of wages and salaries	700,000	140,000
Distribution costs		188,500

Working 3

		£
Wages and salaries	694,200	
	5,800	
70% of wages and salaries	700,000	490,000
Loss on sale		600
Sundry administrative expenses		
(381,000 + 13,600 − 4,900)		389,700
Bad and doubtful debts		
(14,680 + 8,000 − 2,700)		19,980
Depreciation of office equipment		
20% × (214,000 − 40,000 + 48,000)		44,400
Administrative expenses		944,680

46 RESERVES

(a) (i) Reserves are balances in a company's balance sheet forming part of the equity interest and representing surpluses or gains, whether realised or not.

 (ii) **Share premium account**

 The surplus arising when shares are issued at a price in excess of their par value.

 Revaluation reserve

 The unrealised gain when the amount at which fixed assets are carried is increased above cost.

 (Other reserves could be described.)

(b) A **bonus issue** is the conversion of reserves into share capital, with new shares being issued to existing members in proportion to their shareholdings, without any consideration being given by the shareholders.

 A **rights issue** is also an issue of new shares to existing members in proportion to their shareholdings, but with payment being made by the shareholders for the shares allotted to them.

 The fundamental difference between them is that a rights issue raises funds for the company whereas a bonus issue does not.

47 DRAFT FINANCIAL STATEMENTS

(a) SSAP 17 *Post Balance Sheet Events* classifies this type of event as non-adjusting, because it arose as a result of a condition that did not exist at the balance sheet date. Consequently, no change to the figures in the financial statements is required, but there should be a note to ensure that the financial statements are not misleading. The note should state the amount of the loss and the extent of the insurance cover.

(b) A provision should be made for the estimated amount of the liabilities under warranties, as required by FRS 12 *Provisions, Contingent Liabilities and Contingent Assets*. The provision will appear as a liability in the balance sheet and the operating profit will be reduced by the amount of the provision.

(c)   This is an adjusting event according to SSAP 17 *Post Balance Sheet Events*, because the stock was (presumably) in its deteriorated condition as at the balance sheet date. The closing stock should be reduced by £40,000 in the balance sheet and in cost of sales, thus reducing operating profit by this amount, unless it could be shown that the deterioration had taken place after the balance sheet date.

(d)   The goods on sale or return have to be treated as trading stock at 30 September 20X2, applying generally accepted accounting principles. The effect on the profit and loss account and balance sheet will be:

(i)   Sales and trade debtors both reduced by £100,000.

(ii)   Closing stock increased by £80,000.

The combined effect of the two adjustments is to reduce current assets and profit by £20,000.

48   ALPACA LIMITED

Balance Sheet as at 30 April 20X2

	£	£	£
Fixed assets: Cost			1,000,000
Accumulated depreciation			330,000
			670,000
Current assets:			
Stocks		450,000	
Debtors		670,000	
Cash at bank		114,000	
		1,234,000	
less: Creditors: amounts falling due within one year:			
Trade creditors	180,000		
Interest accrued	10,000		
		190,000	
			1,044,000
			1,714,000
less: creditors: amounts falling due after more than one year:			
10% Debentures			200,000
			1,514,000
Capital and reserves			
Issued capital			500,000
Share premium			50,000
Profit and loss account (working)			964,000
			1,514,000

Working for profit and loss account balance

	£	£
Balance at 30 April 20X1		818,000
Sales revenue		4,006,000
Purchases	2,120,000	
Expenses	1,640,000	
Opening stocks	410,000	
Closing stocks		450,000
Interest payable	20,000	
Depreciation	100,000	
Bad debts written off	20,000	
	4,310,000	5,274,000
		4,310,000
Balance at 30 April 20X2		964,000

ACCA marking scheme		
	Available	*Max.*
Accumulated depreciation	1	
Debtors	1	
Issued capital	1	
Share premium	1	
Interest accrued	$\frac{1}{5}$	
Layout and style	$\frac{2}{7}$	7
Profit and loss account		
½ mark per item:	$\underline{4\frac{1}{2}}$	$\underline{4}$
Total	$11\frac{1}{2}$	11

49   ATOK LIMITED

Key answer tips

When adjusting the expenses in the profit and loss account for accruals and prepayments, remember to follow the adjustments through into the balance sheet.

(a)

Profit and loss account for the year ended 30 June 20X9

	£000
Sales revenue (14,800 – 24(sale or return items))	14,776
Cost of sales (W1)	10,280
Gross profit	4,496
Distribution costs	(1,422)
(1,080 + 190 – 120 + 272 depreciation)	
Administrative expenses	(1,742)
(1,460 + 70 – 60 + 272 depreciation)	
Operating profit	1,332
Interest payable (3/12 of 10% × 2,000)	(50)
Profit for the financial year	1,282
Proposed dividend (28 million shares × 2.5 pence)	700
Retained profit	582

Balance sheet as at 30 June 20X9

	£000	£000
Fixed assets		
Tangible assets (W3)		
Land and buildings		17,710
Plant and equipment		7,760
		25,470
Current assets		
Stock (W1)	1,566	
Debtors (4,120 – 24 sale or return items + 180 prepayments)	4,276	
Cash at bank	160	
	6,002	

Less: Creditors: amounts falling due within one year

Trade creditors	(2,240)
Accruals	(310)
(260 expenses + 50 accrued interest)	
Dividend payable	(700)

Net current assets	2,752
Total assets less current liabilities	28,222
Creditors: amounts falling due after more than one year	
10% debentures 20Y8	(2,000)
	26,222

Capital and reserves	
Called up share capital	14,000
Share premium account	4,000
Revaluation reserve (3,000 + 1,500)	4,500
Profit and loss account (3,140 + 582)	3,722
	26,222

(b)   **Statement of movements in reserves**

Year ended 30 June 20X9

	Share premium account	Revaluation reserve	Profit and loss account	Total
	£000	£000	£000	£000
As at 1 July 20X8	2,000	3,000	3,140	8,140
Premium on issue of shares	2,000			2,000
Transfer from profit and loss account of the year			582	582
Surplus on revaluation		1,500		1,500
As at 30 June 20X9	4,000	4,500	3,722	12,222

Workings

(W1)

	£000	£000
Opening stock		1,390
Purchases		8,280
		9,670
Less: Closing stock		
As originally taken	1,560	
Reduction for adjustment (i) to net realisable value	(10)	
Increase for adjustment (ii)	16	
		(1,566)
		8,104
Depreciation in cost of sales (W2)		2,176
Cost of sales		**10,280**

(W2)

	£'000
Depreciation	
Buildings (2% of 8,000)	160
Plant and equipment (20% of 12,800)	2,560
	2,720
Cost of sales (80%)	2,176
Distribution costs (10%)	272
Administrative expenses (10%)	272
	2,720

(W3)

Fixed assets	Land	Buildings	Plant and equipment	Total
	£000	£000	£000	£000
As in the trial balance	10,500	8,000	12,800	31,300
Revaluation	1,500			1,500
	12,000			32,800
Less: depreciation: as at 1 July 20X8		(2,130)	(2,480)	(4,610)
Less: depreciation: charges for year		(160)	(2,560)	(2,720)
	12,000	5,710	7,760	25,470

50   MOORFOOT

Key answer tips

This is a fairly straightforward question calling for the preparation of financial statements for publication.

Make sure that you use the required format (i.e. comply with The Companies Act 1985).

Moorfoot Limited
Profit and loss account for the year ended 30 June 20X1

	£000
Sales revenue (13,600 + 7)	13,607
Cost of sales (W1)	(7,988)
Gross profit	5,619
Distribution costs (W1)	(1,948)
Administrative expenses (W1)	(2,156)
Operating profit	1,515
Interest payable (10% × 1,000)	(100)
Profit for the financial year	1,415
Dividends:	
Interim paid	(360)
Final proposed (48 million shares × 10p)	(480)
Retained profit for the financial year	575

Moorfoot Limited
Balance sheet as at 30 June 20X1

	£000	£000	£000
Fixed assets			
Tangible assets (W2)			
Land			1,510
Buildings			7,114
Warehouse and office equipment			1,240
Motor vehicles			640
			10,504
Current assets			
Stock		1,660	
Trade debtors (810 + 7 – 30 provision for doubtful debts – 6 bad debt)		781	
Prepayments		130	
Cash		140	
		2,711	
Creditors, amounts falling due within one year			
Trade creditors (820 + 18)	838*		
Accruals	360*		
Proposed dividend	480		
		1,678	
			1,033
Total assets less current liabilities			11,537
Creditors, amounts falling due after more than one year			
Debenture loan			(1,000)
			10,537
Capital and reserves			
Called up share capital			1,200
Share premium account			2,470
Profit and loss account (6,292 + 575)			6,867
			10,537

*Alternatively these items may be shown as:

Trade creditors	820
Accruals (360 + 18)	378

Workings

(W1) **Profit and loss account headings**

	Cost of sales £000	Distribution costs £000	Administrative expenses £000
Purchases (8,100 + 18)	8,118		
Stock 1 July 20X0	1,530		
Distribution costs (1,460 + 120 − 60)		1,520	
Administrative expenses (1,590 + 190 − 70)			1,710
Bad debts written off			6
Increase in provision for doubtful debts (30 − 18)			12
Depreciation			
Buildings 2% × 8,300		83	83
Equipment 15% × 1800		135	135
Vehicles 25% × 1,680		210	210
Stock 30 June 20X1	(1,660)		
	7,988	1,948	2,156

(W2) **Tangible assets**

	Land £000	Buildings £000	Warehouse and office equipment £000	Motor vehicles £000
Per trial balance				
Cost	1,510	8,300	1,800	1,680
Accumulated depreciation b/f	–	(1,020)	(290)	(620)
Depreciation for year	–	(166)	(270)	(420)
Net book value at year end	1,510	7,114	1,240	640

51 PRIDE

Balance sheet as at 31 March 20X1

	Cost £000	Accumulated depreciation £000	Net book value £000
Fixed assets			
Land	210		210
Buildings	200	124	76
(accum dep'n = 120 + 2% of 200)			
Plant and equipment (W1)	300	136	164
	710	260	450
Current assets			
Stock		180	
Debtors (146 − 12 provision)		134	
Prepayments		8	
Cash		50	

Total assets		372	
Less: Creditors, amounts falling due within 12 months:			
Creditors	(94)		
Accruals	(4)	(98)	
Net current assets			274
			724
Less: 10% debentures			(100)
			624
Issued share capital:			
700,000 ordinary shares of 50p each			350
Share premium account			240
(180 + (200 × 30p))			
Profit and loss account			34
			624

(W1)

	Cost	Accumulated depreciation
	£000	£000
Plant and equipment		
At 1 April 20X0	318	88
Less: disposal	18	12
	300	76
Depreciation for year		60
		136

ACCA marking scheme	
	Marks
Land	0.5
Buildings	1
Plant and equipment	2
Stock	0.5
Debtors	1
Prepayments	0.5
Cash	0.5
Creditors	0.5
Accruals	0.5
10% debentures	0.5
Share capital	1
Share premium	1
Profit and loss account	0.5
Total	10

52 TAFFORD LIMITED

Tafford Limited
Profit and loss account for the year ended 30 September 20X2

	£000
Turnover	41,600
Cost of sales (W1)	(20,000)
Gross profit	21,600
Distribution costs (W1)	(6,285)
Administrative expenses (W1)	(4,885)
Operating profit	10,430
Interest payable	1,000
Profit on ordinary activities before tax	9,430
Taxation	3,000
Profit for the financial year	6,430

Working

(W1)

	Cost of sales £000	Distribution costs £000	Administrative expenses £000
Opening stock	13,000		
Purchases	22,600		
Distribution costs		6,000	
Administrative expenses			5,000
Bad debts			600
Reduction in provision for doubtful debts			(800)
Depreciation:			
Warehouse machinery		300	
Motor vehicles (see note 1)		125	125
Profit on sale of vehicles (see note 2)		(40)	
Prepayments		(200)	(100)
Accruals		100	60
Closing stock	(15,600)		
	20,000	6,285	4,885

Note 1: Depreciation of motor vehicles = 25% of (1,180 – 180) = 250, divided equally between distribution costs and administrative expenses.

Note 2: The profit on the disposal of the motor vehicles = proceeds of 100 minus net book value of 60.

ACCA marking scheme		
	Marks	*Max.*
Cost of sales	1½	
Distribution costs	3	
Administrative expenses	3	
Interest	1	
Tax	1	
Layout	2	
Total	11½	10

53   HARMONICA

Key answer tips

Pay attention to the requirement in the question to present financial statements in a form suitable for publication.

(a)

Harmonica Limited
Profit and Loss Account for the year ended 31 December 20X5

	£000
Sales	28,600
Cost of sales (W1)	(17,450)
Gross profit	11,150
Distribution costs (W1)	(5,060)
Administrative expenses (W1)	(4,800)
Profit on ordinary activities before interest	1,290
Interest paid (10% × 1,000)	(100)
Profit for year	1,190
Dividends: Interim paid	(40)
Final proposed	(180)
Retained profit for the financial year	970

Harmonica Limited Balance Sheet as at 31 December 20X5

	£000	£000
Fixed assets – Cost (W2)		17,000
Accumulated depreciation (W2)		(4,700)
		12,300
Current assets		
Stock	5,000	
Debtors	6,370	
(6,900 – 400 bad debts – 130 provision)		
Prepayments (70 + 40)	110	
	11,480	
Creditors: amounts falling due within one year		
Trade creditors	(3,800)	
Overdraft at bank	(2,080)	
Accruals (140 + 90)	(230)	
Proposed dividend	(180)	
(4,500,000 shares × 4 pence)		
	(6,290)	
Net current assets		5,190

Total assets less current liabilities	17,490
Creditors: amounts falling due after more than one year	
10% debentures	(1,000)
	16,490
Called up share capital (4,000 + 500)	4,500
Share premium account (1,300 + 1,000)	2,300
Profit and loss account (8,720 + 970)	9,690
	16,490

Workings

(W1) **Expenses**

	Cost of sales £000	Distribution costs £000	Administration expenses £000
Purchases	18,000		
Opening stock	4,500		
Warehouse wages		850	
Salespersons' salaries and commission		1,850	
Administrative salaries			3,070
General administrative expenses			580
General distribution expenses		490	
Directors' remuneration		300	570
Depreciation		1,190	510
(Total 10% of (18,000 − 1,000))			
Profit on sale of fixed assets	(50)		
(150 − 100)			
Closing stock	(5,000)		
Accruals and prepayments (net)		90	140
Prepayments		(40)	(70)
Bad debts written off		400	
Reduction in bad debt provision		(70)	
(200 − 2% of 6,500)			
	17,450	5,060	4,800

(W2) **Fixed assets and accumulated depreciation**

	Fixed assets at cost £000	Accumulated depreciation £000
Per trial balance	18,000	3,900
Disposed of in the year	(1,000)	(900)
	17,000	3,000
Depreciation for year		1,700
Balance sheet amount	17,000	4,700

(b) (i) Authorised share capital is the maximum amount of share capital a company may issue, as stated in its memorandum of association (constitution).It may only be increased by a vote of the shareholders. The issued share capital is that part of the authorised capital which has actually been issued.

The expression 'called up' is the amount of the issued share capital for which payment has so far been demanded from the shareholders.

When shares are issued, the shareholders are usually required to pay the full amount due immediately, and the shares are 'fully called up' on issue. In other cases, the money due may be payable in instalments and the shares are 'partly called up' until the final payment is demanded.

(ii) A capital reserve is not available for distribution as dividend, while a revenue reserve is.

Examples:

Capital reserve:	Revaluation reserve
Revenue reserve:	Profit and loss account balance

(iii) A rights issue is an issue of shares to existing members, usually at a price somewhat below the current market price of the shares, to raise capital for the company. The new shares are offered to existing shareholders in proportion to the size of their shareholding.

A bonus issue is also an issue of shares to existing members, but without cost to them. A bonus issue is made by converting reserves into share capital. No cash is raised. The object is of a bonus issue is to increase the number of shares in issue and, if the shares are traded on a stock market, to reduce the market price per share.

54 ARBALEST

Key answer tips

A four column presentation is required for part (a). Set out the answer neatly using distinct columns. Rule lines if it helps to do so.

(a) (i) **Movements on reserves**

	Share premium	*Revaluation reserve*	*Retained earnings*	*Total*
	£000	£000	£000	£000
At 30.9.X6	400		4,060	4,460
Rights issue	1,000			1,000
Bonus issue	(1,400)		(600)	(2,000)
Revaluation of assets		500		500
Retained profit for year			370	370
At 30.9.X7	nil	500	3,830	4,330

Workings

(W1) Share premium increases on the rights issue by 2 million shares × 50 pence per share.

(W2) The bonus issue is of 4 million shares with a nominal value of £2,000,000. The share premium will be used up entirely, leaving £600,000 to be transferred from the profit and loss reserve account (retained earnings)

(ii) **Movements on fixed assets**

	Land £000	*Cost* Buildings £000	Plant and machinery £000	Total £000
At 30 September 20X6	2,000	1,500	2,800	6,300
Additions	600	2,400	1,600	4,600
Disposals			(1,000)	(1,000)
Revaluation	500			500
At 30 September 20X7	3,100	3,900	3,400	10,400
Depreciation				
At 30 September 20X6	nil	450	1,000	1,450
Charge for year	nil	46	220	266
Disposals			(800)	(800)
At 30 September 20X7	nil	496	420	916
Net book value				
30 September 20X7	3,100	3,404	2,980	9,484

Calculation of depreciation charges

	£000
Buildings:	
2% of 1,500,000	30
2% of 2,400,000 × 4/12	16
	46
Plant and machinery:	
10% of (2,800,000 – 1,000,000)	180
10% of 1,600,000 × 3/12	40
	220

(b) **Share premium account**

The distribution of a dividend implies a profit of some kind out of which the dividend is paid. No profit arises when an issue of shares is made at a premium. The premium is part of the capital of the company.

Revaluation reserve

A gain (profit) does arise when assets are revalued, but it is not realised into cash. It is a generally accepted accounting principle that gains can only be distributed when it is realised, because an unrealised profit can disappear if the value of the revalued asset subsequently drops.

55 HELIOS LIMITED

Helios Limited

Consolidated balance sheet as at 30 June 20X3

	£
Fixed assets:	
Goodwill	68,800
Tangible assets (280,000 + 490,000)	770,000
	838,800
Net current assets (130,000 + 260,000)	390,000
	1,228,800
Share capital	600,000
Share premium account	350,000
Profit and loss account	128,800
	1,078,800
Minority interest	150,000
	1,228,800

Workings

Cost of control

	£		£
Investment in Luna	700,000	Share capital 80%	320,000
		Share premium 80%	160,000
		Profit and loss account	
		80% pre-acq	48,000
		Balance – goodwill	172,000
	700,000		700,000
Balance	172,000	Amortisation 20% × 3 years	103,200
		Balance	68,800
	172,000		172,000

Minority interest

	£		£
Balance for CBS	150,000	Share capital 20%	80,000
		Share premium 20%	40,000
		Profit and loss account 20%	30,000
	150,000		150,000

Profit and loss account

	£		£
Cost of control		Helios	160,000
80% × £60,000	48,000	Luna	150,000
Minority interest			
20% × £150,000	30,000		
Cost of control			
Goodwill amortisation	103,200		
Balance for CBS	128,800		
	310,000		310,000

Alternative workings

	£
Assets in Luna acquired	
(80% of (400,000 + 200,000 + 60,000))	528,000
Cost of acquisition	700,000
Cost of goodwill	172,000

Annual amortisation of goodwill = £172,000/5 years = £34,400.

	£
Cost of goodwill	172,000
Amortisation to 30 June 20X3 (3 years × £34,400)	103,200
Net book value of goodwill	68,800

Minority interest = 20% of £750,000.

Profit and loss account reserve as at	£
30 June 20X3:	
Accumulated profits of Helios	160,000
80% of post-acquisition profits of Luna	
(80% × (150,000 − 60,000))	72,000
	232,000
Less: Amortised goodwill	(103,200)
Consolidated profit and loss account reserve	128,800

56 KOPPA

Key answer tips

The figures in this question are straightforward, requiring few workings. Presentation in a form suitable for publication is important; marks would be lost for incorrect or inadequate presentation.

Koppa Limited
Profit and loss account for the year ended 31 December 20X7

	£000
Sales	8,650
Cost of sales	(5,243)
Gross profit	3,407
Distribution costs	(489)
Administrative expenses	(1,614)
Operating profit	1,304
Interest payable	(120)
Profit for the financial year	1,184
Dividends (200 interim + 600 final)	(800)
Retained profit	384

Movements on reserves

	Share premium £000	Revaluation reserve £000	Profit and loss account £000	Total £000
As at 31 December 20X6	nil	nil	1,272	1,272
Share issue	500			500
Revaluation of land		200		200
Retained profit for year			384	384
As at 31 December 20X7	500	200	1,656	2,356

Koppa Limited
Balance sheet as at 31 December 20X7

	£000	£000	£000
Fixed assets:			
Intangible assets			
Development costs (W2)			219
Tangible assets			
Land and buildings (2,200 + 900 – 100 – 18)			2,982
Office equipment (260 – 60 – 40)			160
Motor vehicles (200 – 90 – 50)			60
			3,421
Current assets			
Stock		880	
Trade debtors		1,360	
Prepayments		40	
Cash		90	
		2,370	
Less:			
Creditors: amounts falling due within one year			
Trade creditors	820		
Accruals	15		
Proposed dividend (3 million shares × 20 pence)	600	1,435	
Net current assets			935
Total assets less current liabilities			4,356
Creditors: amounts falling due after more than one year			
12% debentures			(1,000)
			3,356
Capital and reserves			
Called up share capital			1,000
Share premium account			500
Revaluation reserve			200
Profit and loss account			1,656
			3,356

(W1) Profit and loss account expense headings

	Cost of sales £000	Distribution costs £000	Administrative expenses £000
Purchases	5,010		
Stock 1 January 20X7	990		
Distribution costs		460	
Administrative expenses			1,560
Depreciation:			
Buildings (2% of 900)			18
Office equipment (20% of (260 – 60))			40
Motor vehicles (total 25% of 200)		25	25
Research expenditure	103		
Amortisation of development expenditure	20		
Closing stock	(880)		
Prepayments			(40)
Accruals		4	11
	———	———	———
	5,243	489	1,614
	———	———	———

(W2) Capitalised development costs

	£000
As at 1 January 20X7	180
New expenditure in year	59
	———
	239
Amortised in the year	20
	———
	219
	———

GROUPS OF COMPANIES

57 HANSON

Key answer tips

The percentage holding of preference shares is not relevant in determining the extent of Hanson's control.

Hanson Ltd and its subsidiary
Group balance sheet as at 31 December 20X8

	£	£
Fixed assets		
Intangible (purchased goodwill) (W2)		5,450
Tangible		650,450
		———
		655,900
Current assets		
Stock	214,190	
Debtors	125,430	
Cash at bank	36,450	
	———	
	376,070	

Creditors: amounts falling due within one year	144,550	
Net current assets		231,520
Total assets less current liabilities		887,420
Minority interests (W4)		(103,175)
		784,245
Capital and reserves		
Called up share capital		350,000
Profit and loss account (W3)		434,245
		784,245

Workings

(W1) Shareholdings in Pickford Ltd

	Ordinary %	Preference %
Group	75	25
Minority	25	75
	100	100

(W2) Goodwill

	£	£
Cost of investment		109,150
Less: Share of net assets at acquisition		
Ordinary share capital	100,000	
Profit and loss account	11,000	
	111,000	
	$\times 75\%$	
		(83,250)
Preference share capital	60,000	
	$\times 25\%$	
		(15,000)
Goodwill		10,900
Amount amortised to date $\left(\frac{5}{10} \times 10,900\right)$		5,450
Amount remaining in the balance sheet		
		5,450

(W3) Consolidated reserves

	£
Hanson Ltd:	348,420
Pickford Ltd: 75% of (132,700 − 11,000)	91,275
Less: amortised goodwill	(5,450)
	434,245

(W4) Minority interest

Net assets of Pickford Ltd

	£	£
Ordinary share capital	100,000	
Profit and loss account	132,700	
	232,700	
	× 25%	
		58,175
Preference share capital	60,000	
	× 75%	
		45,000
		103,175

58   PIXIE AND DIXIE

Key answer tips

Note that the goodwill has been fully amortised in the ten year period since acquisition.

Pixie Ltd and its subsidiary
Group balance sheet as at 31 December 20X9

	£	£
Fixed assets		320,600
Current assets	156,500	
Creditors: amounts falling due within one year		
Sundry	102,100	
Net current assets		54,400
Total assets less current liabilities		375,000
Minority interests (W4)		(46,000)
		329,000
Capital and reserves		
Called up share capital		200,000
Profit and loss account (W3)		129,000
		329,000

Workings

(W1) Shareholdings in Dixie Ltd

	Ordinary	Preference
Group	75%	40%
Minority	25%	60%
	100%	100%

(W2) Goodwill

	£	£
Cost of investment		73,000
Less: Share of net assets at acquisition		
Ordinary share capital	50,000	
Profit and loss account	20,000	
	70,000	
	× 75%	
		(52,500)
Preference share capital	40,000	
	× 40%	
		(16,000)
Goodwill – completely amortised over the ten year period since acquisition		4,500

(W3) Consolidated reserves

	£
Pixie Ltd: profit and loss reserve	120,000
Dixie Ltd: 75% of (38,000 – 20,000)	13,500
Less: Goodwill amortised	(4,500)
	129,000

(W4) Minority interest

Net assets of Dixie Ltd

	£	£
Ordinary share capital	50,000	
Profit and loss account	38,000	
	88,000	
	× 25%	
		22,000
Preference share capital	40,000	
	× 60%	
		24,000
		46,000

59 EVON AND ORSET

Cost of control

	£		£
Shares in Orset	180,000	75% share capital	75,000
		75% pre-acquisition profits	45,000
		Profit and loss account:	
		Goodwill written off	
		3/5 × £60,000	36,000
		Balance to CBS	24,000
	180,000		180,000

Note: CBS = consolidated balance sheet.

Minority interest

	£		£
Balance to cbs	57,500	25% share capital	25,000
		25% profit and loss	32,500
	57,000		57,500

Profit and loss account

	£		£
Minority interest 25% × 130,000	32,500	Evon	240,000
Cost of control: 75% × 60,000	45,000	Orset	130,000
Cost of control: goodwill written off	36,000		
Balance to cbs	256,500		
	370,000		370,000

Evon Limited Group
Balance sheet as at 31 March 20X3

	£	£
Goodwill	60,000	
less: amortisation	36,000	24,000
Sundry net assets		790,000
		814,000
Share capital		
500,000 shares of £1 each		500,000
Profit and loss account		256,500
		756,500
Minority interest		57,500
		814,000

Tutorial note: The answer here presents the working in the form of T accounts, but you might prefer to do the calculations differently. For example, Evon acquired 75% of Orset when Orset's net assets were £160,000 (£100,000 + £60,000). The value of the assets acquired were 75% of £160,000 = £120,000. The cost of goodwill is £60,000.

Amortisation = £6,000/5 years

= £12,000/year and so on.

ACCA marking scheme		
		Available
Goodwill	– calculation	3
	– amortisation	1
		4
Minority interest – calculation		3
Profit and loss account		
	Initial profit figures	1
	Minority interest	1
	Cost of control	1
	Goodwill written off	1
		11
Consolidated balance sheet - format		2
Marks available		13
Maximum marks awarded		10

PROFIT AND LOSS ACCOUNTS: FRS 3

60 TOPAZ

Key answer tips

The figures in the question are straightforward. The points being tested are knowledge of FRS 3 presentation requirements and demonstration of understanding of the effects of FRS 3 on users' understanding.

(a) (i)

Topaz Limited
Profit and loss account for the year ended 31 December 20X6

	Continuing operations £m	Discontinued operations £m	Total £m
Sales	68	13	81
Cost of sales	(41)	(8)	(49)
Gross profit	27	5	32
Distribution costs *(Note 1)*	(6)	(1)	(7)
Administrative expenses	(4)	(2)	(6)
Operating profit	17	2	19
Profit on sale of discontinued operations		2.5	2.5
Costs of fundamental reorganisation	(1.8)	—	(1.8)
Profit on ordinary activities before interest	15.2	4.5	19.7
Interest payable			(1)
Profit on ordinary activities before taxation			18.7
Taxation			(4.8)
Profit on ordinary activities after taxation			13.9
Dividends			
Interim paid			(2.0)
Final proposed			(4.0)
Retained profit for the financial year			7.9

Note 1: Distribution costs include a bad debt of £1.9m which arose on the continuing operations.

(ii)

Topaz Limited
Statement of total recognised gains and losses

	£m
Profit for the financial year	13.9
Unrealised surplus on revaluation of properties	4
Total gains recognised since last annual report	17.9

(b) FRS 3 requires separate disclosure of the details relating to sections of the enterprise disposed of during the year, and of the profit or loss arising on the disposal. It also requires details of new acquisitions during the year, as a component of continuing operations.

This extra disclosure assists users in three main ways:

(i) the separate performance of the division sold is disclosed, so that the impact of its profit or loss can be assessed

(ii) the figures provide a better basis for the assessment of future income, because forecasts can be based on the separately disclosed figures for the continuing operations

(iii) exceptional items are clearly defined, and either included in operating profit with disclosure by note, or separately disclosed on the face of the profit and loss account if they are 'super-exceptional' – profits or losses on the sale or termination of an operation, costs of a fundamental reorganisation and profits or losses on the non-routine sale of fixed assets.

61   LARK

(a)

Lark Limited
Profit and loss account for the year ended 31 March 2000

	Continuing operations £000	Discontinued operations £000	Total £000
Sales	14,000	6,000	20,000
Cost of sales	(7,500)	(4,800)	(12,300)
Gross profit	6,500	1,200	7,700
Distribution costs	(1,260)	(840)	(2,100)
Administrative expenses	(2,290)	(700)	(2,990)
Operating profit/(loss)	2,950	(340)	2,610
Cost of fundamental reorganisation	(210)		(210)
Loss on sale of discontinued division		(400)	(400)
Profit/(loss) on ordinary activities before interest	2,740	(740)	2,000
Interest receivable	—	—	1,200
Interest payable			(800)
Profit on ordinary activities before taxation			2,400
Taxation			(480)
Profit for the financial year			1,920

Note: The operating profit on continuing operations of £2,950,000 is after charging an exceptionally large bad debt of £360,000 incurred during the year.

(b)   Two additional statements or notes.

Two from:

(i)   **Statement of total recognised gains and losses.**

This statement contains:

-    profit for the financial year

-    unrealised losses or gains on revaluation of assets

-    prior year adjustments.

(ii)   **Reconciliation of movements in shareholders' funds.**

This statement contains:

-    opening and closing shareholders' funds

-    profit for the financial year

-    dividends paid and proposed for the year

-    new share capital issued

-    goodwill written off.

(iii)   **Note of historical cost profits and losses.**

This note shows what the profit or loss would have been if the profit and loss account had been prepared on a strict historical cost basis.

It contains:

-    reported profit before taxation

-    adjustment to gains on assets sold in the period to include revaluation gains of previous years

-    adjustment to depreciation for difference between actual depreciation charge on revalued assets and what depreciation would have been if calculated on historical cost.

CASH FLOW STATEMENTS: FRS 1

62   PANIEL LIMITED

Paniel Limited
Cash flow statement for the year ended 31 March 20X3

	£	£
Net cash inflow from operating activities		746,000
Returns on investments and servicing of finance:		
Interest paid		(72,000)
Capital expenditure		
Payments to acquire fixed assets (W1)	(1,400,000)	
Receipt from sales of fixed assets	280,000	
		(1,120,000)
Equity dividends paid (W2)		(150,000)
Financing:		
Issuing of ordinary share capital	200,000	
Issuing of debentures	400,000	
		600,000
Increase in cash		4,000

Workings

(W1)

Fixed assets – cost

	£		£
Opening balance	2,140,000	Transfer – disposal	480,000
Purchases (balancing figure)	1,400,000	Closing balance	3,060,000
	3,540,000		3,540,000

(W2) The profit for year was £260,000 and the increase in retained profit was £110,000 (£590,000 - £480,000). Therefore dividends paid were £150,000 (£260,000 - £110,000).

(W3) Share capital and share premium at end of year = £1,100,000 + £900,000 = £2,000,000.

Share capital and share premium at start of year = £1,000,000 + £800,000 = £1,800,000.

So cash raised by issuing new shares = £2,000,000 - £1,800,000 = £200,000.

(W4) Cash raised by issuing new debentures = £1,200,000 - £800,000 = £400,000.

63   MARMOT LIMITED

(a)   **Net cash flow from operating activities – direct method**

	£000	£000
Cash receipts from customers		12,800
Cash paid to suppliers	4,940	
Cash paid to employees	2,820	
Cash paid for expenses	2,270	
		10,030
Net cash flow from operating activities		2,770

(b)   **Net cash flow from operating activities – indirect method**

	£000
Operating profit	2,370
Depreciation charges	880
Increase in stocks	(370)
Decrease in debtors	280
Decrease in creditors	(390)
Net cash from operating activities	2,770

ACCA marking scheme		
		Marks
(a)	1 mark per item	4
(b)	1 mark per item	5
	Agreement of totals	1
Total		10

64   ADDAX LIMITED

(a)

Plant and equipment – cost

20X1		£	20X1		£
1 April	Balance b/d	840,000	10 Dec	Transfer disposal	100,000
20X2			20X2		
1 Oct	Cash	180,000	31 Mar	Balance c/d	920,000
		1,020,000			1,020,000

Plant and equipment – depreciation

20X1		£	20X1		£
10 Dec	Transfer – disposal	60,000	1 April	Balance b/d	370,000
20X2			20X2		
31 Mar	Balance c/d	393,000	31 Mar	Profit & loss account (74,000 + 9,000)	83,000
		453,000			453,000

Plant and equipment – disposal

20X1		£	20X1		£
10 Dec	Transfer – cost	100,000	10 Dec	Transfer – depreciation	60,000
20X2			20X2		
31 March	Profit & loss account	5,000	31 Mar	Cash	45,000
		105,000			105,000

(b)

Addax

Cash flow statement for the year ended 31 March 20X2   (extracts)
Reconciliation of operating profit to operating cash flows   £
Operating profit
Depreciation charges   83,000
Profit on sale of plant   (5,000)

Capital expenditure
    Purchase of plant   (180,000)
    Proceeds of sale of plant   45,000

65   WEASEL PLC

Tutorial note: You are not given the operating profit for the year, so you have to calculate it. Since operating profit is profit before interest and taxation, you can calculate it by taking the increase in retained profit in the year, and then add back dividends on the profits, the taxation charge and the interest charge for the year. Note also that since there have been disposals of plant and machinery, you need to calculate a profit or loss on disposal.

Weasel plc cash flow statement, year ended 31 August 20X9

	£000	£000
Cash flow from operating activities (see below)		2,660
Returns on investments and servicing of finance		
Interest paid (10% of 1,500)		(150)
Taxation (400 opening creditors + 500 annual charge		(400)
− 500 closing creditors)		
Capital expenditure		
Purchase of tangible fixed assets	(2,500)	
Proceeds of sale of tangible fixed assets	250	(2,250)
Equity dividends paid		(500)
Cash outflow before financing		(640)
Financing		
Issue of ordinary share capital (2,200 + 2,540)	400	
− (2,000 + 2,340)		
Issue of debentures	500	
		900
Increase in cash in the period (100 increase in cash in bank + 160 reduction in overdraft)		260

Reconciliation of operating profit to operating cash flow

	£000
Operating profit (W1)	1,710
Depreciation	1,200
Profit on sale of plant (W2)	(50)
Increase in stock (1,400 − 1,200)	(200)
Decrease in debtors (1,400 − 1,500)	100
Decrease in creditors (700 − 800)	(100)
Net cash inflow from operating activities	2,660

Workings

(W1) Calculation of operating profit

	£000
Profit and loss reserve at end of year	2,960
Profit and loss reserve at start of year	2,400
Retained profit for the year	560
Dividends for the year	500
Taxation charge for the year	500
Interest charge for the year (10% of 1,500)	150
Operating profit before interest and taxation	1,710

(W2) Profit on sale of plant

	£000
Net book value of assets disposed of (1,000 − 800)	200
Proceeds of sale	250
Profit on sale	50

66   FINTRY

Key answer tips

There are two requirements for producing a cash flow statement – a knowledge of the format and a methodical approach to calculating the figures needed. Study the workings carefully. The calculation of the cash spent to buy new fixed assets and the depreciation charge for the year can seem quite complex. This question excludes taxation, which is perhaps unusual.

(a)   **Fintry Limited**
Cash flow statement Year ended 30 September 20X2

Reconciliation of operating profit to net cash flow from operating activities

	£000
Operating profit (W3)	628
Depreciation (W2)	460
Profit on sale of fixed assets (55 – 40)	(15)
Increase in stocks (490 – 380)	(110)
Decrease in debtors (380 – 410)	30
Increase in creditors (250 – 200)	50
Net cash inflow from operating activities	1,043

Cash flow statement

	£000	£000
Net cash inflow from operating activities		1,043
Returns on investments and servicing of finance		
Interest paid (10% × 12,000) + 8 bank o'draft interest		(128)
Capital expenditure		
Payments to acquire fixed assets (W1)	(2,055)	
Proceeds of sale of fixed assets	55	
		(2,000)
		(1,085)
Equity dividends paid (W4)		(100)
Financing		
Issue of ordinary shares (1,500 + 800) – (1,000 + 600)	700	
Issue of debentures	500	
		1,200
Increase in cash (W5)		15

Workings

(W1) **Fixed asset purchases**

	£000
Assets at cost/revaluation at start of year	2,740
Revaluation (1,200 – 800)	400
	3,140
Cost of asset disposed of	(200)
	2,940
Assets at cost/revaluation at end of year	4,995
Fixed asset purchases in the year	2,055

(W2) Depreciation charge for the year

	£000
Accumulated depreciation at start of year	700
Accum dep'n on asset disposed of (200 cost – NBV 40)	(160)
	540
Accumulated depreciation at end of year	1,000
Depreciation charge for the year	460

(W3) Calculation of operating profit

	£000
Profit and loss reserve at end of year	780
Profit and loss reserve at start of year	400
Retained profit for the year	380
Dividend charge for the year (40 + 80)	120
Debenture interest charge (12% of 1,000)	120
Bank overdraft interest	8
Operating profit before interest and taxation	628

(W4) Calculation of equity dividends paid

	£000
Dividend payable at start of year	60
Interim dividend (2 million shares × 2 pence)	40
Final dividend proposed	80
	180
Dividend payable at end of year	80
Dividends paid (cash) in the year	100

(W5) Calculation of movement on cash

	£000	£000
Balance at 1 October 20X1		
Cash at bank	10	
Overdraft	(80)	
	—	(70)
Balance at 30 September 20X2		
Cash at bank	15	
Overdraft	(70)	
	—	(55)
Net increase in cash		15

(b)   Under the direct method, operating cash flow would be calculated and shown by deducting cash paid to suppliers and cash paid for salaries, wages and other operating expenses from total cash received from customers.

67   CRASH

Cash flow statement for the year ended 31 March 20X1

	£000	£000
Net cash inflows from operating activities (see below)		1,995
Returns on investments and servicing of finance		
Interest paid (10% × 1,500)		(150)
Capital expenditure		
Purchase of fixed assets (W1)	(2,700)	
Proceeds of sale of fixed assets	375	
		(2,325)
		(480)

Financing
Repayment of debentures (750)
Proceeds of issue of shares 1,200
(3,000 + 1,200) – (2,250 + 750)

450

Decrease in cash (45 increase in cash balance but (30)
75 increase in overdraft)

Note 1: **Reconciliation of operating profit to net cash inflow from operating activities.**

	£000
Operating profit	555
Depreciation (W2)	1,500
Profit on sale of fixed assets (375 – 300)	(75)
Increase in stocks (1,350 – 1,215)	(135)
Decrease in debtors (1,290 – 1,350)	60
Increase in creditors (1,080 – 990)	90
Net cash inflow from operating activities	1,995

Workings

(W1) **Fixed asset purchases**

	£000
Assets at cost/valuation at start of year	9,000
Revaluation	750
	9,750
Cost of asset disposed of	(1,500)
	8,250
Assets at cost/revaluation at end of year	10,950
Fixed asset purchases in the year	2,700

(W2) **Depreciation charge for the year**

	£000
Accumulated depreciation at start of year	3,300
Accum dep'n on asset disposed of	(1,200)
(1,500 cost – NBV 300)	
	2,100
Accumulated depreciation at end of year	3,600
Depreciation charge for the year	1,500

ACCA marking scheme		
	Available	*Maximum*
Cash flow statement:		
Interest paid	1	
Purchase of fixed assets	2	
Proceeds of sale of fixed assets	1	
Repayment of debentures	1	
Issue of shares	1	
	6	
Overall layout	2	
	8	
Note 1		
Depreciation	1	
Profit on sale of fixed assets	1	

Stock	1	
Debtors	1	
Creditors	1	
Total	<u>13</u>	<u>10</u>

68   JANE LTD

Jane Limited
Cash flow statement for the year ended 31 December 20X8

Reconciliation of operating profit to net cash flow from operating activities

	Reference to workings	£000	£000
Operating profit	(W1)		45
Depreciation			100
Loss on sale of plant (60 – 80)			20
Loss on sale of investments (40 – 50)			10
Stock – increase (110 – 80)			(30)
Debtors – increase (180 – 110)			(70)
Creditors – increase (80 – 70)			10
			—
Net cash inflow from operating activities			85
			—

Cash flow statement			
Net cash inflow from operating activities			85
Returns on investments and servicing of finance:			
Interest paid (10% × 150)			(15)
Capital expenditure and financial investment			
Purchase of tangible fixed assets	(W2)	(450)	
Proceeds of sale:			
Tangible fixed assets		60	
Investments		40	(350)
			—
			(280)
Equity dividends paid			(30)
Financing			
Issue of shares		180	
Issue of debentures		50	
			230
Net cash outflow	(W3)		(80)

Workings

(W1)   **Calculation of operating profit**

	£000
Retained profit at start of year	190
Retained profit at end of year	(200)
Reduction in retained profit in the year	(10)
Interest paid	15
Dividend charge for the year (dividend proposed)	40
Operating profit for the year	45

(W2) **Calculation of tangible fixed assets purchased**

	£000
Fixed assets at net book value at start of year	730
Revaluation	100
	830
NBV of asset disposed of	(80)
	750
Depreciation charge for the year	(100)
	650
Fixed assets at net book value at end of year	1,100
Fixed asset purchases in the year	450

(W3) **Calculation of movement on cash**

Balance at 1 January 20X8	20 – 40	(20)
Balance at 31 December 20X8	30 – 130	(100)
Movement for year – net cash outflow		(80)

INTERPRETATION

69   WEDEN LIMITED

(a)

Year ended		*31 March 20X1*		*31 March 20X2*	
(i)	Return on capital employed	500/2,550	19.6%	550/3,900	14.1%
(ii)	Return on owners' equity	400/1,550	25.8%	350/1,900	18.4%
(iii)	Current ratio	1,010/430	2.35:1	1,380/1,480	0.93:1
(iv)	Stock turnover (full credit given for correct answer in days)	2,300/300	7.67 times	3,000/500	6 times
(v)	Creditors' days	380/1,800 × 365	77 days	1,400/3,200 × 365	160 days

(b)   **Comment**

All ratios show a marked deterioration in 20X2 compared with 20X1.

Return on capital employed (ROCE) and return on owners' equity (ROOE) are at reasonable levels in 20X2, but are considerably below the levels in 20X1. A possible cause is the decline in the gross profit percentage caused by reducing prices to increase sales.

ROOE shows a return in excess of ROCE in both years, and well in excess of the interest payable on the loan, showing that the shareholders are continuing to benefit from the gearing effect of the loan.

The current ratio is seriously reduced to a potentially dangerous level. The consequence is the slowness in paying suppliers, which must be eroding suppliers' goodwill, evidenced by the increase in creditors' days from 77 days to 160. In effect, suppliers' money is being used to finance the very heavy purchasing of fixed assets.

The stock turnover ratio has declined, indicating a possible slowing of activity. The decline could be caused simply by a large purchase of goods for stock just before the balance sheet date.

ACCA marking scheme		
		Marks
(a)	1 mark per ratio: 5 × 1	5
(b)	1 mark per comment: 5 × 1	5
Total		10

70   HAWK

Key answer tips

This question requires the calculation of eight accounting ratios for each of two years, plus suggestions for reasons for the changes in them. Some evidence of an understanding of the meaning behind the basic ratios is necessary.

(a)

Year ended 31 March

			20X1	20X2
(i)	Gross profit as percentage of sales			
	600/1,800 × 100		33.3%	
	700/2,500 × 100			28.0%
(ii)	Operating profit as percentage of sales revenue			
	240/1,800 × 100		13.3%	
	250/2,500 × 100			10.0%
(iii)	Return on capital employed			
	190/1,568 × 100		12.1%	
	200/2,122 × 100			9.4%
	Valid alternative calculations also acceptable			
(iv)	Current ratio			
	700 : 518		1.35:1	
	1,230 : 860			1.43:1
(v)	Quick ratio			
	500 : 518		0.96:1	
	870 : 860			1.01:1
(vi)	Stock turnover (days)			
	200/1,200 × 365		60.8 days	
	360/1,800 × 365			73.0 days
(vii)	Trade debtors – sales (days)			
	400/1,440 × 365		101.4 days	
	750/2,000 × 365			136.9 days
(viii)	Trade creditors – purchases (days)			
	210/1,220 × 365		62.8 days	
	380/1,960 × 365			70.8 days

(b)   **Comments on ratios**

(i)   Gross profit percentage on sales has declined from 33.3% to 28.0%, a substantial drop. This could possibly be due to a decision to lower prices in order to increase sales revenue, which has risen by 38.9%. A drop in the gross profit percentage might be an indicator of possible error or fraud if another explanation such as a lowering of prices cannot be found.

(ii)   Net profit to sales is down from 13.3% to 10%, which is also a large drop, but not as large as the drop in the gross profit percentage. A large rise in distribution costs as a percentage of sales helps to explain this poor result.

(iii)   Return on capital employed has declined from 12.1% to 9.4%. This is a reflection of the decline in profitability as shown by ratio (ii) above.

(iv) & (v) The two ratios measuring liquidity have changed little between the two periods, suggesting that the liquidity position is satisfactory at both dates.

(vi)   The stock turnover ratio has increased because the stock level has risen faster than the increases in cost of sales and sales. The higher stock could be a reflection of slowing demand for the company's goods towards the end of the period and/or slackness in the company's stock control procedures.

(vii)   The debtors' days have increased considerably from 101.4 days, a high level, to the even higher level of 136.9 days. The increase suggests slackness in the company's credit control procedures.

(viii) There has been a relatively small increase in the number of days' purchases in trade creditors. The increase is perhaps caused by pressure on the company's liquid resources as a result of the increased stock and trade debtors.

71   CASTOR AND POLLUX

Key answer tips

This question requires the ability to think intelligently about the meaning of accounting ratios. It is possible to score highly, but only by adhering scrupulously to the specific requirements of the question.

(a)   **Five from:**

(i)   A change in the 'mix' of sales revenue. If the sales in the current year include more items with a lower mark-up, the overall gross profit will be reduced.

(ii)   A larger proportion of sales revenue coming from sales made at a reduced price. This reduces the profit on these sales and hence reduces the gross profit percentage..

(iii)   Purchase costs increase and are not passed on in higher sale prices. Costs increase without a corresponding increase in sales revenue.

(iv)   Errors in arriving at year-end stock. If closing stock is understated, cost of sales will be increased and the gross profit as a percentage of sales revenue will fall.

(v)   Theft of stock by customers or staff will reduce closing stock and hence increase cost of sales and reduce the gross profit as a percentage of sales revenue.

(vi)   Defective 'cut-off' procedure. If, for example, a purchase invoice is recorded as a purchase within the period, but the goods concerned remain unsold and are not included in the closing stock, cost of sales will be overstated and gross profit as a percentage of sales understated.

(vii)   Change in analysis. If expenses previously included in distribution costs or administrative expenses are included in cost of sales in the current year, gross profit and the gross profit as a percentage of sales will be reduced.

Other answers considered on their merits.

(b)   **Effect of gearing on profit**

If a company has high borrowings in relation to equity capital, as Castor has, it is likely to show a high return on shareholders' capital when conditions are favourable, and a disproportionately low return for shareholders when conditions turn unfavourable.

At December 20X0, the position of the two companies was:

	Castor		Pollux	
	£000	£000	£000	£000
Shareholders' capital		200		800
Profit for shareholders				
Before interest	100		100	
Less: interest	80	20	20	80
Return on shareholders' capital		10%		10%

In 20X1 the position of the two companies will become:

	Castor		Pollux	
	£000	£000	£000	£000
Shareholders' capital		200		800
Profit for shareholders				
Before interest	200		200	
Less: interest	80	120	20	180
Return on shareholders' capital		60%		22.5%

In 20X2, the position will become:

	Castor		Pollux	
	£000	£000	£000	£000
Shareholders' capital		200		800
Profit for shareholders				
Before interest	50		50	
Less: interest	80	(30)	20	30
Return on shareholders' capital		-15%		3.75%

Castor easily outperforms Pollux in 20X1 from the shareholders' point of view, but when profits fall in 20X2, Castor incurs a loss while Pollux remains modestly profitable.

As long as the money borrowed can be invested by the company to produce a return greater than the rate of interest being paid, gearing increases equity earnings, but if the return drops below the rate of interest, gearing reduces equity earnings.

In addition, when two companies are similar in every respect apart from their gearing, the return on shareholders' capital will rise or fall in the higher-geared company by a much greater percentage amount in response to a given rise or fall in operating profit. Here, the percentage rise or fall in return on shareholders capital is much greater in the higher-geared company Castor than in the lower-geared company Pollux

Note: Credit will be given for other valid methods of expressing gearing.

ACCA marking scheme		
		Marks
(a)	2 marks per valid point	
	Factor	1
	Explanation	1
		10
(b)	Principle explained	4
	Use of figures to present numerical examples	6
Total		20

72   BROOD

(a)

				20X1	20X2
(i)	**Return on total capital employed**				
	5,000 / 48,600	6,500 / 72,300		10.3%	9.0%
(ii)	**Return on owners' equity**				
	3,600 / 28,600	3,700 / 32,300		12.6%	11.5%
(iii)	**Current ratio**				
	38,600 / 28,500	43,000 / 17,400		1.35:1	2.47:1
(iv)	**Quick ratio**				
	22,100 / 28,500	24,600 / 17,400		0.78:1	1.41:1
(v)	**Gearing**				
	20,000 / 48,600	40,000 / 72,300		41.1%	55.3%

Examiners comment

Alternative methods of calculation marked on their merits.

(b)   The return on capital employed and the return on owners' equity both show a decline of over 1 percentage point. Gross profit has remained steady and expenses have not risen in line with increased sales revenue, so the cause is probably that the new capital raised by the debenture issue has not yet been deployed to increase profit.

The current ratio and the quick ratio were somewhat low at 30 April 20X1, because of the high bank overdraft. About half of the funds raised by the debenture issue has been used to reduce the overdraft, resulting in a movement to unnecessarily high ratios by 30 April 20X2. Expansion of the business as funds are deployed in the future development of the business should mean that these ratios return to a lower level.

The gearing ratio has risen from a fairly high level to a very high level as a result of the debenture issue. This means that the business is vulnerable to a downturn in profits as almost half of the current operating profit is absorbed by interest.

ACCA marking scheme			
		Available	*Max.*
(a)	5 ratios	5	5
(b)	Comment		
	ROCE and ROOE	2	
	CA/CL and QA/CL	2	
	Gearing	2	5
Total		11	20

73 OVERTRADING

(a) (i) Longer payment period for trade creditors

(ii) A rising bank overdraft

(iii) Increasing stocks

(iv) Deterioration in the quick ratio (acid test ratio)

(v) Rapid increase in sales and trade debtors

(b) Three from:

(i) Raise additional long-term capital (equity or loan) – this would introduce more cash into the current assets without increasing the current liabilities, thus improving the working capital position.

(ii) Negotiate an increased overdraft facility.

(iii) Attempt to clear stocks by sales at reduced prices – this would generate more cash to pay suppliers and speed up the working capital cycle.

(iv) Offer cash discounts to customers to encourage prompt payment – this too would generate more cash to pay suppliers and speed up the working capital cycle.

(v) Negotiate longer payment periods from suppliers – this would ease the pressure on the enterprise and allow it to pay suppliers from proceeds of profitable sales in due course.

(vi) Sell non-essential assets – this would realise cash to increase working capital.

Examiners comment

Other items marked on their merits.

ACCA marking scheme		
		Marks
(a)	1 mark per item	4
(b)	1 mark per item	3
	1 mark per explanation of effect	3
Total		10

74 APILLON

(a)

			Year ended 31 March	
			20X2	*20X3*
(i)	Current ratio	990,000/430,000	2.3:1	
		1,420,000/860,000		1.65:1
(ii)	Quick ratio	450,000/430,000	1.05:1	
		700,000/860,000		0.81:1
(iii)	Stock turnover	540,000/1,900,000 × 365	104 days	
		720,000/2,400,000 × 365		109 days
(iv)	Debtors' collection period			
		450,000/2,800,000 × 365	59 days	
		700,000/3,700,000 × 365		69 days
(v)	Creditors' payment period			
		410,000/2,080,000 × 365	72 days	
		690,000/2,580,000 × 365		98 days

Note: The debtors' collection period has been calculated by comparing year-end debtors with the total credit sales in the year. Credit sales are total sales minus cash sales.

(b)   **Comments**

(i)   The current ratio and quick ratio are both down by over 20%. The drop in the quick ratio to below 1:1 could indicate liquidity problems, especially in view of the rise in the bank overdraft from £20,000 to £170,000.

(ii)   The increase in sales, and hence in debtors purchases and creditors, is placing strain on the working capital. This is evidenced by the increase in the debtors' and creditors' payment periods.

(iii)   The business is one requiring large holdings of stock, but stock control appears to have deteriorated slightly between the two years.

(iv)   Cash sales have decreased considerably in 20X3. Making more sales for cash could contribute to an improvement in the current and quick ratios because this would reduce the bank overdraft.

The examiner stated that other comments would be considered on their merits.

ACCA marking scheme	
	Marks
1 mark per pair of ratios (5 ratio pairs × 1)	5
1 mark per valid comment (4 × 1)	4
	9

Section 5

MOCK EXAMINATION QUESTIONS

SECTION A – ALL 25 QUESTIONS ARE COMPULSORY AND MUST BE ANSWERED

EACH QUESTION IN SECTION A IS WORTH 2 MARKS

1   **W is a sole trader and has a year-end of 31 December. The balance sheets as at 31 December 20X4 and as at 31 December 20X3 are shown below. Drawings by W for the year to 31 December 20X4 were £1,500.**

	31 December 20X4	31 December 20X3
	£	£
Fixed assets	5,400	4,700
Stock	1,200	1,400
Debtors	1,950	2,050
Cash	170	340
Creditors	2080	2150

What was the profit for the year ended 31 December 20X4?

A   £1,200

B   £1,340

C   £1,660

D   £1,800

2   **Financial statements are prepared on the assumption that the business will continue in existence for the foreseeable future.**

What does the above statement describe?

A   Accrual concept

B   Fair value concept

C   Going concern concept

D   Capital maintenance concept.

3   **F prepares his accounts to 31 December each year. On 1 January 20X3 the amount prepaid for insurances was £360.**

He paid £240 on 1 April 20X3 for Type one insurance for year ended 31 March 20X4. On 1 June 20X3 he paid £960 for Type two insurance for year ended 31 May 20X4.

What was the charge to the profit and loss account in 20X3 for insurances?

A   £740

B   £820

C   £920

D   £1,100

4   **A suspense account had been created to cater for B's difference on his trial balance.**

It was then discovered that an invoice for £512 from the sales day book had been debited to the accounts receivable control account as £152, and the petty cash balance of £20 had been omitted from the trial balance. The suspense account was reduced to zero on correction of these errors.

What was B's difference on his trial balance?

A   Credits exceeded debits by £340

B   Debits exceeded credits by £340

C   Credits exceeded debits by £380

D   Debits exceeded credits by £380.

5   **A suspense account had been created to cater for D's difference on his trial balance.**

The following errors were then discovered:

1   Cash received from H Smith had been credited to the account of G Smith in the sales ledger.

2   Cash paid for repairs to the building had been debited to the fixed asset account.

3   Discounts allowed had been debited in error to discounts received.

4   Sales returns of £400 have been debited to the sales ledger control account.

5   The balance on the rental account had been omitted from the trial balance.

Which of the above errors would require an entry being made to the suspense account as part of the correction?

A   1, 2 and 3 only

B   3, 4 and 5 only

C   3 and 4 only

D   4 and 5 only.

6   **Which of the following errors will NOT result in the sales ledger control account disagreeing with the total of the account balances in the sales ledger?**

A   Addition error in a customer's account.

B   Sales returns being debited to the sales ledger control account.

C   Purchase credited to C's account in the sales ledger.

D   Posting of a sales invoice to F's account in the sales ledger instead of K's account.

7   **G's purchase ledger control account had a closing balance of £540.**

During the period purchases amounted to £19,670; cash paid to suppliers was £19,068; returns inwards were £350; and returns outwards were £250.

What was the opening balance on the purchase ledger control account?

A   £188

B   £288

C   £1,392

D   £1,492

8 On 1 June 20X3, R's cash account showed a debit balance of £90. It was then discovered that deposits of £100 did not appear on the bank statement until 7 July 20X3.

On 7 June 20X3, a cheque for a supplier had been entered into the cash book as £69 instead of £96. On 4 July 20X3, R received a bank statement showing an overdraft balance of £50 as at 31 June 20X3. The cash account reconciled to the bank statement after making these adjustments together with an amendment for bank charges.

What was the amount for bank charges?

A £13

B £40

C £67

D £113

9 P's cash account showed a debit balance of £240.

It was then discovered that cheques amounting to £290 had not yet been presented at the bank. Bank charges of £50 had not been entered in the cash account. Deposits of £370 had not yet appeared on the bank statement. The cash account reconciled to the bank statement after making these adjustments.

What was the balance on the bank statement?

A £110

B £160

C £210

D £270

10 A's purchases for the year were £33,140. Opening stock was valued at £10,192, whilst closing stock was valued at £9,780. The company operates a standard gross margin of 20% on sales.

What was the value of sales for the year?

A £40,262

B £41,940

C £63,734

D £66,390

11 F manufactures one product for which 60 units remain in stock at the year-end.

Each unit cost £4.50 to manufacture and is sold for £5 with a 15% prompt payment discount. To improve sales, F decided to repackage the product and spent a further £0.60 per unit on repackaging.

What should be the value per unit of the closing stock?

A £3.65

B £4.25

C £4.40

D £4.50

12   **D Limited had ordinary shares of 50p each at 31 December 20X2.**

The amount of authorised share capital was £500,000 and issued share capital was £300,000. The company has a large share premium account in its reserves. On 1 January 20X3, when the market price of the shares was 80p each, the company made a bonus issue of 1 for every 4 shares previously held.

What were the correct entries following the issue of shares?

A   Debit Bank £75,000, Credit Share capital £75,000

B   Debit Bank £120,000, Credit Share capital £75,000, Credit Share premium £45,000

C   Debit Share premium £120,000, Credit Share capital £120,000

D   Debit Share premium £75,000, Credit Share capital £75,000.

13   **An intangible asset can be recognised for development costs may provided that certain conditions are met. According to SSAP 13, which of the following must be demonstrated in order to recognise development costs as an intangible asset?**

1   Expenditure is separately identifiable.

2   There should be a clearly defined project.

3   The total costs of development must not be expected to exceed the total future benefits or revenues.

4   Total expected future revenues from the project are not expected to be outweighed by the related future costs.

5   The project's outcome can be considered to be technically feasible.

A   Items 1, 2 and 5 only

B   Items 1, 3 and 5 only

C   Items 2, 3 and 4 only

D   Items 1, 2, 4 and 5 only.

14   **R Ltd acquired a building on 1 January 20X1.**

The buildings was re-valued for the first time on 30 September 20X3 to £120,000. R has a policy of depreciating buildings at 2% straight line basis with a proportionate charge in the year of acquisition and assuming no residual value. The transfer to R's revaluation reserve for the building, for the year ending 31 December 20X3, was £16,050.

What was the acquisition cost of the asset on 1 January 20X1?

A   £97,350

B   £103,950

C   £109,667

D   £110,000

15   **Q sold a motor vehicle on 1 September 20X4 for £8,000. The motor vehicle had originally cost £24,000 on 1 January 20X1.**

It is the company's policy to provide depreciation at 20% on the straight line basis, on assets held at the year end.

What was the resulting profit/(loss) on disposal?

A   £2,000 profit

B   £1,600 profit

C   £1,600 loss

D   £2,000 loss

16   **A customer of L Ltd, is taking legal action for faulty workmanship.**

L Ltd is refusing to accept liability for the customer's loss. The court case will not be heard until August 20X4. The lawyers representing L think it possible that the customer will be successful in his claim, which is for a material sum.

What should be the correct treatment for the claim in the accounts for the year ended 31 December 20X3?

A   Do not recognise the loss, and no disclosure is necessary in the financial statements

B   Do not recognise the loss, but disclose details of the customer's claim by way of a note to the accounts.

C   Recognise the loss, and report it as a provision in the balance sheet

D   Recognise the loss and recognise it as an accrual in the balance sheet

17   **What is the correct order for presentation of the following items in the balance sheet?**

1   Prepayments

2   Reserves

3   Intangible fixed assets

4   Trade creditors

5   Interest-bearing borrowings

A   3, 4, 1, 5, 2

B   3, 1, 4, 5, 2

C   3, 1, 2, 5, 4

D   3, 1, 4, 2, 5

18   **E had an operating profit of £70,000. The increases in stock, debtors and trade creditors, were £10,000, £5,000 and £8,000 respectively. Depreciation for the year amounted to £22,000. There was a profit on disposal of a fixed asset of £4,000.**

What figure should appear in the cash flow statement for net cash inflow from operating activities?

A   £65,000

B   £81,000

C   £89,000

D   £111,000

19   **V had a profit before tax of £8,000. Income taxes paid amounted to £3,000. The depreciation charge for the year was £7,000.**

There was an increase in stock of £2,000, a decrease in debtors of £1,500 and a decrease in trade creditors of £3,600. The interest paid was £1,400.

What, according to FRS 1, is the net cash inflow from operating activities?

A   £6,500

B   £9,500

C   £10,900

D   £14,700

20   **A, B and C set up in partnership on 1 January 20X3.**

Their agreement was to share profits in the ratio of 2:3:4 (for A, B and C respectively), after taking account of salaries of £26,500 for A and £18,500 for C. B has made a loan of £300,000 to the partnership, on which interest is paid at 3% each year. Profits for the year ended 31 December 20X3 amounted to £99,000.

What was the share of profit between partners for the year?

A   £22,000 for A, £33,000 for B and £44,000 for C

B   £36,500 for A, £24,000 for B and £38,500 for C

C   £38,500 for A, £18,000 for B and £42,500 for C

D   £38,500 for A, £27,000 for B and £42,500 for C

21   **N Limited had a corporation tax liability of £27,000 brought forward from 20X1.**

During 20X2, the profit and loss account showed a charge of £19,000 for corporation tax and the corporation tax liability shown under current liabilities in the balance sheet was £22,000.

What figure should be shown for corporation tax paid in the cash flow statement for the year 20X2?

A   £14,000

B   £19,000

C   £24,000

D   £41,000

22   **B Limited made a return on capital employed of 25.5%. Its profit before interest and taxation amounted to £60,000. The asset turnover ratio (calculated as sales/capital employed) was 85%.**

What was the value of sales revenue?

A   £70,588

B   £100,840

C   £200,000

D   £276,817

23   **C is making a payment to a supplier. At the moment, the current ratio of C is higher than 1.0 and C does not have a bank overdraft.**

What will happen to the current ratio when the payment has been made (assuming that no other transactions occur)?

A   The current ratio will increase.

B   The current ratio will be unchanged.

C   The current ratio will fall.

D   The ratio might rise, fall or remain the same, depending on the values involved.

24 **B Limited acquired 70% of the share capital of C Limited on 1 January 20X3. At that date, C's accumulated profits were £5,000 and its share capital was £20,000.**

At 31 December 20X3, C's share capital was £20,000 and its profit and loss reserve was £7,000. The consolidated profit and loss account for the year to 31 December 20X3 showed goodwill of £1,000. Goodwill is being amortised over five years by the straight-line method.

What was the correct value of the purchase consideration?

A   £13,900

B   £19,900

C   £22,500

D   £23,900

25 **C Limited acquired 80% of the share capital of T Limited on 31 December 20X2 for £500,000.**

The goodwill is being amortised by the straight line method over five years. The share capital can reserves of C and T were as follows.

	C Ltd		T Ltd	
	31 December 20X2	31 December 20X5	31 December 20X2	31 December 20X5
	£000	£000	£000	£000
Share capital	1,200	1,200	200	200
Other reserves	800	800	–	–
P & L account reserves	900	1,500	300	400

What (in £000s) was the profit and loss account reserve in the consolidated balance sheet as at 31 December 20X5?

A   3,480

B   3,520

C   3,760

D   3,820

SECTION B – ALL QUESTIONS ARE COMPULSORY AND MUST BE ATTEMPTED

1   FINANCIAL STATEMENTS

Financial statements are normally prepared on the basis of a number of accounting concepts or principles, including:

(i)   Going concern

(ii)   Accruals

(iii)   Consistency

Required:

Explain what you understand by each of these concepts and give an example of how each is applied in the preparation of financial statements.   **(10 marks)**

2   C, L, P, N AND V

At 31 December 20X0, C had trade receivables totalling £58,174, a specific provision for doubtful debts of £490 (relating to N) and a general provision for doubtful debts equating to 1% of those debts not specifically provided against. During 20X1, the following occurred.

(i)   L went bankrupt owing £765.

(ii)   P paid £350. His debt had been written off several years earlier.

(iii)   £190 was paid by N but he refused to pay the remaining balance. It was decided that the difference should be written off.

(iv)   It was agreed that a specific provision should be created for 40% of a debt of V. He owed a total of £2,000.

(v)   It was decided that a general provision equal to 1% of those debts not specifically provided against should be maintained.

(vi)   Total trade debtors at 31 December 20X1 were £62,427.

(vii)   Payments received from credit customers in 20X1, including the money from P, totalled £379,000.

Required:

Prepare the debtors control account, bad debt account and provision for doubtful debts account. Show in the accounts the double entry for each item, and carry forward the balances at the end of the year.   **(10 marks)**

3   P LIMITED

P Limited had the following fixed asset register as at the year ended 31 December 20X4.

Asset number	Asset type	Date purchased	Original value (£)
0037	Motor vehicle	30/09/20X1	17,000
0038	Office equipment	01/01/20X2	2,500
0039	Office equipment	31/12/20X3	3,000
0040	Motor vehicle	31/12/20X3	10,400
0041	Office equipment	01/01/20X4	4,300
0042	Motor vehicle	30/11/20X4	11,600

Additional information:

1   The company provides depreciation on motor vehicles at 25% each year on the straight line basis, with a proportionate charge in the year of acquisition. On office equipment, it provides for depreciation at 20% each year on the reducing balance basis.

2   Asset 0042 replaced a vehicle purchased for £9,600 on 01/01/20X2 and then sold on 01/01/20X4 for £2,800.

Required:

Prepare the profit and loss account and balance sheet extracts relating to these fixed assets for the year ended 31 December 20X4. Your extracts should be accompanied by appropriate disclosure notes as required by accounting standards.   **(10 marks)**

4   ROCK GROUP

At 31 December 20X3, the balance sheets for the parent company and subsidiary company of the Rock Group were as follows:

	Rock Ltd £000	Subsidiary £000
Total assets, excluding investment in Subsidiary	1,100	530
Investment in Subsidiary	330	-
	1,430	530
Total liabilities	(320)	(150)
	1,110	380
Equity and liabilities		
Capital and reserves		
Issued capital	800	290
Share premium	100	-
P & L account reserve	210	90
	1,110	380

Rock had acquired 80% of Subsidiary on 31 December 20X1 for a purchase consideration of £330,000. It had been decided that any goodwill arising on consolidation should be amortised over a five-year period. The balance sheet of Subsidiary at the date of acquisition showed share capital of £290,000 and a P & L account reserve of £30,000.

Required:

Prepare a consolidated balance sheet for the Rock Group as at 31 December 20X3.

(10 marks)

5   M LIMITED

The following ratios have been prepared for M Limited for the years ended 31 December 20X1 and 20X2.

	20X2	*20X1*
Gross profit %	15.4%	12.3%
Quick ratio (acid test ratio)	0.8:1	0.7:1
Stock turnover days	25 days	20 days
Debtor days	35 days	47 days
Gearing %	50%	55%

Required:

Analyse the performance of M over the two-year period, suggesting possible causes of the changes in each ratio shown above, between 20X1 and 20X2.   **(10 marks)**

Section 6

ANSWERS TO MOCK EXAMINATION QUESTIONS

SECTION A

1   D

		£
Net assets at 31 December 20X4	(5,400 + 1,200 + 1,950 +170 - 2,080)	6,640
Net assets at 31 December 20X3	(4,700 + 1,400 + 2,050 + 340 – 2,150)	6,340
Increase in net assets		300
Drawings		1,500
Profit for the year		1,800

2   C

This is a simple definition of the going concern concept. As long as an enterprise is a going concern, it is acceptable to value assets at cost or fair value, rather than at a break-up disposal value.

3   D

The prepayment for insurances at 31 December 20X3 is $(3/12 \times £240) + (5/12 \times £960)$ = £460.

Insurance expense

Date		£	Date		£
1.1	Opening bal	360	31.12	P & L account	1,100
1.4	Bank	240		(balancing figure)	
1.6	Bank	960	31.12	Closing bal	460
		1,560			1,560

4   D

The corrections needed are:

Debit:	Debtors (512 – 152)	£360	
Credit:	Suspense account		£360
Debit:	Petty cash	£20	
Credit:	Suspense account		£20

The balance on the suspense account, and so the difference between the total amount of debits and the total amount of credits, is £360 + £20 = £380. The balance on the suspense account is a credit balance, which means that without the suspense account, total debits must exceed total debits.

5   D

The necessary corrections are:

1   The wrong account has been credited, so debit T account and credit S account with the amount of the payment. In any case, unless the receivables ledger is a part of the double entry system, the error would not be relevant to the trial balance.

2   Debit Repairs account, Credit Fixed asset (land and buildings) account.

3   Debit Discounts allowed, credit Discounts received

4   Credit Sales ledger control account £800, debit Suspense account $800

5   Debit Rental account, credit Suspense account.

Only corrections 4 and 5 involve a suspense account.

6   D

In the case of D, only the individual accounts of F and K are affected, but the total of the balances on the accounts in the sales ledger will be unaffected. The error therefore does not result in the balance on the sales ledger control account disagreeing with the accounts totals in the sales ledger.

7   A

Creditors

	£		£
Bank	19,068	Opening balance	**188**
Returns inwards	250	(balancing figure)	
Closing balance	540	Purchases	19,670
	19,858		19,858

8   A

	£
Cash book balance	90
Deposits not on bank statement	(100)
	(10)
To correct error in cash book (96 – 69)	(27)
	(37)
Bank statement balance	(50)
Bank charges	13

9   A

	£
Cash account balance	240
Cheques not yet presented at bank	290
	530
Deposits not yet on bank statement	(370)
Bank charges	(50)
Bank statement balance	110

10   B

	£
Opening stock	10,192
Purchases	33,140
	43,332
Closing stock	9,780
Cost of sales	33,552
Sales = Cost of sales × 100/(100/80)	41,940

11   C

Net realisable value is the estimated selling price less the estimated costs of completion and the estimated costs necessary to make the sale. The prompt payment discount is neither a completion cost nor a selling cost, and should therefore not be included in the calculation of NRV.

NRV = £5.00 - £0.60 = £4.40. This is lower than cost, and should be the balance sheet valuation of the stock items.

12   D

The bonus issue involves the issue of (600,000/4) 150,000 new shares with a nominal value of £75,000. The company can use its share premium account for the issue, so we reduce (debit) the share premium account and increase (credit) the share capital account. No cash is raised in a bonus issue.

13   D

SSAP 13 specifies several items that must be demonstrated. They include items 1, 2, 4 and 5 in the question, but not item 2. (If the net future benefits from the development project are less than the costs incurred to date, the development cost could still be shown in the balance sheet, but valued at the lower of cost or NRV.)

14   D

The building was revalued after 2.75 years, at which time accumulated depreciation on the building was 2.75 × 2% = 5.5% of the cost of the asset. The net book value of the asset was therefore 94.5% of cost.

	£
Revalued amount	120,000
Transfer to revaluation reserve	16,050
Net book value at date of revaluation (= 94.5% of cost)	103,950
Cost of asset (103,950 × (100/94.5))	110,000

15   C

Depreciation is charged at 20% on the fixed assets held at the end of the year. In this example, this means that there is accumulated depreciation for three full years at the time of disposal.

	£
Cost of asset	24,000
Depreciation (20X1, 20X2 and 20X3)	
60% of $24,000	14,400
Net book value at time of sale	9,600
Sale price	8,000
Loss on sale	1,600

16   B

The outcome of the legal dispute is not wholly within the control of L, and an unfavourable outcome is only possible, not probable. The claim by the customer is therefore a contingent liability. A contingent liability is a possible obligation arising from a past event, whose existence or non-existence will only be confirmed by the occurrence of an uncertain future event that is not wholly within the control of the enterprise. A contingent liability should not be recognised as a loss in the profit and loss account, but the business should disclose the nature of the contingent liability and, if practicable an estimate of its financial effect and an indication of the uncertainties relating to the amount of timing of any payment (FRS 12).

17   B

Fixed assets (intangible asset) are followed by current assets (prepayment), then current liabilities (trade creditors) then non-current liabilities (interest-bearing borrowings) and finally capital and reserves.

18   B

	£
Net profit before taxation	70,000
Adjustments for:	
Depreciation	22,000
Profit on disposal	(4,000)
	88,000
Increase in stocks	(10,000)
Increase in debtors	(5,000)
Increase in trade creditors	8,000
Net cash inflow from operations	81,000

19   C

	£
Net profit before taxation	8,000
Adjustment for:	
Depreciation	7,000
	15,000
Increase in stock	(2,000)
Decrease in debtors	1,500
Decrease in trade creditors	(3,600)
Net cash inflow from operations	10,900

20   C

The interest on the loan to B is an interest charge in the income statement, and is not an appropriation of the partnership profit.

	A £	B £	C £	Total £
Salaries	26,500		18,500	45,000
Share of residual profit	12,000	18,000	24,000	54,000
Total profit share	38,500	18,000	42,500	99,000

21   C

	£
Opening tax liability	27,000
Tax charge for the year	19,000
	46,000
Closing tax liability	(22,000)
Corporation tax paid in the year	24,000

22   C

Profit before interest and taxation = £60,000

Return on capital employed = 25.5%

Capital employed = £60,000/25.5% = £235,294

Asset turnover ratio = Revenue/capital employed = 85%

Revenue = 85% × £235,294 = £200,000.

23   A

The current ratio (current assets dividend by current liabilities) is above 1.0 before the payment of cash to the supplier. As a result of the payment, there will be an equal reduction in current assets (cash reduced) and current liabilities (trade payables). Mathematically, the effect of the payment must be to increase the current ratio.

24   C

	£
Net assets acquired: 70% of (20,000 + 5,000)	17,500
Purchased goodwill (£1,000 × 5 years)	5,000
Purchase consideration	22,500

25   B

	£000
Acquired: 80% of (200 + 300)	400
Acquisition cost	500
Goodwill arising on acquisition	100
Accumulated amortisation (× 3/5)	60

	£000
Share capital of C	1,200
Reserves of C	800
P & L reserves of C	1,500
	3,500
80% of post-acquisition accumulated profits of T (= 80% of (400 − 300))	80
Amortised goodwill	(60)
Accumulated profits on consolidation	3,520

SECTION B

1 FINANCIAL STATEMENTS

(i)   *Going concern*. This refers to the accounts being prepared on the assumption that the business will continue in operation into the foreseeable future. It is therefore assumed that the business will not have to liquidate its operations, or cut them back significantly.

If this assumption of a going concern is applied, assets and liabilities can be valued accordingly. For example, a fixed asset might be valued at cost less accumulated depreciation, on the assumption that this represents the fair value of the asset if it is to be used until the end of its useful economic life. If a going concern basis cannot be assumed, it would be appropriate to value the asset in a different way, for example at its immediate disposal value.

(ii) *Accruals concept*. Under this basis of accounting, the effects of transactions are recognised as they occur, and not when the cash payment or received for the transaction occurs. The transactions are then reported in the financial statements of the period to which they relate. This means, for example, that if a business incurs an obligation to pay cash in the future, the accrued expense will be recognised in the profit and loss account as an expense and in the balance sheet as an accrual, before the cash is paid.

An example of the application of the accruals concept is that a business might incur an expense in Year 1, but not receive the invoice by the end of year 1. If so, the expense will be included in the profit and loss account for year 1 and be reported as an accrued expense in the balance sheet as at the end of year 1. Similarly, if a business makes an annual rental payment in advance on 1 July, and its financial year ends on 31 December, one half of the rental payment will be treated as a prepayment, and will not be charged against profit in the profit and loss account for the year when the rental payment is made. The prepayment will be included as a current asset in the balance sheet at the year-end.

(iii) *Consistency*. The presentation and classification of items in the financial statements should be retained from one period to the next. This is to allow users of financial statements to make comparisons with financial performance between different accounting periods. A change in presentation is permissible or required when:

(1)   a significant change in the nature of the operations of the business makes an alternative form of presentation of financial statements appropriate, or

(2)   a change in presentation is required by a new FRS.

For example, a business might decide to value its stock using the FIFO method. If so, it should not in a subsequent year change to an average cost method of valuation.

2 C, L, P, N, AND V

Debtors

	£		£
Opening balance	58,174	Bad debts – L	765
Sales	383,968	Bad debts – N (490 - 190)	300
(balancing figure)		Bank (379,000 – 350)	378,650
		Closing balance	62,427
	442,142		442,142

The provision at the start of the year is £490 for N + 1% of £(58,174 – 490) = £1,066.

The provision at the end of the year is (40% of £2,000) = £800 for V + 1% of £(62,427 – 800) = £1,416.

Provision for doubtful debts

	£		£
		Opening balance (see above)	1,066
Closing balance	1,416	Bad debts	350
	1,416		1,416

Bad debts

	£		£
Debtors – L	765	Bank: debt recovered	350
Debtors – N	300	Profit and loss account	715
	1,065		1,065

3   P LIMITED

Workings

Motor vehicles

Annual depreciation charges

0037: £17,000/4 = £4,250

0040: £10,400/4 = £2,600

0042: £11,600/4 = £2,900

Replaced vehicle: £9,600/4 = £2,400

Depreciation charge on vehicle 0042 in 20X4 = 1/12 × £2,900 = £242.

Annual depreciation charge 20X4 = £4,250 + £2,600 + £242 = £7,092.

Accumulated depreciation at 31 December 20X3

0037: £4,250 × 2.25 years = £9,563

0040: £0

Replaced vehicle: 2 × £2,400 = £4,800

Net book value at 31 December 20X3

		£
0037	(£17,000 – 9,563)	7,437
0040		10,400
Replaced vehicle	(£9,600 – 4,800)	4,800
		22,637

Accumulated depreciation at 31 December 20X4

0037: £4,250 × 3.25 years = £13,813
0040: £2,600
0042: £242

Net book value at 31 December 20X4

		£
0037	(£17,000 – 13,813)	3,187
0040		7,800
0042	(£11,600 – 242)	11,358
		22,345

Loss on disposal of vehicle = Sale price minus net book value at time of sale

= £2,800 - £4,800 = loss of £2,000.

Office equipment

	Cost	Dep'n 20X2	Dep'n 20X3	Dep'n 20X4	NBV 31.12.X3	NBV 31.12.X4
0038	2,500	(500)	(400)	(320)	1,600	1,280
0039	3,000	–	–	(600)	3,000	2,400
	5,500					
0041	4,300	–	–	(860)	-–	3,440
	9,800	(500)	(400)	(1,780)	4,600	7,120

Solution

Balance sheet extract

Fixed assets:

Office equipment	£7,120
Motor vehicles	£22,345

Note to the profit and loss account

Profit from operations is after charging:

Depreciation	£7,120
Loss on disposal	£2,000

Note: Fixed assets

	Motor vehicles £	Office equipment £	Total £
Cost			
Balance b/f	37,000	5,500	42,500
Additions	11,600	4,300	15,900
Disposals	(9,600)	–	(9,600)
Balance c/f	39,000	9,800	48,800
Depreciation			
Balance b/f	14,363	900	15,263
Charge for the year	7,092	1,780	8,872
Disposals	(4,800)	–	(4,800)
Balance c/f	16,655	2,680	19,335
Net book value			
Balance b/f	22,637	4,600	27,237
Balance c/f	22,345	7,120	29,465

4 ROCK GROUP

Consolidated balance sheet as at 31 December 20X3

	£000	£000
Fixed assets		
Goodwill (working 1)	74.0	
Amortisation (working 1)	29.6	
		44.4
Other assets (1,100 + 530)		1,630.0
		1,674.4
Liabilities (320 + 150)		(470.0)
Total assets less liabilities		1,204.4
Minority interest (working 3)		(76.0)
		1,128.4
Capital and reserves		
Issued capital		800.0
Reserves		100.0
P & L reserve (working 2)		228.4
		1,128.4

Workings

1

	£000
Net assets acquired: 80% of (290,000 + 30,000)	256
Cost of acquisition	330
Goodwill arising on acquisition	74

Annual charge for amortisation	£14,800
Accumulated amortisation at 31.12.X3 (2 years)	£29,600

2

	£000
P & L reserves of Rock	210.0
Post-acquisition retained profits of S	48.0
(80% of (90,000 – 30,000))	
	258.0
Amortised goodwill	29.6
	228.4

3   Minority interest = 20% of £(290,000 + 90,000) = £76,000.

5   M LIMITED

Gross profit percentage

The percentage has gone up in 20X2 compared with 20X1. This could be due to higher sales volume, increased selling prices or cost reductions.

Quick ratio (acid test ratio)

This has improved as the current assets, excluding stocks, of the business are higher relative to its current liabilities. This indicates improved liquidity. The change could be due to an improved cash position as a result of higher profits. Another reason might have been that the company now holds less stocks, so that the cash tied up in stocks had been released. However, the increase in stock turnover days shows that this is unlikely to be the case here.

Stock turnover days

This ratio has worsened as it now takes 25 days to convert stock into sales revenue, compared with just 20 days in the previous year. This could be due to a special build-up of stocks, for example for a marketing campaign at the start of the ext year. A concern for management is that the cause could be greater difficulty in selling stocks, or perhaps poor stock control management (allowing stock levels to rise to an unnecessarily high level.)

Debtor days

This ratio has improved as it now takes less time to collect in the cash due from credit customers. This could be due to improvements in credit control and debt collection procedures. The company might also have begun to offer attractive discounts for early payment, which many customers are taking.

Gearing

This ratio has gone down, indicating that a lower proportion of long-term finance of the company is now provided by long-term debts, and a greater proportion is financed by equity. The improvement could be due to the repayment of some debt financing or the increase in financing from equity/ordinary shareholders. In view of the rise in gross profit, it seems likely that the total profits have been quite high, and a proportion of those profits have been retained. This would increase total equity financing and reduce the gearing ratio.

Section 7

DECEMBER 2003
EXAMINATION QUESTIONS

Section A – ALL 25 questions are compulsory and MUST be attempted

Each question within this section is worth 2 marks.

1   At 1 July 20X2 the doubtful debt provision of Q Limited was £18,000.

During the year ended 30 June 20X3 debts totalling £14,600 were written off. It was decided that the doubtful debt provision should be £16,000 as at 30 June 20X3.

What amount should appear in the company's profit and loss account for bad and doubtful debts for the year ended 30 June 20X3?

A   £12,600

B   £16,600

C   £48,600

D   £30,600.

2   A company's trial balance totals were:

Debit   £387,642

Credit   £379,511

A suspense account was opened for the difference.

Which ONE of the following errors would have the effect of reducing the difference when corrected?

A   The petty cash balance of £500 has been omitted from the trial balance

B   £4,000 received for rent of part of the office has been correctly recorded in the cash book and debited to Rent account

C   No entry has been made in the records for a cash sale of £2,500

D   £3,000 paid for repairs to plant has been debited to the plant asset account.

3   The bookkeeper of Peri Limited made the following mistakes:

Discount allowed £3,840 was credited to Discounts Received account.

Discount received £2,960 was debited to Discounts Allowed account.

Discounts were otherwise correctly recorded.

Which of the following journal entries will correct the errors?

		Dr	Cr
		£	£
A	Discount allowed	7,680	
	Discount received		5,920
	Suspense account		1,760
B	Discount allowed	880	
	Discount received	880	
	Suspense account		1,760
C	Discount allowed	6,800	
	Discount received		6,800
D	Discount allowed	3,840	
	Discount received		2,960
	Suspense account		880

4 **The following bank reconciliation statement has been prepared by a trainee accountant:**

	£
Overdraft per bank statement	3,860
less: Outstanding cheques	9,160
	5,300
add: Deposits credited after date	16,690
Cash at bank as calculated above	21,990

What should be the correct balance per the cash book?

A £21,990 balance at bank as stated

B £3,670 balance at bank

C £11,390 balance at bank

D £3,670 overdrawn.

5 **The following sales ledger control account has been prepared by a trainee accountant:**

20X3		£	20X3		£
1 Jan	Balance	284,680	31 Dec	Cash received from	179,790
31 Dec	Credit sales	189,120		credit customers	
	Discounts allowed	3,660		Contras *	800
	Bad debts written off	1,800			
	Sales returns	4,920		Balance	303,590
		484,180			484,180

* = Contras against amounts owing by company in purchases ledger

What should the closing balance on the account be when the errors in it are corrected?

A £290,150

B £286,430

C £282,830

D £284,430.

6 **Which of the following calculations could produce an acceptable figure for a trader's net profit for a period if no accounting records had been kept?**

A   Closing net assets plus drawings minus capital introduced minus opening net assets

B   Closing net assets minus drawings plus capital introduced minus opening net assets

C   Closing net assets minus drawings minus capital introduced minus opening net assets

D   Closing net assets plus drawings plus capital introduced minus opening net assets.

7 **A company with an accounting date of 31 October carried out a physical check of stock on 4 November 20X3, leading to a stock value at cost at this date of £483,700.**

Between 1 November 20X3 and 4 November 20X3 the following transactions took place:

(1)   Goods costing £38,400 were received from suppliers.

(2)   Goods that had cost £14,800 were sold for £20,000.

(3)   A customer returned, in good condition, some goods which had been sold to him in October for £600 and which had cost £400.

(4)   The company returned goods that had cost £1,800 in October to the supplier, and received a credit note for them.

What figure should appear in the company's financial statements at 31 October 20X3 for closing stock, based on this information?

A   £458,700

B   £505,900

C   £508,700

D   £461,500.

8 **In preparing its financial statements for the current year, a company's closing stock was understated by £300,000.**

What will be the effect of this error if it remains uncorrected?

A   The current year's profit will be overstated and next year's profit will be understated

B   The current year's profit will be understated but there will be no effect on next year's profit

C   The current year's profit will be understated and next year's profit will be overstated

D   The current year's profit will be overstated but there will be no effect on next year's profit.

9 **A sole trader took some goods costing £800 from stock for his own use. The normal selling price of the goods is £1,600.**

Which of the following journal entries would correctly record this?

		Dr £	Cr £
A	Stock account	800	
	Purchases account		800
B	Drawings account	800	
	Purchases account		800
C	Sales account	1,600	
	Drawings account		1,600
D	Drawings account	800	
	Sales account		800

10   A company's gross profit percentage on sales has decreased by 5% in 20X2 compared with 20X1.

Which one of the following matters could have caused the decrease?

A   The level of sales in 20X2 is lower than that in 20X1

B   There have been more bad debts in 20X2 than in 20X1

C   Stock at the end of 20X2 is lower than that at the end of 20X1

D   Theft of stock by staff and customers has increased.

11   A sole trader fixes his prices to achieve a gross profit percentage on sales revenue of 40%. All his sales are for cash. He suspects that one of his sales assistants is stealing cash from sales revenue.

His trading account for the month of June 20X3 is as follows:

	£
Recorded sales revenue	181,600
Cost of sales	114,000
Gross profit	67,600

Assuming that the cost of sales figure is correct, how much cash could the sales assistant have taken?

A   £5,040

B   £8,400

C   £22,000

D   It is not possible to calculate a figure from this information.

12   P, after having been a sole trader for some years, entered into partnership with Q on 1 July 20X2, sharing profits equally.

The business profit for the year ended 31 December 20X2 was £340,000, accruing evenly over the year, apart from a charge of £20,000 for a bad debt relating to trading before 1 July 20X2 which it was agreed that P should bear entirely.

How is the profit for the year to be divided between P and Q?

	P £000	Q £000
A	245	95
B	250	90
C	270	90
D	255	85

13   Part of the reconciliation of operating profit to net cash inflow from operating activities from a company's draft cash flow statement is shown below:

	£000
Operating profit	8,640
Depreciation charges	(2,160)
Proceeds of sale of fixed assets	360
Increase in stock	(330)
Increase in creditors	440

The following criticisms of the above extract have been made:

(1)   Depreciation charges should have been added, not deducted.

(2)   Increase in stock should have been added, not deducted.

(3)   Increase in creditors should have been deducted, not added.

(4)   Proceeds of sale of fixed assets should not appear in this part of the cash flow statement.

Which of these criticisms are valid?

A   2 and 3 only

B   1 and 4 only

C   1 and 3 only

D   2 and 4 only.

14   In preparing a company's cash flow statement complying with FRS 1 Cash Flow Statements, which, if any, of the following items could form part of the calculation of cash flow from financing?

(1)   Proceeds of sale of premises

(2)   Dividends received

(3)   Bonus issue of shares

A   1 only

B   2 only

C   3 only

D   None of them.

15   Which of the following assertions about cash flow statements is/are correct?

(1)   A cash flow statement prepared using the direct method produces a different figure for operating cash flow from that produced if the indirect method is used.

(2)   Rights issues of shares do not feature in cash flow statements.

(3)   A surplus on revaluation of a fixed asset will not appear as an item in a cash flow statement.

(4)   A profit on the sale of a fixed asset will appear as an item under Capital Expenditure in a cash flow statement.

A   1 and 4

B   2 and 3

C   3 only

D   2 and 4.

16   Which of the following statements concerning the accounting treatment of research and development expenditure are true, according to SSAP 13 Accounting for Research and Development?

(1)   Development costs recognised as an asset must be amortised over a period not exceeding five years.

(2)   Research expenditure, other than capital expenditure on research facilities, should be recognised as an expense as incurred.

(3)   In deciding whether development expenditure qualifies to be recognised as an asset, it is necessary to consider whether there will be adequate finance available to complete the project.

(4) Development projects must be reviewed at each balance sheet date, and expenditure on any project no longer qualifying for capitalisation must be amortised through the profit and loss account over a period not exceeding five years.

A 1 and 4

B 2 and 4

C 2 and 3

D 1 and 3.

17 Which of the following statements about accounting concepts and policies is/are correct?

(1) The effect of a change to an accounting policy should be disclosed as an extraordinary item if material.

(2) Information in financial statements should be presented so as to be understood by users with a reasonable knowledge of business and accounting.

(3) Companies should create hidden reserves to strengthen their financial position.

(4) Consistency of treatment of items from one period to the next is essential to enhance comparability between companies, and must therefore take precedence over other accounting concepts such as prudence.

A 1 and 4

B 2 and 3

C 3 and 4

D 2 only.

18 A company is considering the following changes when preparing its financial statements:

(1) Changing the basis of charging depreciation on plant and machinery from the straight line method to the reducing balance method.

(2) Including in administration expenses some overhead costs previously shown within cost of sales.

(3) Capitalising new development expenditure when such expenditure had previously been written off as incurred.

Which of these changes would qualify as a change of accounting policy according to FRS18 Accounting Policies?

A 1 and 2 only

B 1 and 3 only

C 2 and 3 only

D All three changes.

19 Which of the following statements about company financial statements is/are correct, according to accounting standards and company law?

(1) A material profit or loss on the sale of part of the entity must appear in the profit and loss account as an extraordinary item.

(2) Dividends paid and proposed should not be included in the profit and loss account, but in the reconciliation of movements in shareholders' funds only.

(3) The profit and loss account must show separately any material profit or loss from operations discontinued during the year.

(4) The statement of total recognised gains and losses must not include unrealised gains or losses.

A 1, 2 and 3

B 2 and 4

C 3 only

D 1 and 4.

20 Which of the following items are required to be disclosed in a limited company's financial statements?

(1) Directors' remuneration

(2) Auditors' remuneration

(3) Staff costs

(4) Depreciation and amortisation

A 1, 2 and 3 only

B 1, 2 and 4 only

C 2, 3 and 4 only

D All four items.

21 At 30 June 20X2 a company's capital structure was as follows:

	£
Ordinary share capital	
500,000 shares of 25p each	125,000
Share premium account	100,000

In the year ended 30 June 20X3 the company made a rights issue of 1 share for every 2 held at £1 per share and this was taken up in full. Later in the year the company made a bonus issue of 1 share for every 5 held, using the share premium account for the purpose.

What was the company's capital structure at 30 June 20X3?

	Ordinary share capital £	Share premium account £
A	450,000	25,000
B	225,000	250,000
C	225,000	325,000
D	212,500	262,500

22 At 30 June 20X2 a company had £1m 8% debentures in issue, interest being paid half-yearly on 30 June and 31 December.

On 30 September 20X2 the company redeemed £250,000 of these debentures at par, paying interest due to that date.

On 1 April 20X3 the company issued £500,000 7% debentures, interest payable half-yearly on 31 March and 30 September.

What figure should appear in the company's profit and loss account for interest payable in the year ended 30 June 20X3?

A £88,750

B £82,500

C £65,000

D £73,750.

23 Which of the following material events occurring after the balance sheet date, and before the financial statements are approved by the directors, should be adjusted for in those financial statements?

(1) A valuation of property providing evidence of impairment in value at the balance sheet date.

(2) Sale of stock held at the balance sheet date for less than cost.

(3) Discovery of fraud or error affecting the financial statements.

(4) The insolvency of a debtor with a balance owing at the balance sheet date which is still outstanding.

A All of them

B 1, 2 and 4 only

C 3 and 4 only

D 1, 2 and 3 only.

24 A company's summarised financial statements, ignoring tax, are shown below:

Profit and loss account		Balance sheet	
	£m		£m
Profit before interest	200	Fixed assets	1,000
Interest paid	(80)	Net current assets	1,600
Profit after interest	120		2,600
Dividends	(40)	less: Loan capital	(800)
Retained profit	80		1,800
		Ordinary share capital	1,000
		Reserves	800
			1,800

What is the correct calculation of return on shareholders' capital employed?

A 120/1,800 = 6.7%

B 200/2,600 = 7.7%

C 40/1,800 = 2.2%

D 120/1,000 = 12.0%

25 The capital of a limited company is made up as follows:

	£m
Issued ordinary share capital	1,000
Share premium account	500
Profit and loss account	3,000
8% debentures	1,500

Which of the following calculations of the company's gearing ratio, based upon these figures, is correct?

A 1,500/6,000 = 1 25%

B 4,500/1,500 = 300%

C 4,500/6,000 = 1 75%

D 1,500/1,000 = 150%

(50 marks)

Section B – ALL FIVE questions are compulsory and must be attempted

1   ABRADOR

(a)   At 31 December 20X2 the following balances existed in the accounting records of Abrador plc:

	Reference to notes	£
Issued share capital –		
2,000,000 ordinary shares of 50p each	1	1,000,000
Share premium account	1	400,000
Suspense account	1	800,000
Profit and loss account	2	7,170,000
Deferred development costs		570,000
Tangible fixed assets – cost		5,000,000
depreciation at 31 December 20X1	3	1,000,000
Stock at 31 December 20X2		3,900,000
Trade debtors	4	3,400,000
Overdraft at bank		100,000
Trade creditors		1,900,000
Provision for doubtful debts at 31 December 20X1	4	100,000
6% debentures	5	400,000

Notes

1   On 31 December 20X2 the company issued for cash 1,000,000 ordinary shares at a premium of 30p per share. The proceeds have been debited to cash and credited to the suspense account.

2   The profit for the year is included in the figure of £7,170,000 above but does not include adjustments for Notes 3 and 4 below.

3   Depreciation is to be provided at 25% per year on the reducing balance basis.

4   Debts totalling £400,000 are to be written off and the provision for doubtful debts adjusted to 3% of the debtors.

5   The 6% debentures are due for redemption on 31 December 20X3 and the obligation is not to be refinanced. All interest due to 31 December 20X2 has been paid.

Required:

Prepare the company's balance sheet as at 31 December 20X2 for publication, using the format in the Companies Act 1985.

Note: The information in (b) below is not relevant for this part of the question.

(8 marks)

(b)   The deferred development costs of £570,000 in (a) above are made up as follows:

	£	£
Project A		
Completed by 31 December 20X1		
Balance of costs as at 31 December 20X1	400,000	
Amortised 20X2	(100,000)	
		300,000
Project B		
In progress		
Total costs as at 31 December 20X1	150,000	
Further costs in 20X2	120,000	
Balance as at 31 December 20X2		270,000
		570,000

The charge in the profit and loss account for 20X2 was £185,000 made up as follows:

	£
Project A: Amortisation	100,000
Project C: Research costs written off	85,000

Required:

State the figures for the disclosure note summarising this information required by SSAP13 Accounting for Research and Development. A statement of the company's policy for research and development expenditure is NOT required. **(4 marks)**

(Total: 12 marks)

2 RIFFON

The accounting records of Riffon Limited included the following balances at 30 June 20X2:

		£
Office buildings	– cost	1,600,000
	– accumulated depreciation (10 years at 2% per year)	320,000
Plant and machinery	– cost (all purchased in 20X0 or later)	840,000
	– accumulated depreciation (straight line basis at 25% per year)	306,000

During the year ended 30 June 20X3 the following events occurred:

20X2

1 July	It was decided to revalue the office building to £2,000,000, with no change to the estimate of its remaining useful life.

1 October 20X3	New plant costing £200,000 was purchased.
1 April	Plant which had cost £240,000 and with accumulated depreciation at 30 June 20X2 of £180,000 was sold for £70,000.

It is the company's policy to charge a full year's depreciation on plant in the year of acquisition and none in the year of sale.

Required:

Prepare the following ledger accounts to record the above balances and events:

(a) Office building: cost/valuation
     accumulated depreciation
     revaluation reserve. **(6 marks)**

(b) Plant and machinery: cost
     accumulated depreciation
     disposal. **(6 marks)**

(Total: 12 marks)

3   EAGLE AND OXER

On 1 November 20X0 Eagle plc acquired 70% of the share capital of Oxer Limited for £180,000. At this date the profit and loss account balance of Oxer Limited amounted to £150,000.

The balance sheets of the two companies at 31 October 20X4 were as follows:

	Eagle plc £	Oxer Limited £
Investment in Oxer Limited	180,000	
Sundry net assets	490,000	410,000
	670,000	410,000
Ordinary share capital	220,000	100,000
Profit and loss account	450,000	310,000
	670,000	410,000

Eagle plc's policy is to amortise goodwill arising on consolidation over five years.

Required:

Prepare the consolidated balance sheet of Eagle plc and its subsidiary at 31 October 20X4.

(8 marks)

4   ALUKI

The directors of Aluki Limited, a fashion wholesaler, are reviewing the company's draft financial statements for the year ended 30 September 20X3, which show a profit of £900,000 before tax.

The following matters require consideration:

(a)   The closing stock includes:

    (i)   3,000 skirts at cost £40,000. Since the balance sheet date they have all been sold for £65,000, with selling expenses of £3,000.

    (ii)   2,000 jackets at cost £60,000. Since the balance sheet date half the jackets have been sold for £25,000 (selling expenses £1,800) and the remainder are expected to sell for £20,000 with selling expenses of £2,000.   **(2 marks)**

(b)   An employee dismissed in August 20X3 began an action for damages for wrongful dismissal in October 20X3. She is claiming £100,000 in damages. Aluki Limited is resisting the claim and the company's solicitors have advised that the employee has a 30% chance of success in her claim.

The financial statements currently include a provision for the £100,000 claim.

(4 marks)

(c)   In October 20X3 a fire destroyed part of the company's warehouse, with an uninsured loss of stock worth £180,000 and damage to the building, also uninsured, of £228,000. The going concern status of the company is not affected.

The financial statements currently make no mention of the fire losses.   **(3 marks)**

Required:

Explain to the directors how these matters should be treated in the financial statements for the year ended 30 September 20X3, stating the relevant accounting standards.   **(9 marks)**

5   HISTORICAL COST BASIS

The use of historical cost as a basis for accounting is widespread.

Required:

(a)   Explain THREE ways in which the use of historical cost accounting may mislead users of financial statements.   **(6 marks)**

(b)   Briefly state THREE reasons why historical cost accounting remains in use in spite of its limitations.   **(3 marks)**

(Total: 9 marks)

Section 8

ANSWERS TO DECEMBER 2003 EXAMINATION QUESTIONS

SECTION A

1 A

	£
Provision at 30 June 20X2	18,000
Provision at 30 June 20X3	16,000
Reduction in provision	(2,000)
Bad debts written off	14,600
Bad and doubtful debts expense	12,600

2 B

The suspense account would be opened as follows.

	£		£
		Opening balance	8,131

To reduce the balance, the correction of the error requires a debit entry in the suspense account and a corresponding credit entry in one or more other ledger accounts. Only error B meets this requirement. To correct error B requires the following entries:

	Dr £	Cr £
Suspense account	4,000	
Rent (expense) account		4,000
Suspense account	4,000	
Rental income account		4,000

3 B

The required corrections are:

	Dr £	Cr £
Discounts allowed	3,840	
Discounts received	3,840	
Suspense account		7,680
Suspense account	5,920	
Discounts allowed		2,960
Discounts received		2,960

The net effect is to debit the Discounts allowed and Discounts received accounts each with £880 and to credit the suspense account with £1,760.

4   B

	£	
Bank statement balance	3,860	overdraft
In cash book but not yet in bank statement:		
(1) Cheques not yet presented	9,160	
	13,020	overdraft
(2) Deposits not yet credited	16,690	
Cash book balance (= correct)	3,670	

5   C

Sales ledger control account

20X3		£	20X3		£
1 Jan	Balance b/d	284,680	31 Dec	Cash	179,790
31 Dec	Sales	189,120		Contras	800
				Discounts allowed	3,660
				Bad debts	1,800
				Sales returns	4,920
				Balance c/d	**282,830**
		473,800			473,800
20X4					
1 Jan	Balance b/d	**282,830**			

6   A

Profit = Increase in net assets minus New capital introduced + Drawings taken out

= (Closing net assets – Opening net assets) – New capital + Drawings

7   D

Item		£
	Stock at 4 November	483,700
(1)	Less: Goods received after 30 October	(38,400)
(2)	Plus: Goods sold after 30 October, at cost	14,800
(3)	Less: Goods returned after 30 October, at cost	(400)
(4)	Plus: Purchase returns after 30 October	1,800
	Stock valuation at 30 October	461,500

8   C

Current year

Closing stock under-valued, therefore cost of sales over-stated and profit under-stated.

Next year

Opening stock under-valued, therefore cost of sales under-stated and profit over-stated.

9   B

Stock items withdrawn by the owner of the business are accounted for as drawings. The drawings should be recorded at the purchase cost of the items taken, not their sales price. The effect of taking stock as drawings is to reduce the amount of purchases in the period; therefore debit drawings, credit purchases.

10 D

Since theft of stock cannot be measured, the effect of theft is to increase the cost of sales and reduce the gross profit and the gross profit as a percentage of sales. Answer D is therefore correct. It could be argued that answer A is also correct, on the grounds that the cost of sales includes some fixed costs; therefore lower sales increases the unit cost of sale and reduces the gross profit/unit. However, this was not the examiner's intention. Answer B is not correct because bad debts do not affect the cost of sales and gross profit (they reduce net profit). Answer C is not correct because lower stock levels are caused by purchase quantities of stocks being less than sales quantities, which has no relevance to gross profit in the period.

11 B

The gross profit is 60% of sales revenue, but the figure for sales revenue is unreliable because it is an amount after deduction of suspected money stolen.

Since the gross profit is 40% of expected sales revenue, it is also 40/60 (= 40/(100 − 40)) of the cost of sales.

	£
Cost of sales	114,000
Gross profit (× 40/60)	76,000
Expected sales receipts	190,000
Actual sales receipts	181,600
Cash shortfall	8,400

12 B

	£
Profit before bad debt (340,000 + 20,000)	360,000
Profit each half year, before bad debt	180,000
Profit in first six months to 30 June (180,000 − 20,000)	160,000
Profit in second six months to 31 December	180,000

	Total £	P £	Q £
1st six months	160,000	160,000	0
2nd six months	180,000	90,000	90,000
Total	340,000	250,000	90,000

13 B

Depreciation charges should be added, not subtracted, when calculating the cash flow from operating activities. The profit on disposal of fixed assets should be subtracted in the same part of the statement: however, the proceeds (i.e. the cash received) from such disposals are cash flows from capital expenditure items, and should be shown elsewhere in the cash flow statement. Therefore criticisms (1) and (4) are valid.

14 D

Proceeds from the sale of premises would be included in the capital expenditure section of the cash flow statement. Dividends received are usually included as returns on investments and servicing of finance. A bonus issue of shares does not give rise to any cash flows, and so is not included at all.

15   C

Statement (4) is incorrect. The *proceeds* from the sale of a fixed asset appears under Capital Expenditure, but the *profit or loss* reported on the disposal is an adjustment in reconciling operating profit to the net cash flow from operating activities. Statements (1) and (2) are also incorrect. Only statement (3) is correct.

16   C

Statements (2) and (3) only are correct. There is no requirement in SSAP13 for capitalised development costs to be amortised over a period of five years or less.

17   D

This question mainly tests your awareness of the ASB's *Statement of principles for financial reporting*. Only statement (2) is correct: the *Statement of principles* comments on the capabilities of users that: 'Those preparing financial statements are entitled to assume that users have a reasonable knowledge of business and economic activities and a willingness to study with reasonable diligence the information provided.' Statement (1) is incorrect: disclosure is required of the effect of a change in accounting policy, but not as an extraordinary item. Statement (3) is incorrect: the *Statement of principles* states that companies should not create hidden reserves, because this would make the financial information unreliable. Statement (4) is also incorrect: the *Statement of principles* states that 'consistency is not an end in itself, nor should it be allowed to become an impediment to the introduction of improved accounting practices. Consistency can also be useful in enhancing comparability between entities, although it should not be confused with a need for absolute uniformity.'

18   C

FRS18 defines an accounting policies as those principles, rules and practices that specify (1) how assets, liabilities, gains or losses are recognised (2) how measurement bases for them are selected, and (3) how assets, liabilities, gains or losses are presented in the financial statements. Accounting policies are distinguished from estimation techniques, which implement the measurement aspects of accounting policies.

An Appendix to FRS18 presents some examples. Changing the basis of depreciation from one method to another does not involve a change of measurement basis (measurement basis = historical cost), only a change in the estimation technique used. This is therefore not a change in accounting policy.

Changing certain overheads from cost of sales to administration expenses involves a change of presentation, and so is a change in accounting policy.

Capitalising an item that had previously been treated as a revenue expense does not affect how the cost is measured, but it does involve a change in recognition (the cost is now a fixed asset rather than an expense) and consequently it also involves a change in the way it is presented. Therefore this is a change in accounting policy.

The correct answer is therefore C.

19   C

Statement (3) is correct. Separate disclosure of the profit or loss in the period from discontinued operations is a requirement of FRS3. Statement (1) is incorrect: extraordinary items are extremely rare and relate to abnormal events. Statement (2) is incorrect: it is usual practice in the UK to include dividends paid and proposed in the profit and loss account. Statement (4) is incorrect: an example of unrealised gains in the Statement of total Recognised Gains and Losses (STRGL) is a revaluation surplus recorded on the revaluation of a fixed asset.

20   D

These disclosures are requirements of the Companies Act 1985. The Companies Act was amended in 2002 by the directors' Remuneration Reporting Regulations, which require extensive disclosures of directors' remuneration.

21   B

	Ordinary share capital £	Share premium £
At 30 June 20X2	125,000	100,000
Rights issue (75p premium/share)	62,500	187,500
	187,500	287,500
1 for 5 bonus issue	37,500	(37,500)
At 30 June 20X3	225,000	250,000

22   D

Interest is calculated on an accruals basis.

Interest payable:	£
On £250,000 8% debentures redeemed 30 September ($£250,000 \times 8\% \times 3/12$)	5,000
On £750,000 8% debentures ($£750,000 \times 8\%$)	60,000
On £500,000 7% debentures ($£500,000 \times 7\% \times 3/12$)	8,750
Total interest payable in the year	73,750

23   A

An adjusting post balance sheet event is something that is discovered after the balance sheet date (and before the financial statements are approved by the board of directors) but which existed before/at the balance sheet date. All four of the events in the question are therefore adjusting post-balance sheet events.

24   A

The return on *shareholders'* capital (ROSC) is the profit attributable to shareholders as a percentage of ordinary share capital and reserves. ROSC = (120/1,800) = 6.7%.

25   A

Although gearing can be calculated in several ways, interest-bearing debt capital is always 'above the line'. Two common methods of calculating gearing are:

(a)   Long-term debt capital/(ordinary share capital and reserves).

Here this is 1,500/(1,000 + 500 + 3,000) = 1,500/4,500 = 33.3% - not an available Answer.

(b)   Long-term debt capital/(ordinary share capital and reserves plus long-term debt capital).

Here this is 1,500/(4,500 + 1,500) = 1,500/6,000 = 25% (Answer A).

SECTION B

1   ABRADOR

(a)

Abrador plc
Balance sheet as at 31 December 20X2

	£	£	£
Fixed assets			
Intangible			
Development costs		570,000	
Tangible (W1)		3,000,000	
			3,570,000
Current assets			
Stock	3,900,000		
Debtors (W2)	2,910,000		
		6,810,000	
Creditors: amounts falling due within one year			
Trade creditors	1,900,000		
Overdraft at bank	100,000		
6% debentures	400,000		
		(2,400,000)	
			4,410,000
			7,980,000
Capital and reserves			
Called up share capital (W4) (1,000,00 + 500,000)			1,500,000
Share premium account (W4) (400,000 + 300,000)			700,000
Profit and loss account (W3)			5,780,000
			7,980,000

Workings

(W1) *Tangible fixed assets*

	£
At cost	5,000,000
Accumulated depreciation to 31 December 20X1	(1,000,000)
Net book value at 31 December 20X1	4,000,000
Depreciation in the year to 31 December 20X2 (25%)	(1,000,000)
Net book value at 31 December 20X2	2,000,000

(W2) *Debtors and provision for doubtful debts*

	£
As stated in the question	3,400,000
Bad debts written off	(400,000)
Adjusted debtors	3,000,000
Provision for doubtful debts (3%)	90,000
Debtors as stated in the balance sheet	2,910,000

	£
Provision for doubtful debts at 31 December 20X1	100,000
Provision for doubtful debts at 31 December 20X2	90,000
Reduction in the provision	10,000

(W3) *Profit and loss account (accumulated profits)*

	£	£
As stated in the question		7,170,000
Items not yet accounted for:		
Depreciation (W1)	1,000,000	
Bad debts written off	400,000	
Reduction in doubtful debt provision (W2)	(10,000)	
		1,390,000
Adjusted profit and loss account		5,780,000

(W4) *Share capital and share premium*

The proceeds of the share issue have added (1,000,000 × 50p) £500,000 to called up share capital and (1,000,000 × 30p) £300,000 to the share premium account.

Note

The 6% debentures are repayable within 12 months and so are shown as a current liability in the balance sheet.

(b)

Movements on deferred development expenditure during the year	£
Balance at 31 December 20X1	550,000
New expenditure in 20X2	120,000
	670,000
Amortisation for the year	(100,000)
Deferred development expenditure at 31 December 20X2	570,000

Total expenditure on research and development charged in profit and loss account	£
Current expenditure	85,000
Amortisation of deferred development costs	100,000
	185,000

ACCA marking scheme	
(a)	*Marks available*
Development costs correctly displayed	0.5
Tangible fixed assets (2 × 0.5)	1.0
Debtors (2 × 0.5)	1.0
Debentures in current liabilities	0.5
Called up share capital	1.0
Share premium	1.0
Profit and loss account (3 × 0.5)	1.5
Layout	2.0
	8.5
Maximum awarded for part (a)	8.0
(b) Movements in deferred development expenditure	
Opening balance	1.0
Movements (2 × 1)	2.0
Profit and loss account (2 × 0.5)	1.0
Marks for part (b)	4.0
Total	12.0

2   RIFFON

(a)

Office building at cost/valuation

20X2		£	20X3		£
1 July	Balance b/d	1,600,000			
	Revaluation	400,000	30 June	Balance c/d	2 000,000
		2 000,000			2,000,000
20X3					
1 July	Balance b/d	2,000,000			

Office building - accumulated depreciation

20X2		£	20X2		£
1 July	Revaluation reserve	320,000	1 July	Balance b/d	320,000
20X3			20X3		
30 Jun	Balance c/d	50,000	30 June	Profit and loss a/c (W1)	50,000
		370,000			370,000
			20X3		
			1 July	Balance b/d	50,000

Revaluation reserve

20X3		£	20X2		£
			1 July	Office building at cost/valuation	400,000
			1 July	Office building – accum. depreciation	320,000

(b)

Plant and machinery at cost

20X2		£	20X3		£
1 July	Balance b/d	840,000	1 April	Disposal a/c	240,000
1 Oct	Bank	200,000	30 June	Balance c/d	800,000
		1,040,000			1,040,000
20X3					
1 July	Balance b/d	800,000			

Plant and machinery - accumulated depreciation

20X3		£	20X2		£
1 April	Disposal a/c	180,000	1 July	Balance b/d	306,000
			20X3		
30 Jun	Balance c/d	326,000	30 June	Profit and loss a/c (W2)	200,000
		506,000			506,000
			20X3		
			1 July	Balance b/d	32,000

Plant and machinery – disposal account

20X3		£	20X3		£
1 April	Transfer - cost	240,000	1 April	Transfer – accumulated depreciation	180,000
30 June	Profit and loss a/c (profit on disposal)	10,000		Bank	70,000
		250,000			250,000

Workings

(W1) *Depreciation of office building*

Depreciation = 2% per annum straight line, therefore the asset is depreciated over 50 years.

Remaining life after revaluation = 50 – 10 = 40 years

Depreciation charge for the year to 30 June 20X3

= Revalued amount/Remaining life

= £2 million/40 = £50,000.

(W2) *Depreciation of plant and machinery*

25% × (£840,000 - £240,000 + £200,000) = £200,000.

ACCA marking scheme	
(a)	*Marks available*
Office building:	
Cost/valuation (2 × 0.5)	1.0
Accumulated depreciation:	
calculations	1.0
entries (4 × 0.5)	2.0
Revaluation reserve (2 × 1)	2.0
(b)	
Plant and machinery	
Cost	2.0
Accumulated depreciation	2.0
Disposal	2.0
Total	12.0

3   EAGLE AND OXER

Workings

(W1)

Goodwill	£
Value of net assets in Oxer acquired	
(70% of (£100,000 + £150,000)	175,000
Cost of the investment	180,000
Goodwill on acquisition	5,000
Annual amortisation (over 5 years)	1,000
Accumulated amortisation to 31 October 20X4	4,000
Goodwill in consolidated balance sheet (£5,000 - £4,000)	1,000

(W2) *Minority interest*

Minority interest in Oxer = 30% × £410,000 = £123,000.

(W3)

Consolidated profit and loss reserve	£	£
Profit and loss reserve of Eagle		450,000
Profit and loss reserve of Oxer, 31 October 20X4	310,000	
Profit and loss reserve of Oxer, 31 October 20X4	150,000	
Post-acquisition retained profits of Oxer	160,000	
Group share (= 70%)		112,000
less: Amortised goodwill		(4,000)
Consolidated profit and loss reserve		558,000

Eagle Group
Consolidated balance sheet as at 31 October 20X4

	£
Goodwill (W1)	1,000
Sundry net assets (490,000 + 410,000)	900,000
	901,000
Ordinary share capital	220,000
Profit and loss account (W3)	558,000
	778,000
Minority interest (W2)	123,000
	901,000

ACCA marking scheme	
	Marks available
Goodwill (5 × 0.5)	2.5
Minority interest (2 × 0.5)	1.0
Profit and loss account (5 × 0.5)	2.5
Share capital	0.5
Sundry net assets	1.0
Heading	0.5
Total	8.0

4   ALUKI

(a)   The basic principle for the valuation of stock according to SSAP 9 Stock and Long-term Contracts is to take the lower of cost and net realisable value.

The 3,000 skirts should therefore be included at cost £40,000, since their NRV is £62,000 (£65,000 - £3,000).

The jackets should be valued at net realisable value, which is lower than cost. (Cost = £30,000 for each half of the stock):

	£
£25,000 less £1,800	23,200
£20,000 less £2,000	18,000
Net realisable value of skirts	41,200

Tutorial note: All the skirts must be valued, since the sale of the items occurred after the balance sheet date.

(b)   FRS 12 Provisions, Contingent Liabilities and Contingent Assets requires contingent liabilities of this kind and degree of probability be disclosed by note, detailing the nature of the contingent liability and an estimate of the financial effect.

The £100,000 provision should therefore be removed from the balance sheet and the note substituted. However, a provision should be made for legal expenses to be incurred, since some legal costs will be incurred whatever the outcome of the dispute.

(c)   SSAP17 *Accounting for Post Balance Sheet Events* classifies this as a non-adjusting event, since it occurred after the balance sheet date. It should not be included in the financial statements to 30 September, but a note giving details of the event and its financial effect (a loss of £180,000 plus £228,000 = £408,000) is required as the item is material enough to influence a reader of the financial statements.

ACCA marking scheme		
		Marks available
(a)	*Stock*	
	SSAP 9 mentioned	1.0
	Valuation	1.0
(b)	*Contingent liability*	
	FRS 12 mentioned	1.0
	Disclose by note stating nature and financial effect	1.0
	Remove £100,000 and replace with note	1.0
	Provide for legal expenses	1.0
(c)	*Post balance sheet event*	
	SSAP 17 mentioned	1.0
	Non-adjusting	1.0
	Note required detailing event and financial effect	<u>1.0</u>
Total		<u>9.0</u>

5 HISTORICAL COST BASIS

(a)

(i) **Profit on a sale** is calculated by taking the difference between historical cost and sale proceeds. When prices are rising, the 'holding gain' arising while the goods were held in stock is included as part of the profit, ignoring the fact that it will cost more to replace the stock item.

(ii) **Depreciation** based on the historical cost of fixed assets understates the real value of the benefit obtained from the use of these assets if prices have risen since the assets were acquired. Profit is thus overstated.

(iii) The use of **historical values for fixed assets** in the balance sheet understates their actual value. This can mislead shareholders when the balance sheet value of the business is used when calculating return on capital employed.

Tutorial note: It is now common for public companies to revalue some fixed assets regularly, particularly land and buildings.

(b)

(i) It is simple and cheap

(ii) Figures used are objective and verifiable.

(iii) A widely-acceptable, sound and acceptable alternative does not exist.

ACCA marking scheme	
	Marks available
Part (a): (3 × 2)	6.0
Part (b): (3 × 1)	<u>3.0</u>
Total	<u>9.0</u>